I0800252

IMAGES
of America

POMPANO PARK HARNESS TRACK

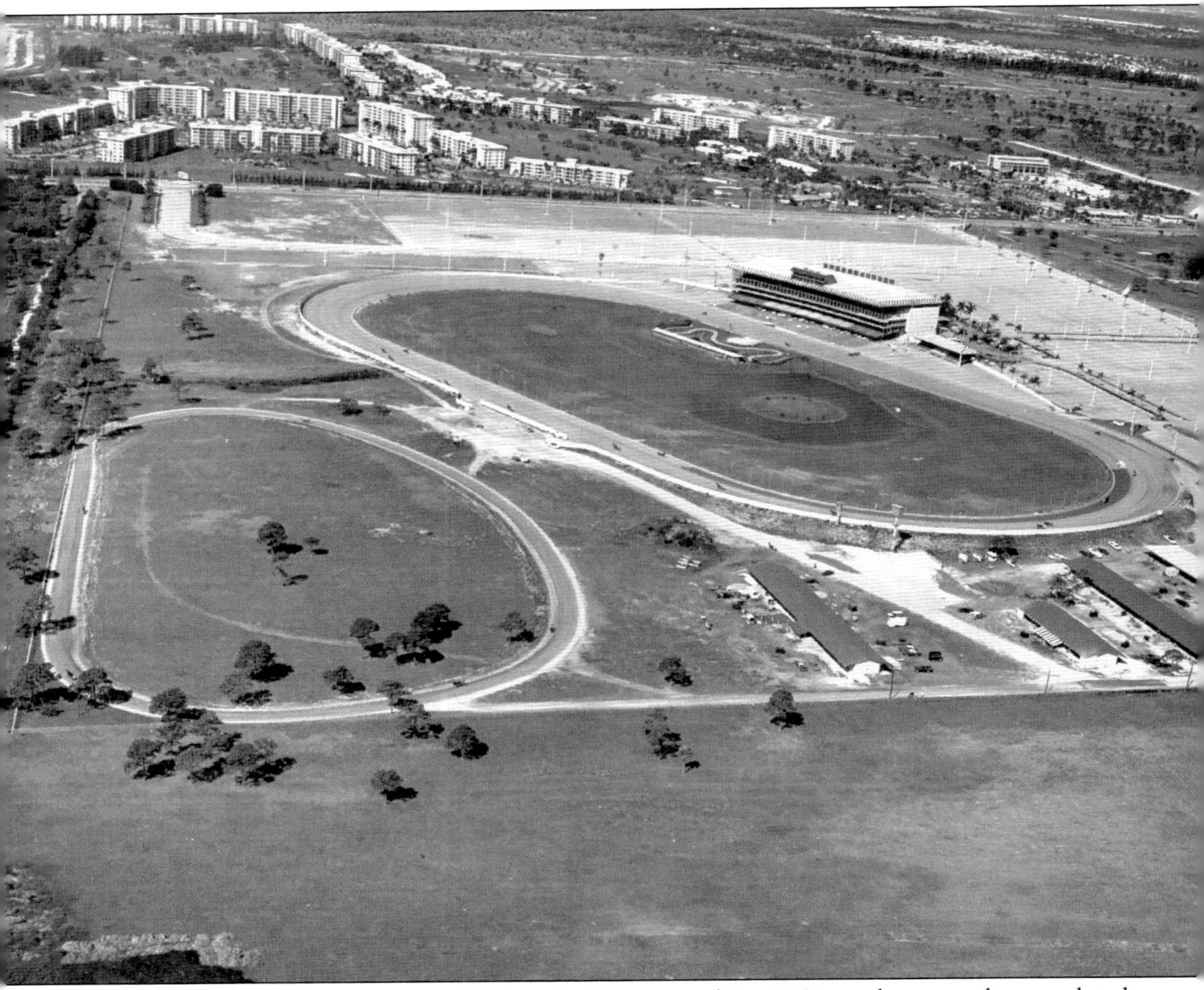

An impressive, panoramic aerial view looks westward in 1964 at the recently completed Pompano Park Harness Track. The present training track is at left. The Palm Aire community can be seen in the background at left, off Powerline Road. To the right of the grandstand is the main entrance coming off Racetrack Road (SW 3rd Street).

IMAGES
of America

POMPANO PARK HARNESS TRACK

Frank J. Cavaioli

ARCADIA

ISBN 0-7385-1750-X

Published by Arcadia Publishing
Charleston SC, Chicago IL, Portsmouth NH, San Francisco CA

Printed in Great Britain

Library of Congress Catalog Card Number: 20041122431

For all general information contact Arcadia Publishing at:
Telephone 843-853-2070
Fax 843-853-0044
E-mail sales@arcadiapublishing.com
For customer service and orders:
Toll-Free 1-888-313-2665

Visit us on the internet at http://www.arcadiapublishing.com

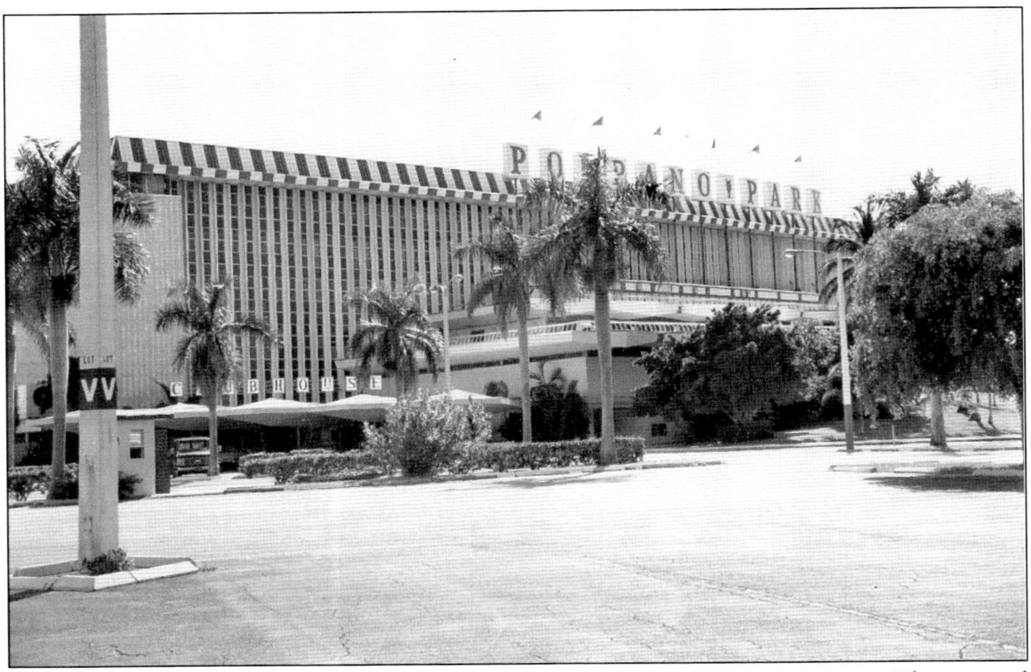

Pompano Park Pink (a paint pigment) was the favorite color of the van Lenneps. The original design of the building featured alternating pink and white vertical lines. Today, green and white lines adorn Pompano Park. In this image, the clubhouse entrance can be seen at left, as the view is taken from the south parking lot.

Contents

ACKNOWLEDGMENTS

Thanks go to the following whose help made this book possible: John Berry, Aime Choquette, Dan Gawlas, Don Daniel, Dick Feinberg, Bud Garner, Harness Racing Museum and Hall of Fame, Debbie Schaut, United States Harness Writers Association, United States Trotting Association, and Steven J. Wolf.

INTRODUCTION

Known as the "Winter Capital of Harness Racing," Pompano Park has long been a fixture for championship harness racing in South Florida. It opened its gates on February 4, 1964, for a 46-night inaugural season at its 331-acre site east of Powerline Road and south of Atlantic Boulevard in Pompano Beach. It was not the first Florida harness race track. Short, unsuccessful race meets were held at Ponce de Leon Raceway near Jacksonville in 1959 and at Seminole Raceway outside Orlando in 1963. The Pompano Beach property on which harness racing now takes place was once a failed 1926 Thoroughbred racetrack. During World War II, the old grandstand was dismantled and used to build part of the Gulfstream Park Racetrack structure. Stock car races took place at the original track in the late 1940s.

The property was purchased in 1953 by New York advertising executive Frederick L. van Lennep (1911–1987), a Philadelphia native and a 1933 Princeton graduate. He was determined to build a grand harness track in Pompano Beach. He had barns built as well as a half-mile training track. He used the track for winter horse training during the next decade. He and his wife, Frances Dodge van Lennep, were the owners of the second-largest Standardbred breeding farm in the world, Castleton Farm in Lexington, Kentucky. Frances was the daughter of John Dodge, co-founder of the Dodge automobile company. While running their track, the van Lenneps wintered at their oceanfront Delray Beach, Florida home. They shipped their horses down by railroad. Other owners followed.

Before the track opened in 1964, a legal battle began, as competing racing interests organized to prevent the van Lenneps from building their racetrack in Pompano Beach, whose 1960 population was 15,992. After all the legal battles were settled and all the minor hurdles overcome, Pompano Park Harness Track opened on February 4 amid much acclaim, and at a cost of $5.5 million. Despite the two inches of rain that fell on opening night, attendance reached 4,011, with a handle of $108,154. The inaugural season lasted until March 28, 1964. That first season Pompano Park had five nationally known champions on the grounds: Speedy Scot, Race Time, Coffee Break, Country Don, and Kentucky Belle—over a million dollars in horse flesh! The leading driver was John Chapman. The leading trainer was Tom Merriman.

The original 1926 group of promoters had organized to construct a Thoroughbred racetrack in the southwest section of what was then the city of Pompano (later to be merged in 1947 with the eastern coastal area to become the city of Pompano Beach), where the present track stands. The track cost $1.25 million and provided stables and service buildings for 1,000 horses. The grandstand could accommodate upwards of 7,000 people. The track was a one-mile oval, 100 feet wide, and was surfaced with sand and clay.

Those promoters of 1926 had hoped to conduct pari-mutuel betting at the Thoroughbred track. But the track was shut down after one day of racing because pari-mutuel betting was illegal. Florida governor John Martin called the Pompano track "a center of lawbreakers" and threatened to send in the military to plow under the track. Pompano was then a rural community with a 1930 population of 2,614.

Since 1964, however, Pompano Park has grown to host appearances and record-breaking performances of harness racing's greatest horses, trainers, and drivers from around the world. When 1979 and 1980 Horse of the Year Niatross, trained and driven by Clint Galbraith, raced on December 27, 1980, a record crowd of 18,451 was in attendance, while more than 5,000 fans were turned away for lack of parking. On November 13, 1987, Mack Lobell, driven by John Chapman, set a world record in the prestigious Breeders Crown Championship with a 1:54.1 victory. During the 2004 winter season, the $250,000 Isle of Capri Series was held, as well as the $125,000 Mack Lobell Trotting Series. Stanley Dancer, Billy Haughton, Delvin Miller, Bill Popfinger, Lucien Fontaine, Buddy Regan, Jerry Silverman, Howard Beissinger, George Sholty, Clint Hodgins, Gene Sears, Herve Filion, and Ralph Baldwin are just some of the great drivers who made their "mark at the Park." Current leading drivers are Bruce Ranger, Wally Hennessey, Kevin Wallis, Mickey McNichol, Marc Aubin, George Napolitano, David Ingraham, Walter Ross Jr., John Kakaley, Gaston Lareau, and Joe Pavia Jr.

Through the 1980s, Pompano Park was the only harness track in the country to have a complete golf course within its boundaries. Flanking the main entrance, a regulation par-60 course measuring almost 3,000 yards challenged golfers on every one of the 18 holes. The modern clubhouse contained a well-stocked pro shop and golf carts. Visitors could golf in the afternoon, then cross the parking lot for harness racing in the evening.

For the silver anniversary in the 1988–1989 season, a complete renovation of Pompano Park's second-floor trackside level provided new floor tiling, a regional bright color scheme, and increased television accessibility. An owner's lounge (now the Niatross Room) was established for horse owners and their guests. Saturday morning barn-area tours and nightly handicapping seminars were conducted. The present owners, Isle of Capri Casinos, Inc., purchased the racetrack on June 30, 1995.

Pompano Park conducts many charitable events and is the home of the Broward County Fair. The track has sheltered horses during hurricanes. The Park is a complete entertainment destination with live racing, simulcasting, poker play, and fine dining all year. It can accommodate 20,000 spectators, 12,000 cars, and more than 1,000 horses. It is the only harness track nighttime facility in Florida. Regular visitors included Frank Sinatra, Jackie Gleason, Walter Matthau, Mickie Mantle, Whitey Ford, Lorne Greene, Bobby Riggs, Lee Elder, Lyle Waggoner, George Steinbrenner, Barbara McNair, Joe Garagiola, Kay Stevens, Roy White, Charley Keller, Lou Worsham, Ed Sullivan, Sam Bowie, Dennis Martinez, Arnold Palmer, Sammy Davis Jr., Ed Kranepool, Tony Segreto, and Rodney Dangerfield.

The purebred American miniature horses are based at the track and serve as ambassadors of the Park and harness racing. They entertain and educate those interested in the sport. Miniature horses, which originated in Western Europe, served as pets and pulled carriages. They were brought to the United States in the 1880s and were used in coalmines. The Pompano Park "minis" are popular with children, who get to hug, pet, and ride with them. Every month these miniature horses are featured at the track.

One

The Beginning

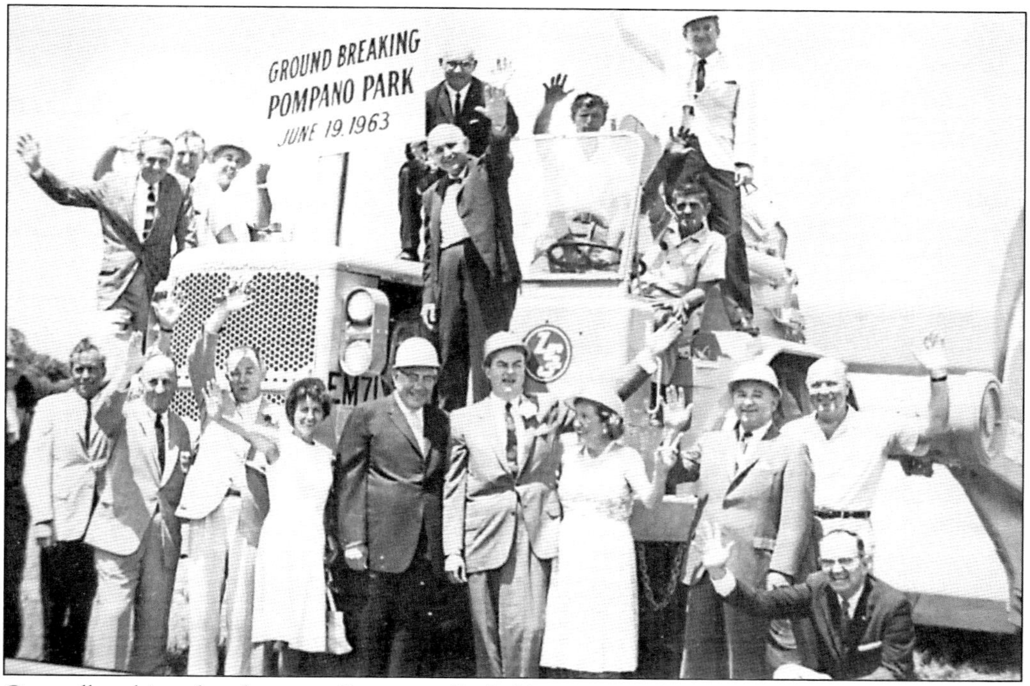

Groundbreaking for the new Pompano Park Harness Track took place on June 19, 1963. Frederick L. van Lennep, seventh from the left in the front row, was the driving force to bring harness racing to South Florida. His wife, Frances Dodge van Lennep, joined him in this endeavor. The van Lenneps owned Castleton Farm in Lexington, Kentucky, and Wolverine Raceway in Detroit, Michigan.

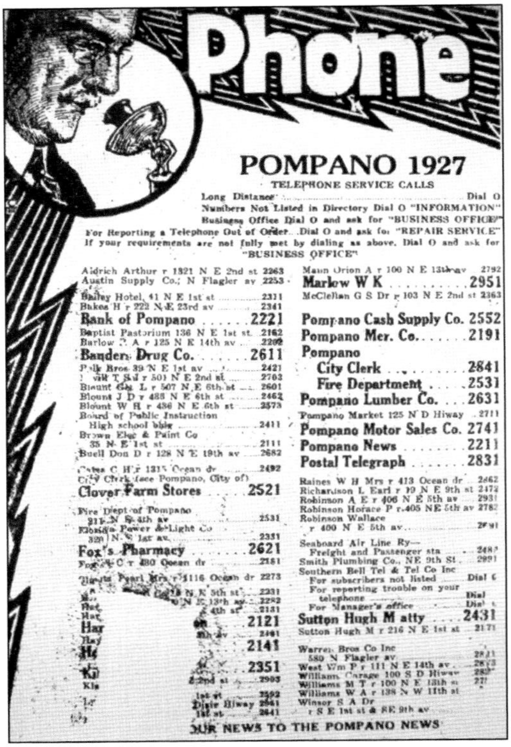

Phone

POMPANO 1927

TELEPHONE SERVICE CALLS

Long Distance .... Dial O
Numbers Not Listed in Directory Dial O "INFORMATION"
Business Office Dial O and ask for "BUSINESS OFFICE"
For Reporting a Telephone Out of Order...Dial O and ask for "REPAIR SERVICE"
If your requirements are not fully met by dialing as above, Dial O and ask for "BUSINESS OFFICE"

Aldrich Arthur r 1821 N E 2nd st 2263
Austin Supply Co.; N Flagler av 2253
Bailey Hotel, 41 N E 1st st 2311
Bakes H r 222 N E 23rd av 2341
Bank of Pompano 2221
Baptist Pastorium 136 N E 1st st 2162
Barlow [illegible] A r 125 N E 14th av 2202
Banders Drug Co. 2611
[illegible] Bros 39 N E 1st av 2421
[illegible] T [illegible] r 501 N E 2nd st 2703
Blount [illegible] L r 507 N E 6th st 2601
Blount J D r 488 N E 6th st 2462
Blount W H r 436 N E 6th st 2573
Board of Public Instruction
High school bldg 2411
Brown Elec & Paint Co
35 N E 1st st 2111
Buell Don D r 128 N E 19th av 2682
[illegible] C H r 1315 Ocean dr 2492
City Clerk (see Pompano, City of)
Clover Farm Stores 2521
Fire Dept of Pompano
[illegible] N E 4th av 2531
Florida Power & Light Co
[illegible] N E 1st av 2331
Fox's Pharmacy 2621
[illegible] C r 480 Ocean dr 2181
[illegible] Pearl Mrs r 1116 Ocean dr 2273
[illegible]

Mann Orion A r 100 N E 13th av 2792
Marlow W K 2951
McClellan G S Dr r 103 N E 2nd st 2363
Pompano Cash Supply Co. 2552
Pompano Mer. Co. 2191
Pompano
City Clerk 2841
Fire Department 2531
Pompano Lumber Co. ... 2631
Pompano Market 125 N D Hiway 2711
Pompano Motor Sales Co. 2741
Pompano News 2211
Postal Telegraph 2831
Raines W H Mrs r 413 Ocean dr 2662
Richardson L Earl r 19 N E 9th st 2472
Robinson A E r 406 N E 5th av 2931
Robinson Horace P r 405 NE 5th av 2782
Robinson Wallace
r 400 N E 5th av [illegible]
Seaboard Air Line Ry—
Freight and Passenger sta [illegible]
Smith Plumbing Co., NE 9th St 2991
Southern Bell Tel & Tel Co Inc
For subscribers not listed Dial [illegible]
For reporting trouble on your telephone Dial
For Manager's office Dial [illegible]
Sutton Hugh M atty ... 2431
Sutton Hugh M r 216 N E 1st st [illegible]
Warren Bros Co Inc
580 N Flagler av [illegible]
West Wm P r 111 N E 14th av [illegible]
Williams Garage 100 S D Hiway [illegible]
Williams M T r 100 N E 13th st [illegible]
Williams W A r 138 N W 11th st
Winsor S A Dr
r S E 1st st & SE 9th av

[illegible]UR NEWS TO THE POMPANO NEWS

The Southern Bell Telephone Company directory consisted of a single page of listings for Pompano in 1927, a year after a failed attempt to bring Thoroughbred racing to South Florida. The official 1930 population of the city of Pompano was 2,614. This telephone directory is a reminder of an earlier period in local history.

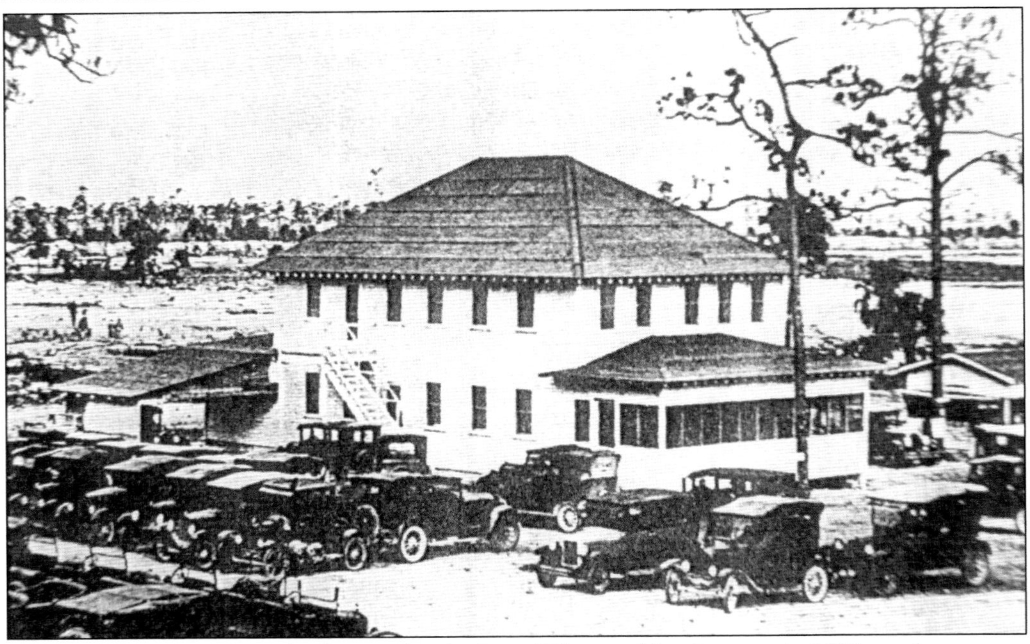

This rare image captures the first and only day of Thoroughbred racing in 1926 on the present site of Pompano Park. Betting was illegal then. The original clubhouse (center) and track (in the background) were built at a cost of $1.25 million. The track was a one-mile oval 100 feet wide. Stock car races were held there briefly in the late 1940s, before it was torn down.

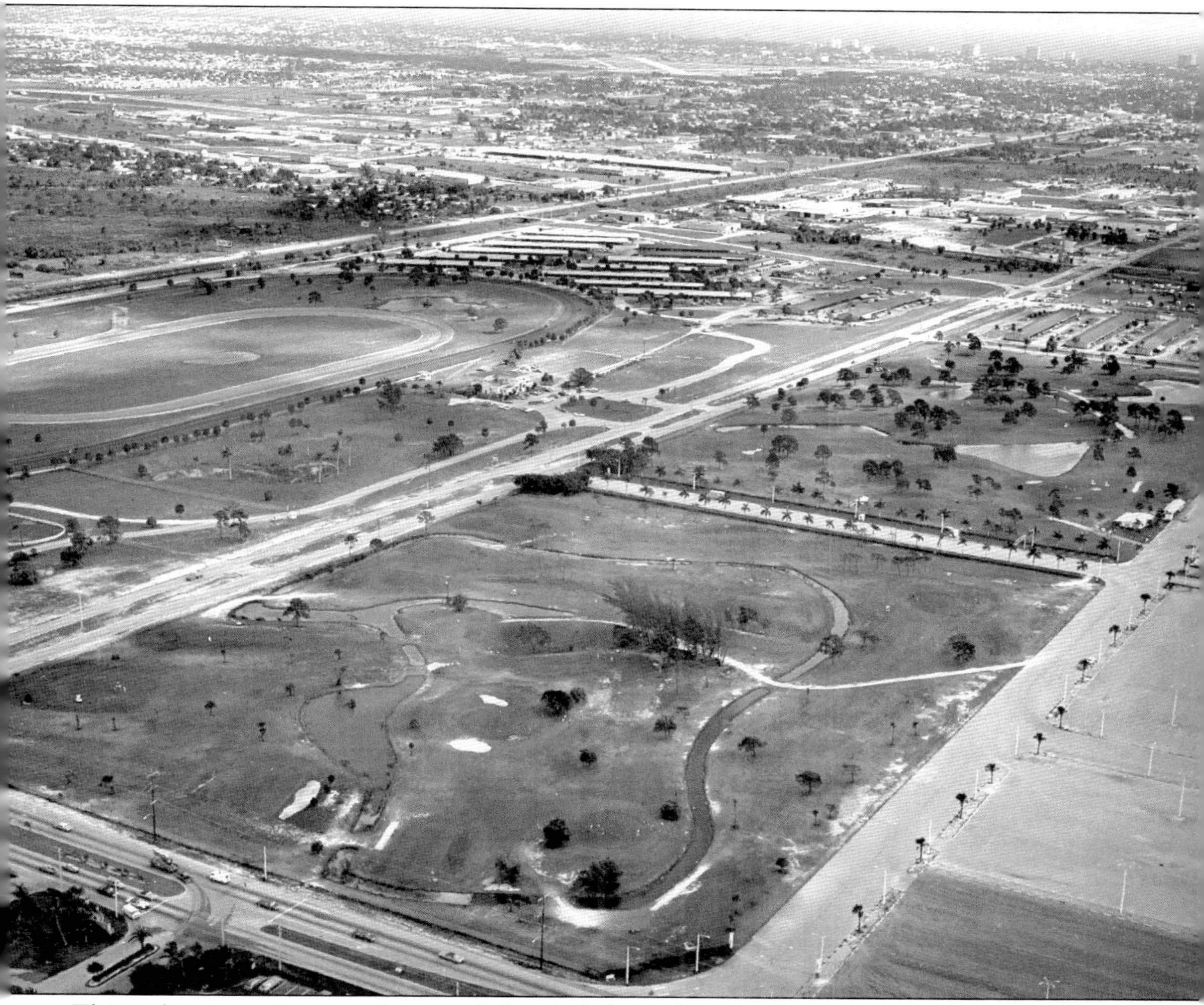

This is the new training track, upper left with Atlantic Boulevard just above it, that was built by Frederick L. van Lennep after he bought the property in 1953. The old clubhouse is in the center. In the distant center background, Pompano Beach Airfield is barely visible, and the lone long, flat building is the Farmers Market just north of Atlantic Boulevard. Racetrack Road (SW 3rd Street) is at center, running left to right.

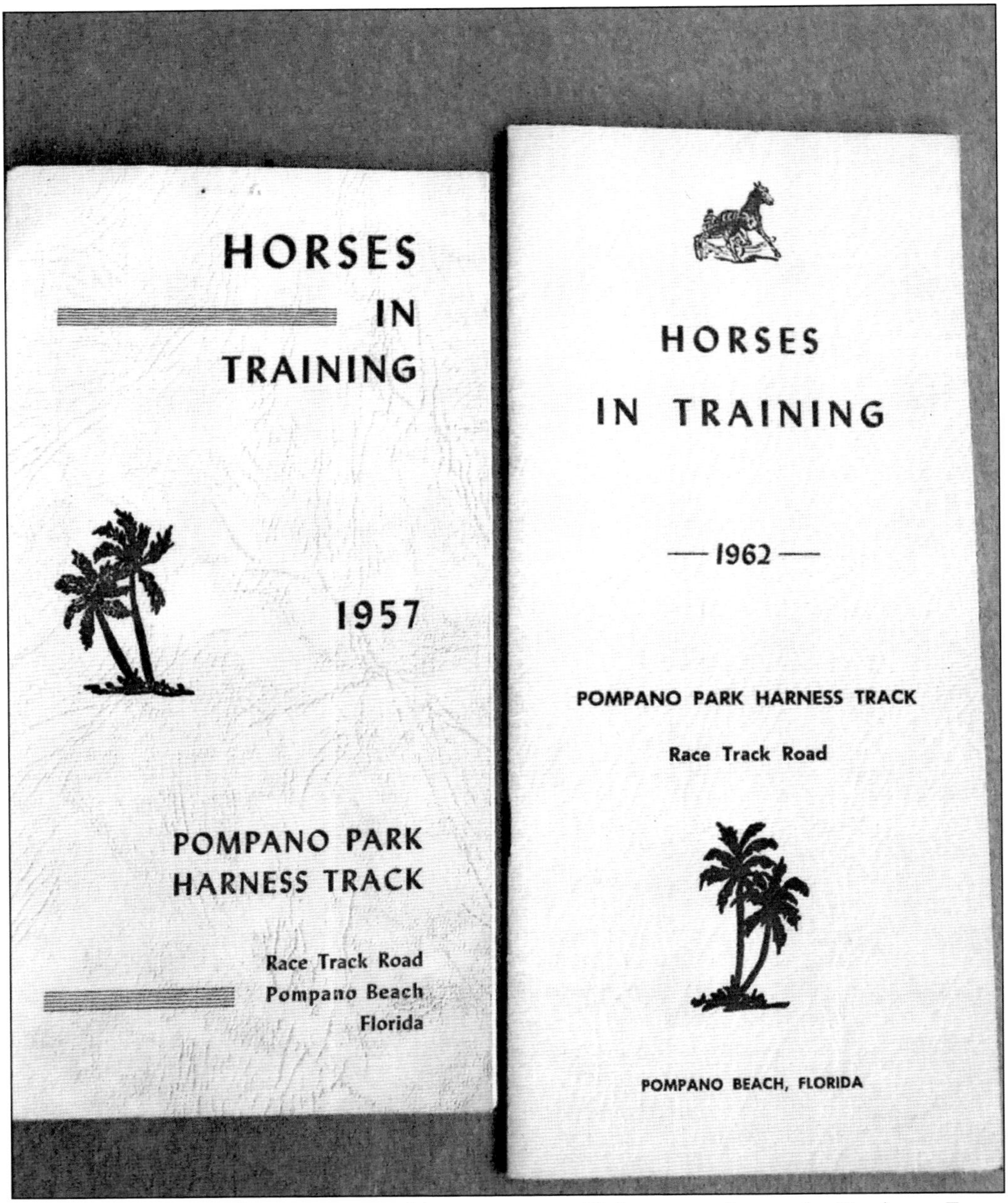

In 1957, there were four training stables containing 77 horses at the track: Castleton Farm, Frank Ervin, Arden Homestead, and W.W. Vandeveer. The training stables had increased to 14 with 137 horses in residence by the winter season of 1962. The spacious grounds and facilities were owned and maintained by the van Lenneps. These booklets listed the "Horses in Training" for those years. Horse-training viewing was open to the public from 7:00 a.m. to noon, Monday through Saturday.

Before pari-mutuel betting on Standardbred racing began in 1964, harness-horse exhibitions were held at the Pompano Park training track, as this 1955 program indicates. Frederick L. van Lennep served as master of ceremonies to explain trotting and pacing. The van Lenneps lobbied hard to prepare the state and community for harness racing.

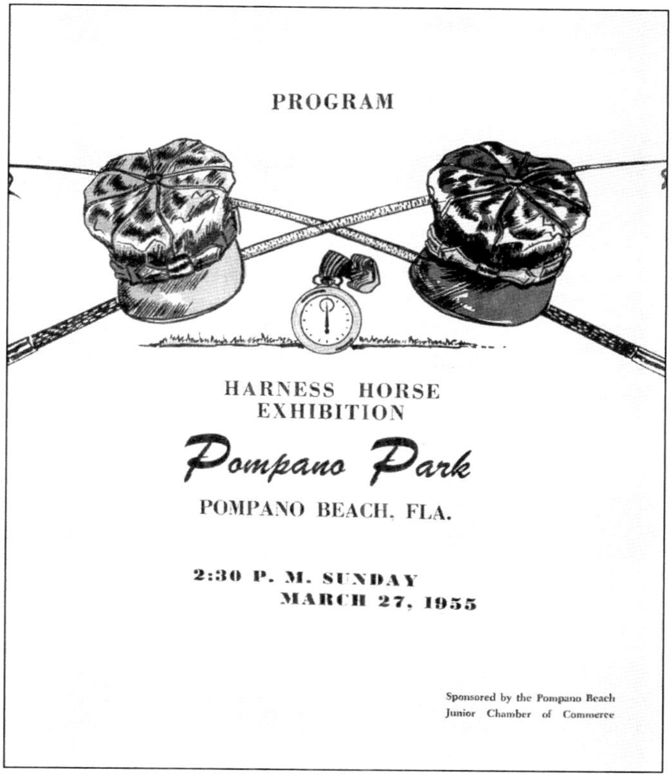
PROGRAM

HARNESS HORSE EXHIBITION

Pompano Park

POMPANO BEACH, FLA.

2:30 P. M. SUNDAY
MARCH 27, 1955

Sponsored by the Pompano Beach Junior Chamber of Commerce

Ducks play gracefully on the spacious grounds at the training track south of Atlantic Boulevard in 1960, before the permanent track was built four years later. The fenced-in training track can be seen in the background. On these grounds, the van Lenneps built a public golf course.

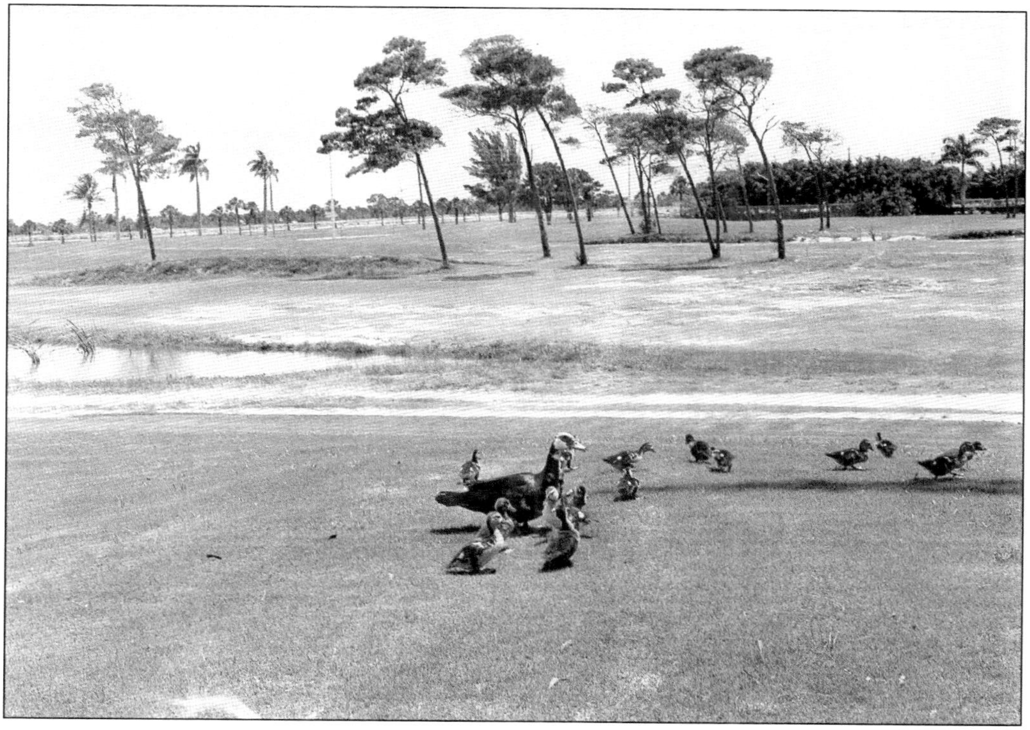

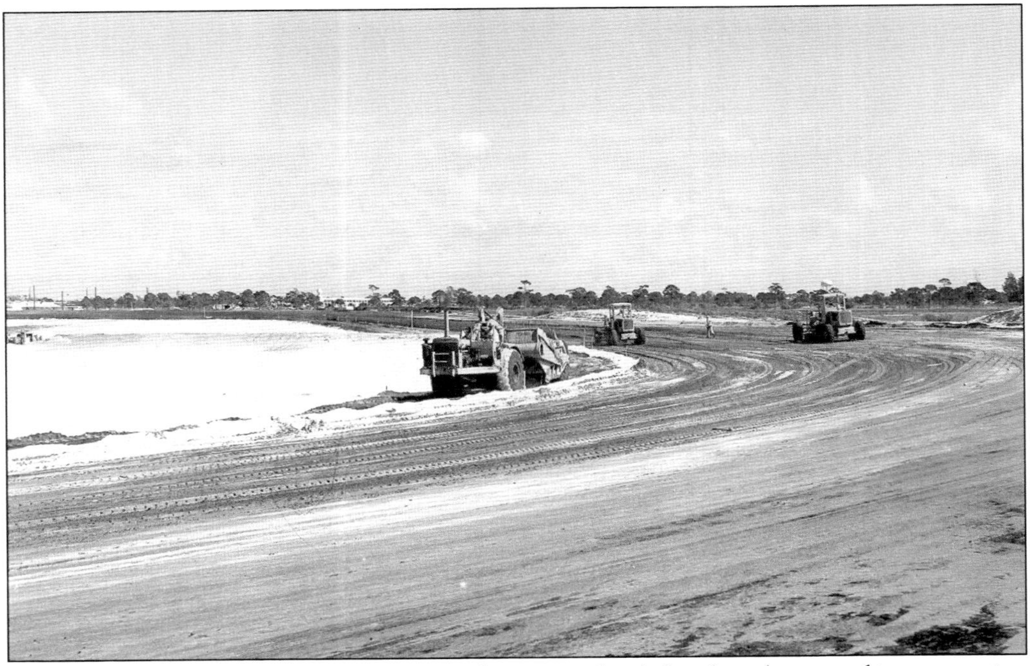
Construction has finally begun in 1963. Work crews are busily leveling the ground in preparation for surfacing the track and for building railings and fences. Note the lack of development beyond the track.

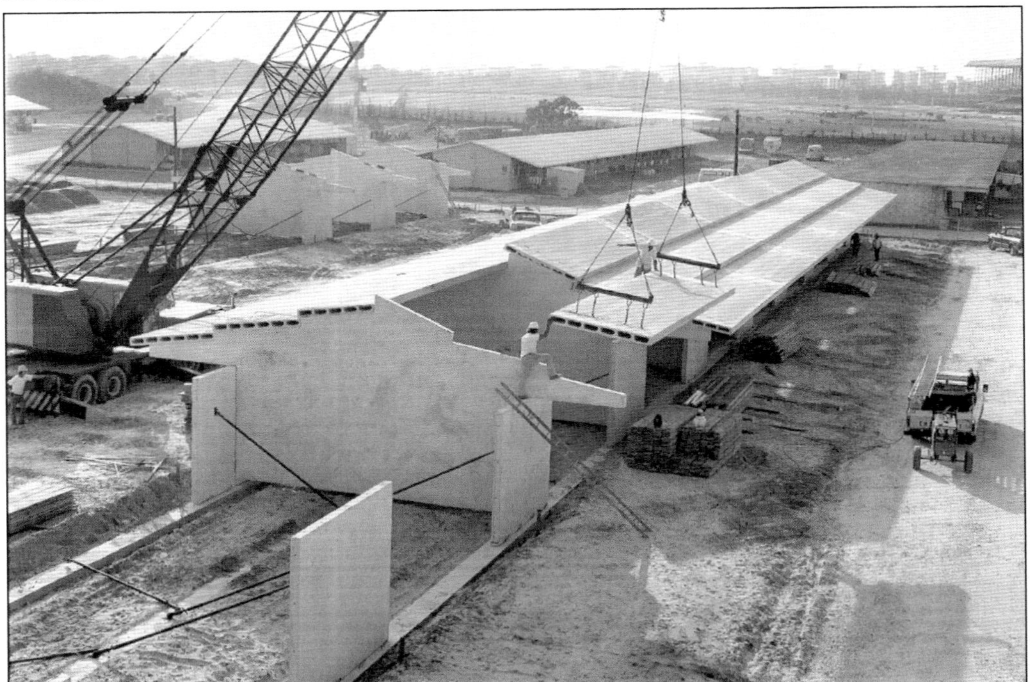
Workmen are completing the construction of the paddock area. To the far right, the grandstand facility appears to be ready for the 1964 inaugural season.

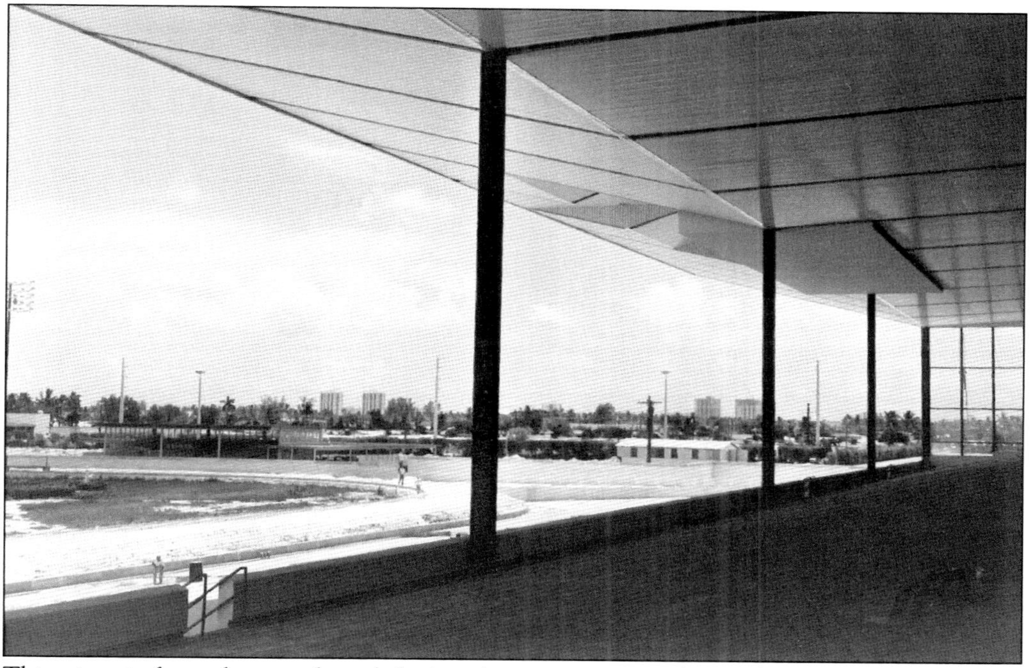

This view is from the grandstand during the construction phase of Pompano Park. In the distance to the east, at right, lies the beach, three miles away. The landscape at the time was not dotted with many high-rise condominiums.

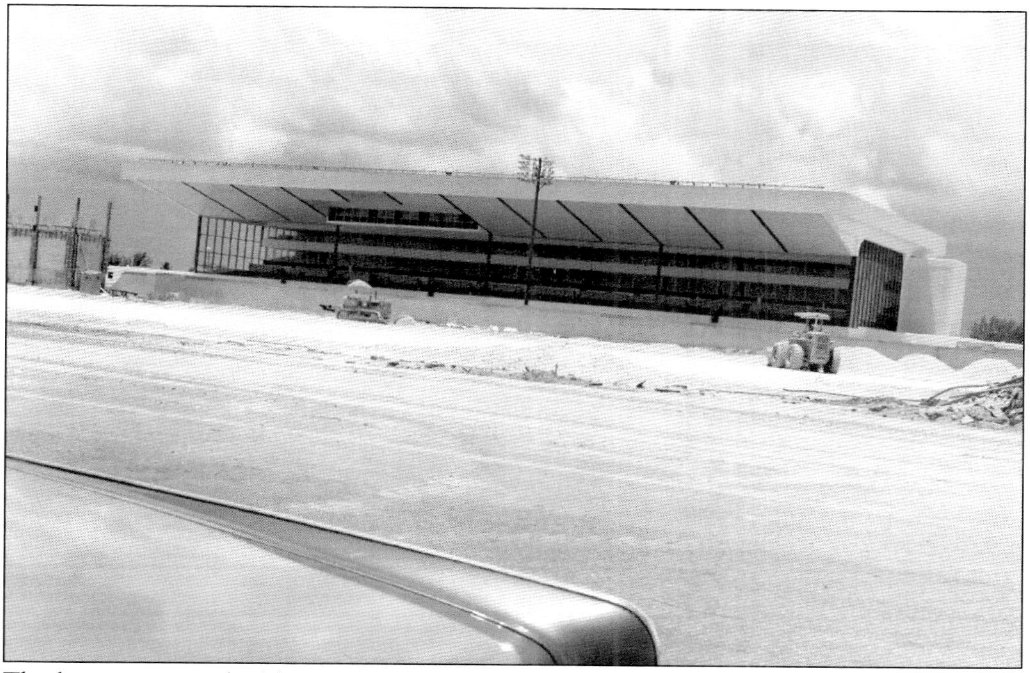

The basic structure had been completed in 1963, although the finishing touches had to be added later. Pompano Park Harness Track would become the first and only Standardbred racing facility in Florida. It would take on the title of the "Winter Capital of Harness Racing."

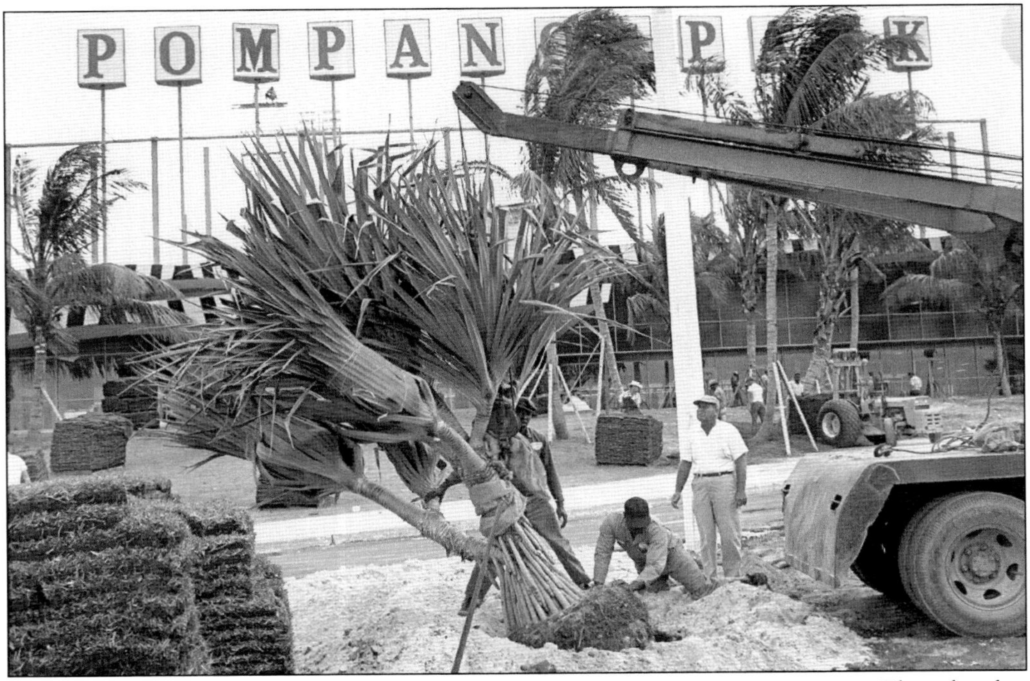

Palm trees and sod are being planted during the landscape phase of construction. Though a few items remained to be completed, opening night on February 4, 1964, was a success, with an attendance of 4,011. The first race was won by Sea Eagle, driven by Lenford Waugh, in 2:13.2.

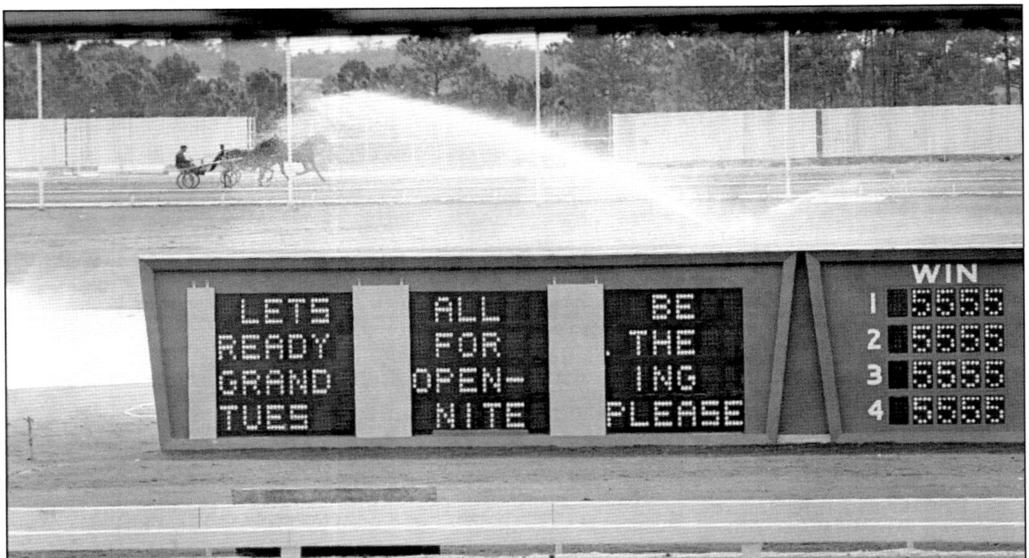

The brand-new tote board announces the grand opening of Pompano Park Harness Track. Horses and drivers are warming up in the background. There are no advertisements on the billboards. Notice the original fence and rails.

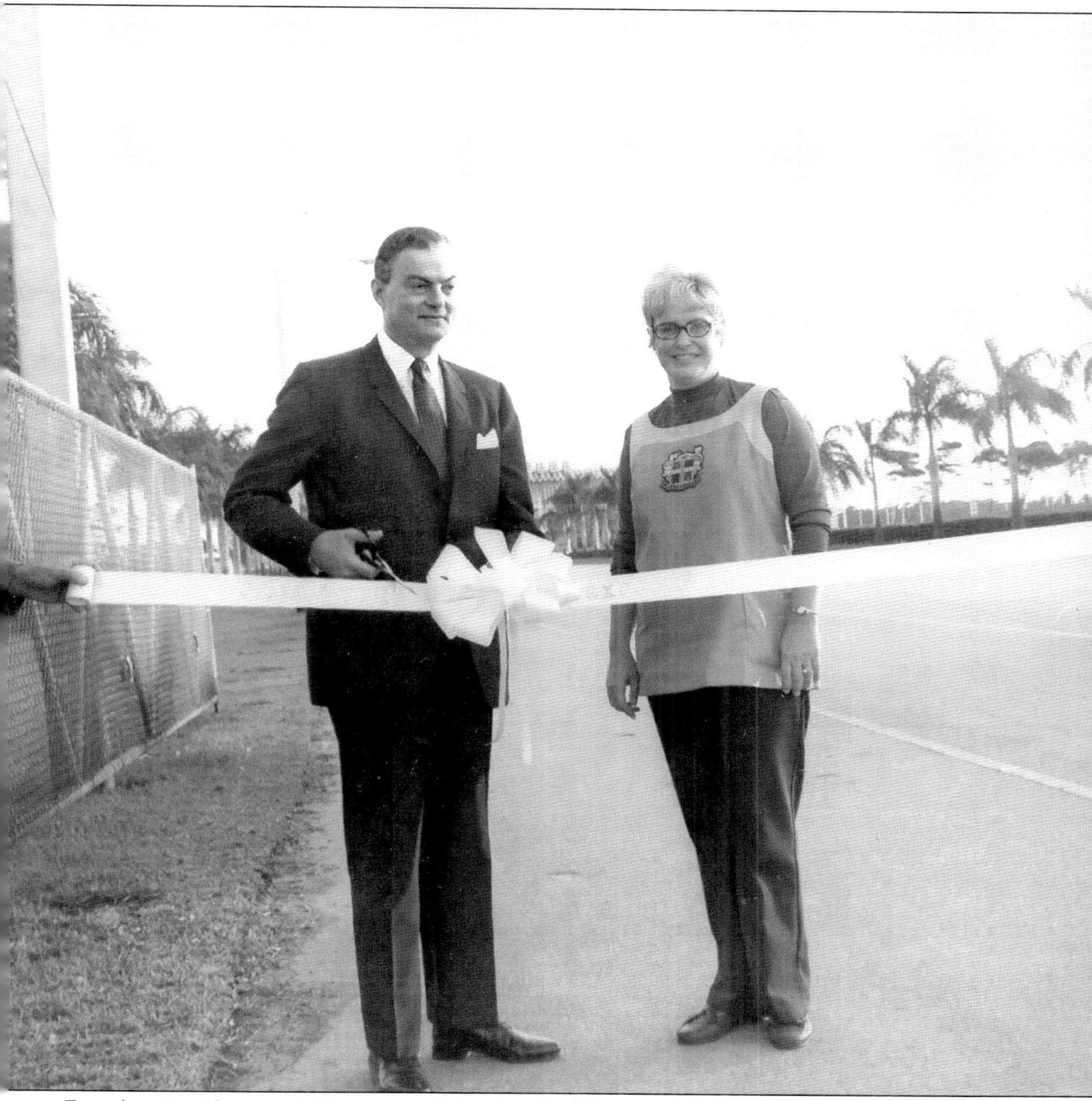

Founder, President, and Chairman of the Board of Pompano Park Frederick L. van Lennep prepares to cut the ceremonial ribbon at the main entrance on opening day, February 4, 1964. For that first season, there were eight races on weekdays and nine on Saturdays. The only wagering was Win, Place, Show, and the Daily Double. Exotic bets had not yet arrived.

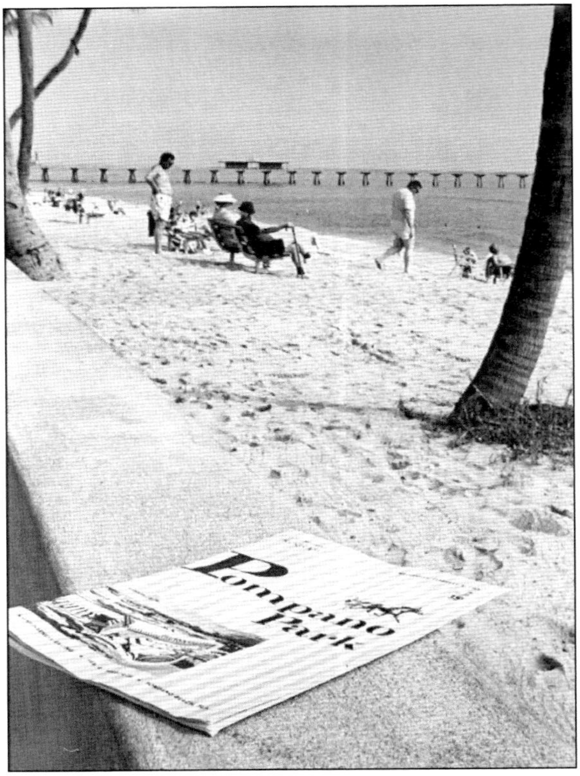

The first Pompano Park racing program rests on a barrier wall at the beach after opening day. The fishing pier is being constructed in the background. In the distance, at the extreme upper left, historic Hillsborough Lighthouse can be seen.

A group of fans at the clubhouse entrance wait for their cars to be delivered to them by valets at the close of racing on the first night. Fashion at the track was more formal in the 1960s than today, especially the mink stoles worn by the women.

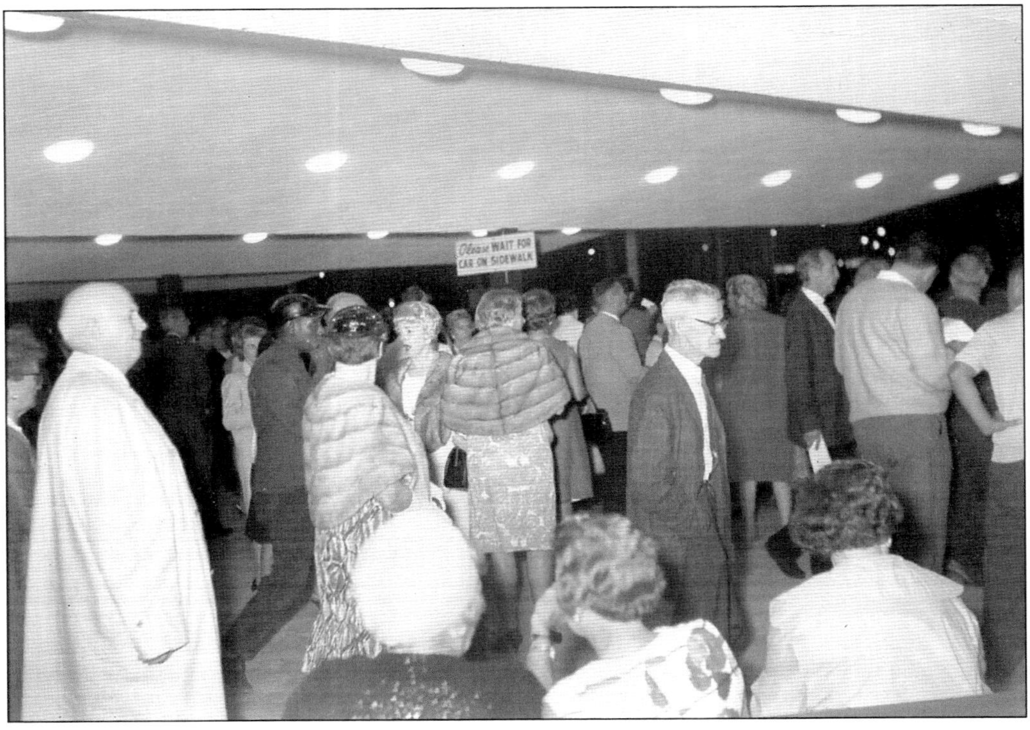

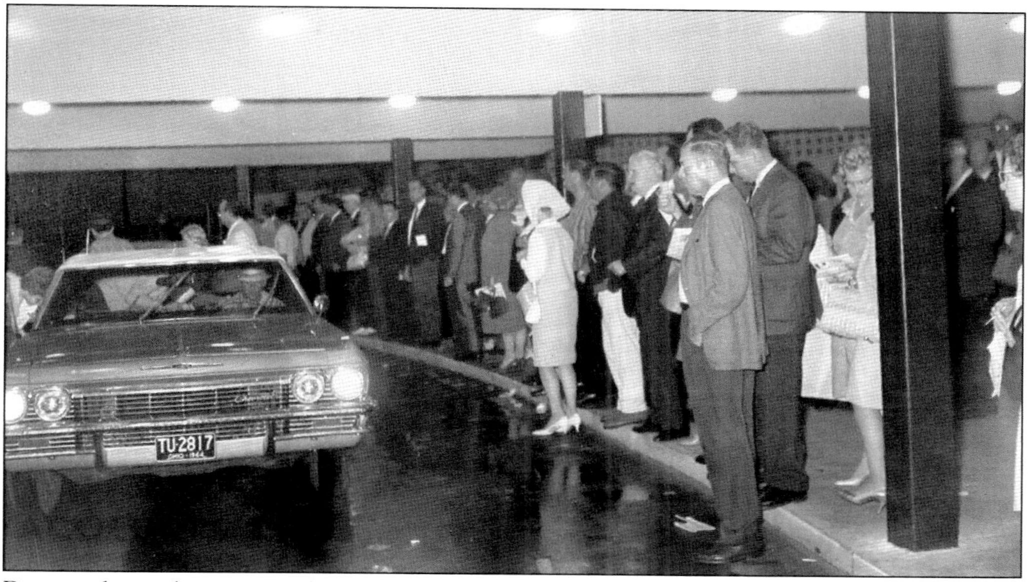

Despite the inclement weather on opening night, 4,011 people attended the historic event, some of whom are waiting for valets. John Chapman was the leading driver at the 46-night meet. The first equine darling of the fans was Music Box, a free-legged pacing daughter of Victory Song.

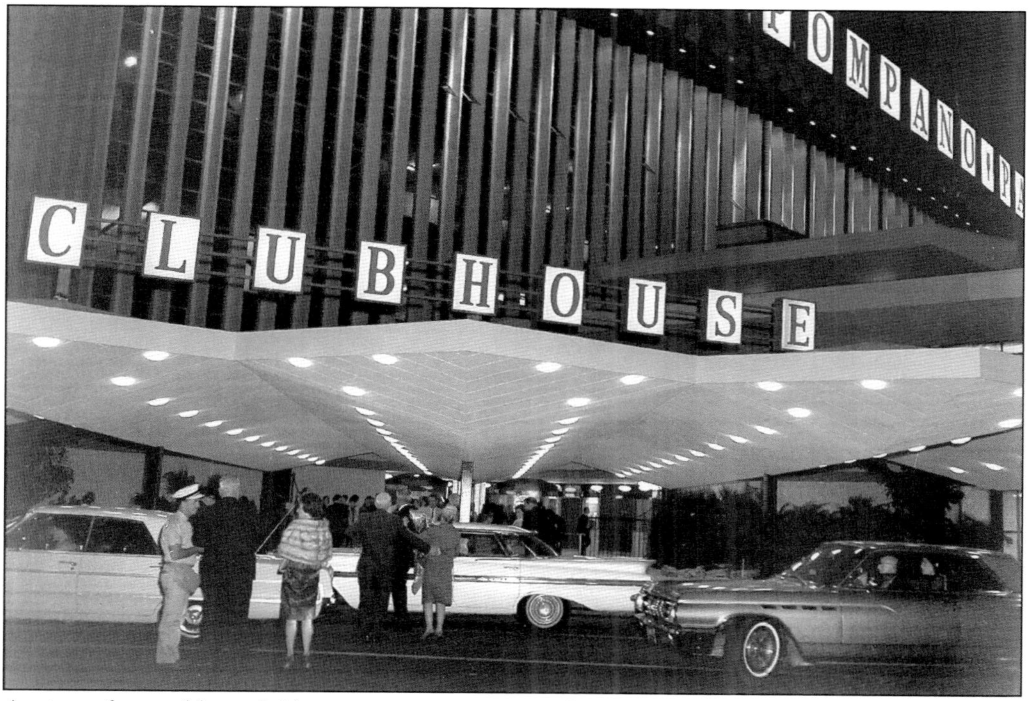

A view of a sparkling clubhouse entrance receives fans upon arriving on opening night. The second season continued in this fashion and featured an official theme song, "Up In Pompano," adapted from "Down in Florida," an original tune written by driver/trainer Roger Brown and recorded by the Sammy Spear Band from the Jackie Gleason Show.

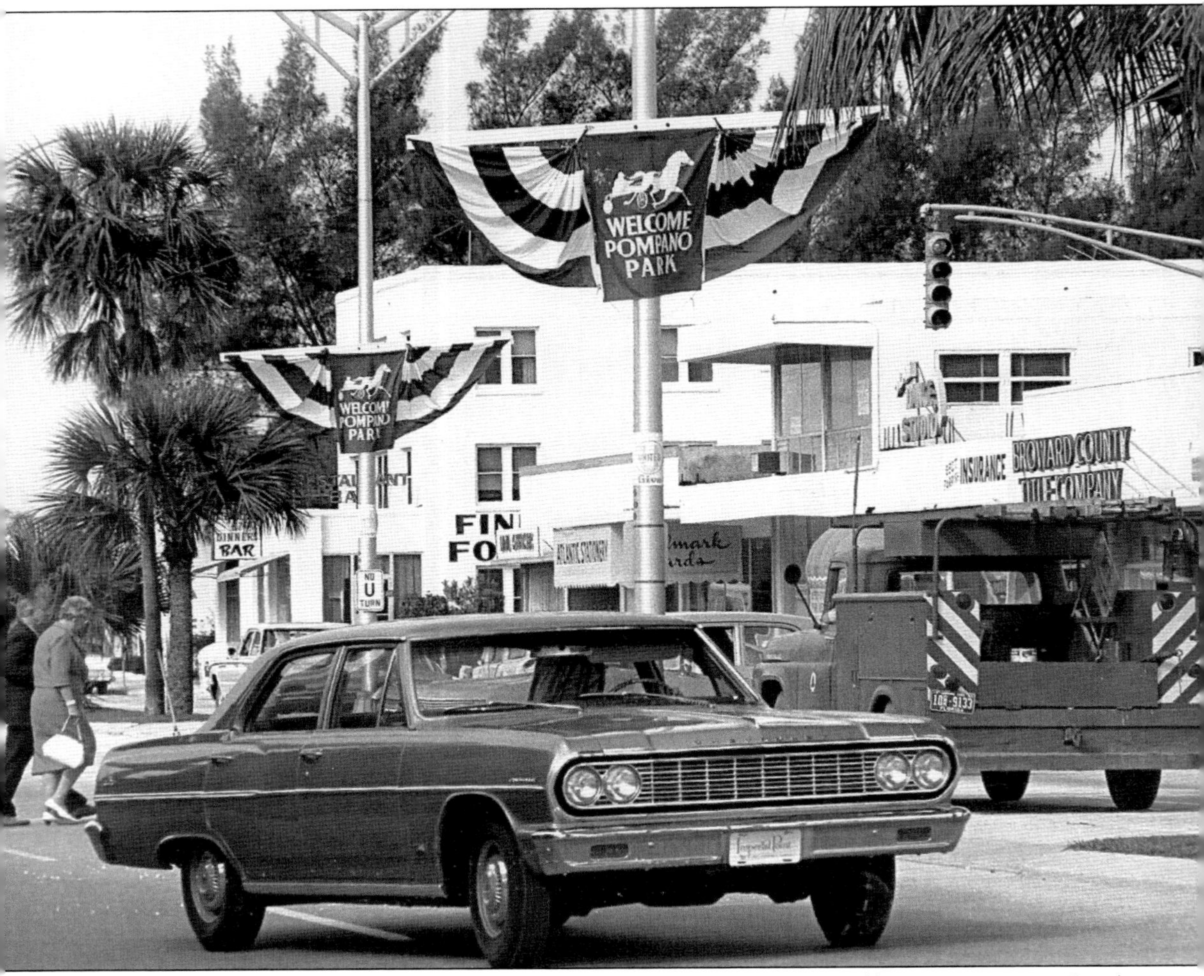

The city of Pompano Beach joined in celebrating the inauguration of harness racing in South Florida. Welcome banners are prominently placed on utility poles on the north side of Atlantic Boulevard east of U.S. Highway 1 (Federal Highway). Pompano Park, located three miles west of the beach, has contributed to the development of the region by attracting tourists during the winter season.

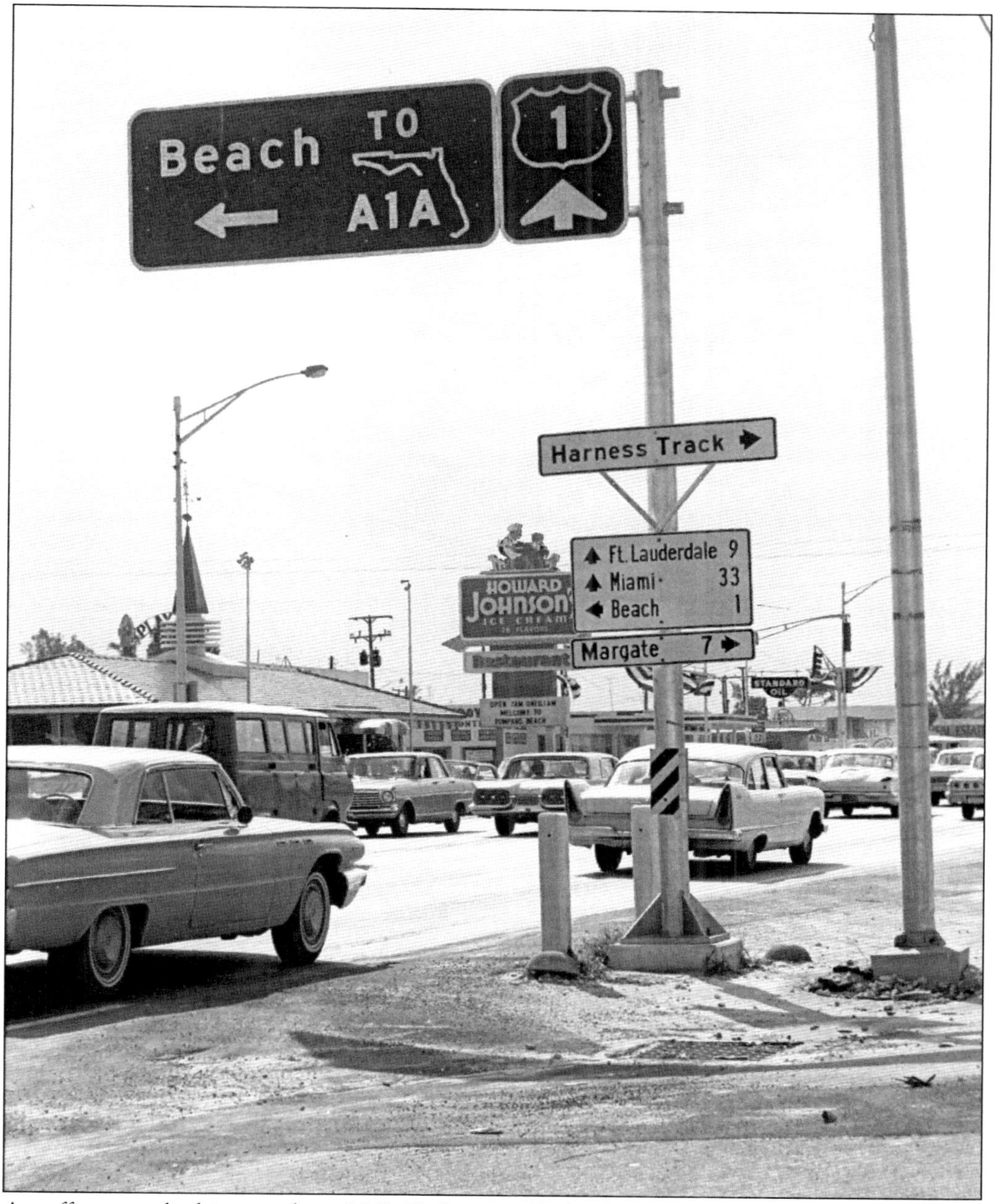

A traffic scene looking south on U.S. Highway 1 (Federal Highway) shows a sign pointing to the harness track, west via Atlantic Boulevard, and another sign pointing east to the beach, also by way of Atlantic Boulevard. The Howard Johnson restaurant at this intersection has been replaced by Waldenbooks. Note the barely-visible price of gasoline below the Standard Oil sign at right near the welcome banner.

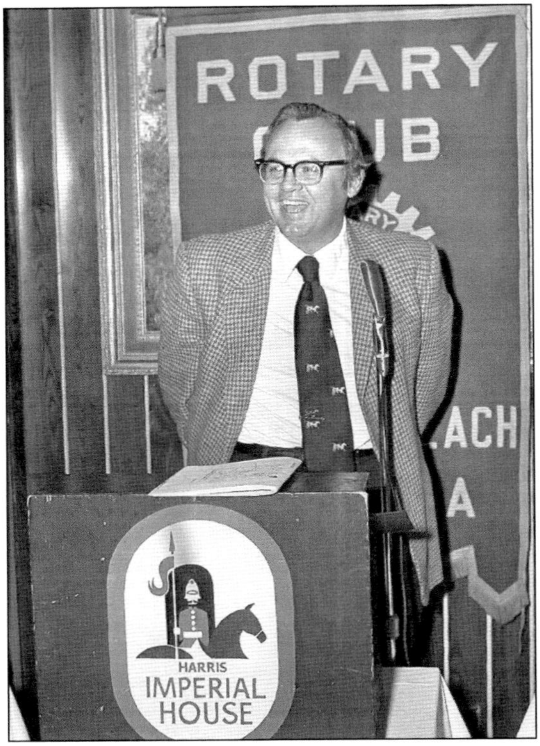

Hector van Lennep, eldest son of Frederick L. van Lennep, addresses one of the weekly meetings of the Rotary Club at the old Harris Imperial House in Pompano Beach in 1975. His topic was the early history of harness racing in South Florida. He served as vice president and general manager in the 1970s and early 1980s.

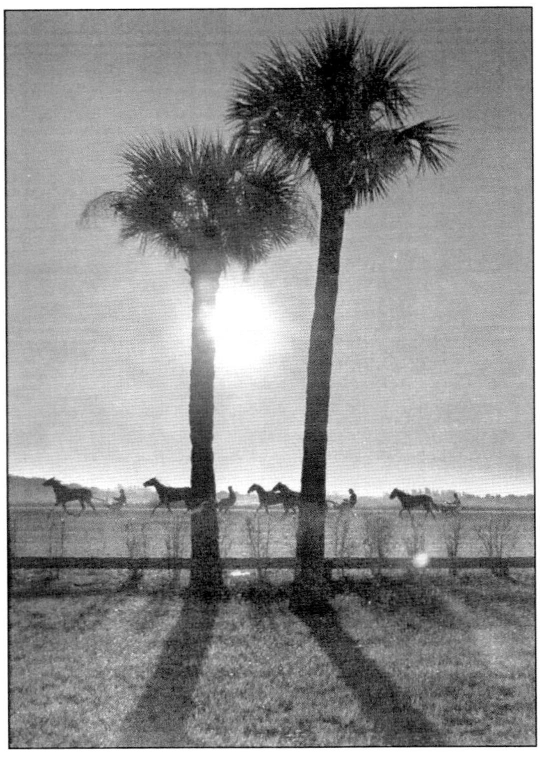

This postcard captures drivers and horses during a training session at the "Winter Capital of Harness Racing" in Florida, where the most prestigious racing events take place. The sport developed in the 19th century to become America's first national pastime; it is now enjoyed by millions throughout the world.

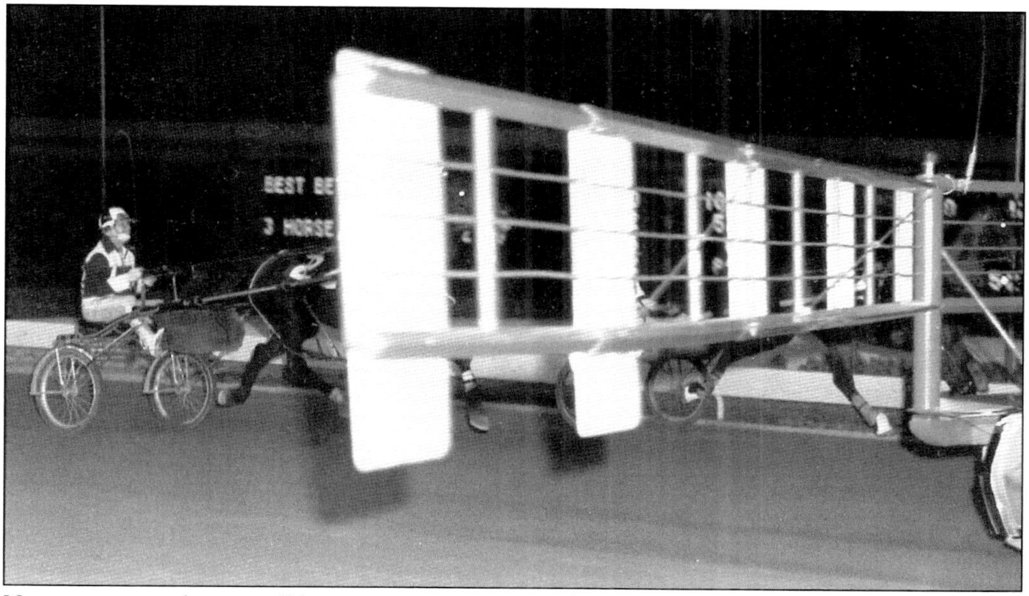

Horses can race, but not all horses can trot or pace. This makes harness racing unique. The start also differs from Thoroughbred racing because in Standardbred racing it is a moving start. A gate, above, is attached to a car that takes all the horses to the start. When the gate is opened the race begins.

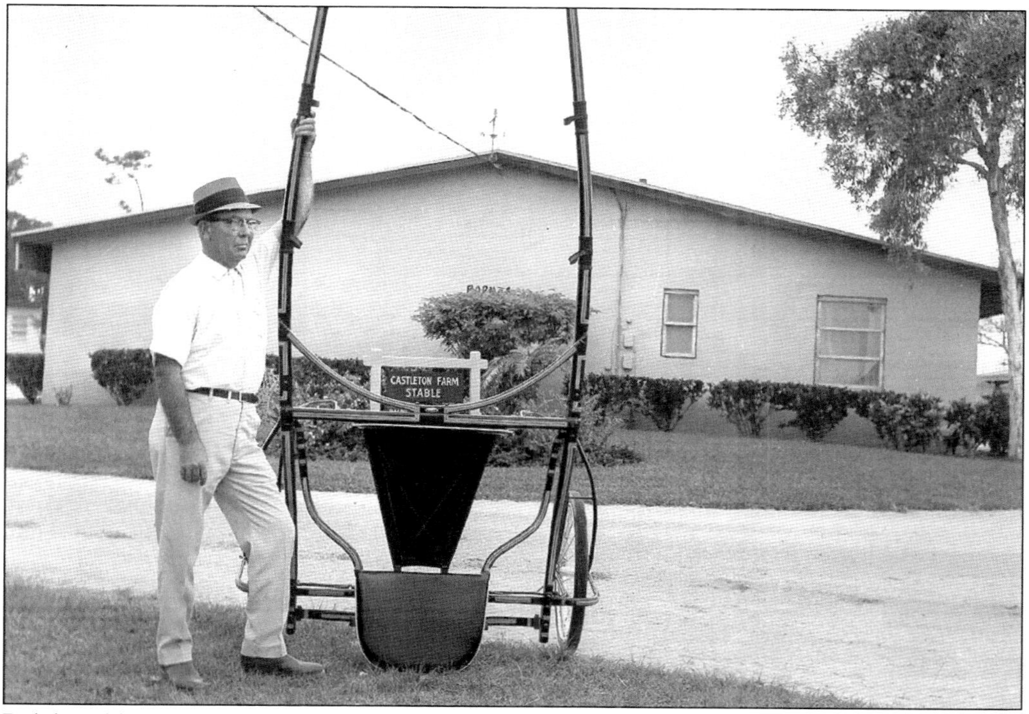

Ralph Baldwin, who trained Castleton Farm horses at Pompano Park, stands next to a jog cart that is used for training horses; it is heavier than a sulky. The sulky is a driver's cart or "bike" used in harness races.

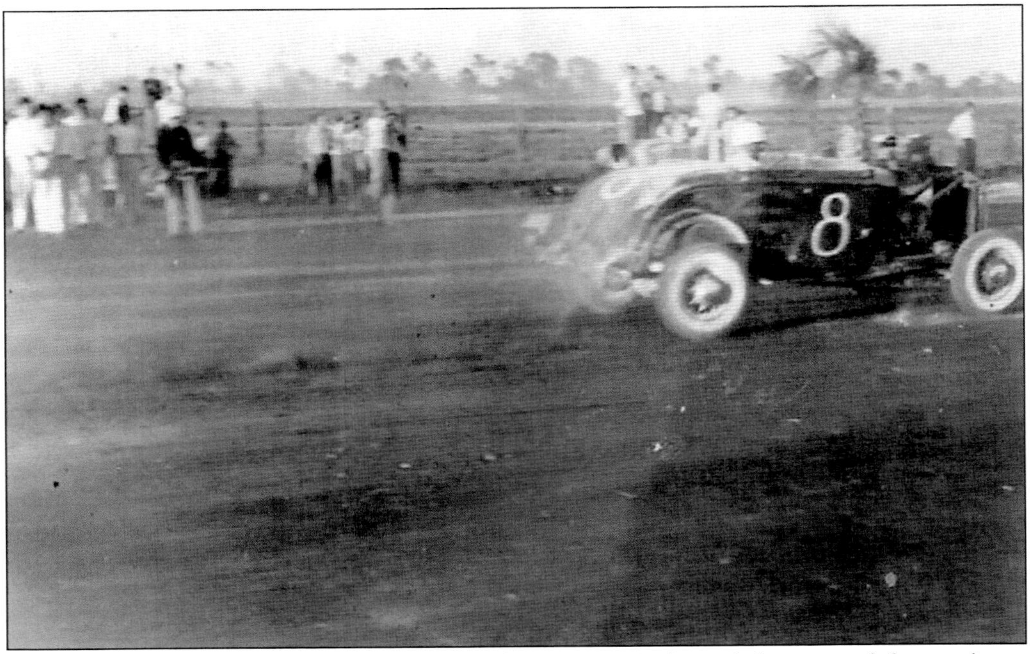

This rare surviving image shows the original Pompano Park track being used for stock car racing in 1947. Though popular in the late 1940s, and very popular today, automobile racing eventually yielded to harness racing in Pompano Beach. (Courtesy of Bud Garner.)

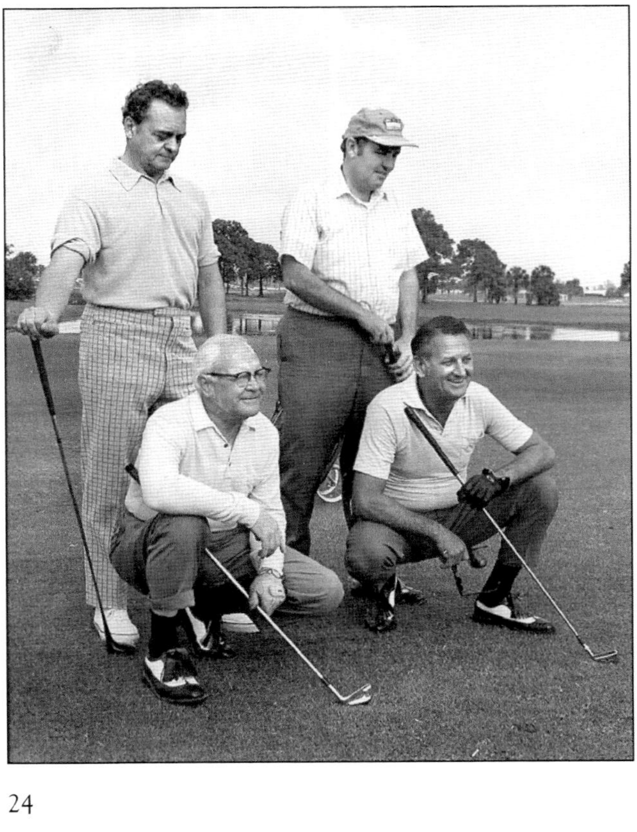

These four golfers are enjoying the day on the course at Pompano Park in 1970. The course was located on both sides of the main entrance and north of the racetrack. It was the only golf course at a racetrack in the country. It does not exist today.

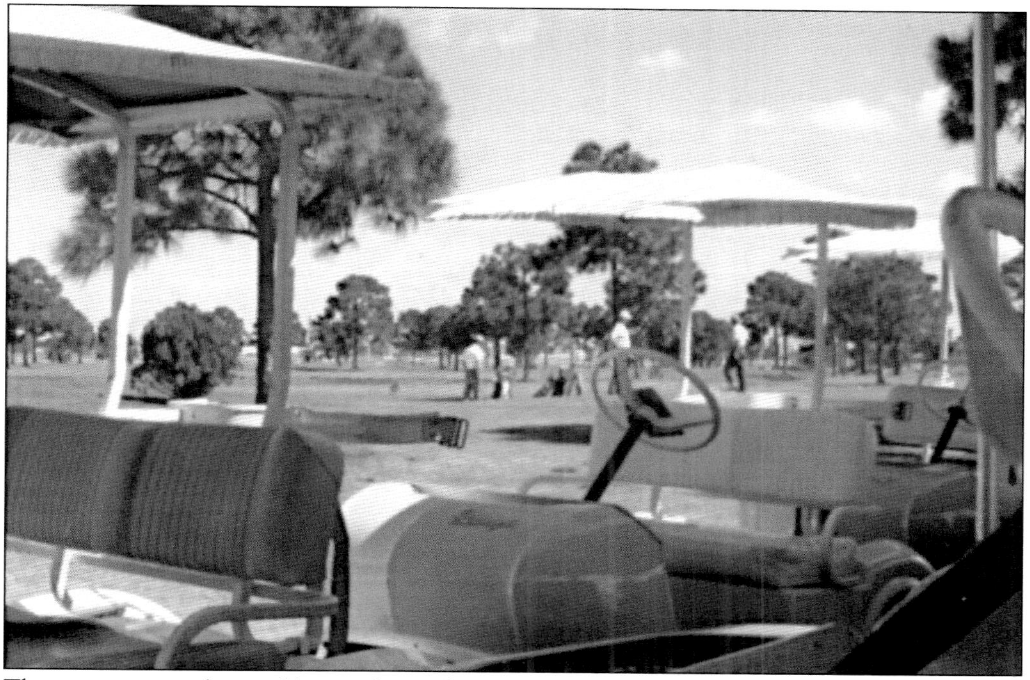

These rare scenes show golfers at play at the 18-hole, par-60 golf course measuring almost 3,000 yards. The van Lenneps built the golf course, which was open to the public. Ray Daly was the attending golf pro. Golfers could play a round of golf and then go to the track to wager on harness racing. This land is still a part of the original property, but today it is covered over with trees and shrubs.

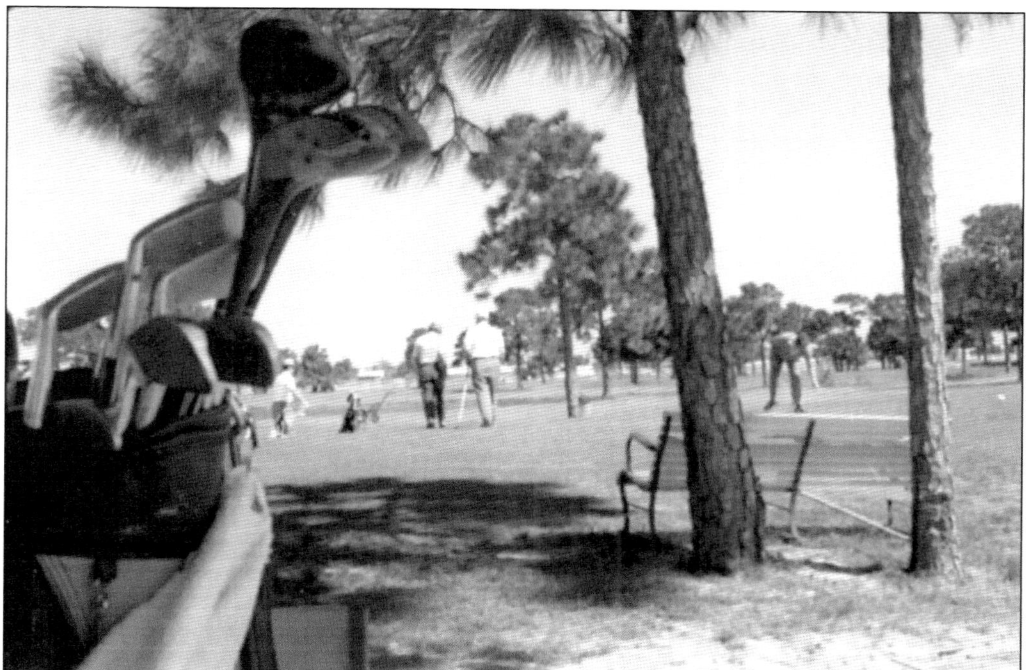

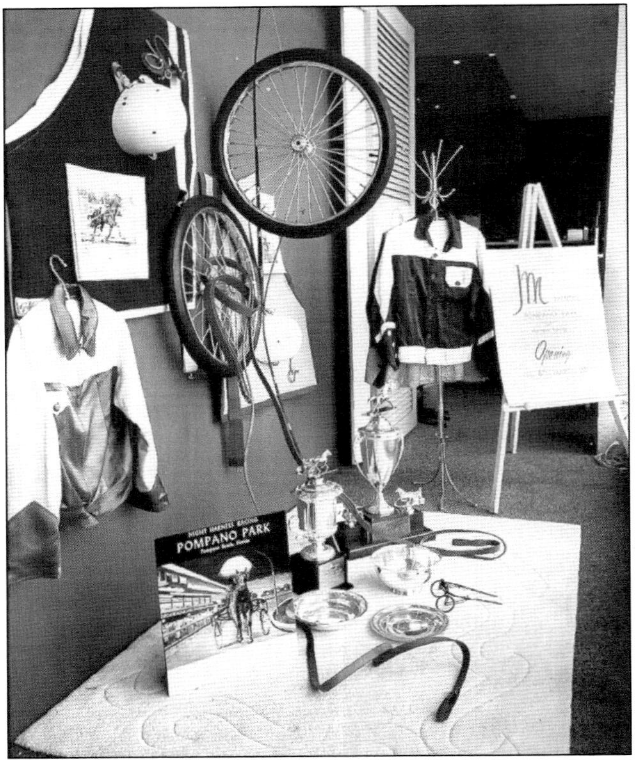

The Jordan Marsh Department Store of Miami participated in the 1964 inaugural ceremonies of Pompano Park with this display of harness racing equipment, riding colors, and trophies. There were actually two openings: one on February 4 and the second one on February 6, as indicated on the sign at the right.

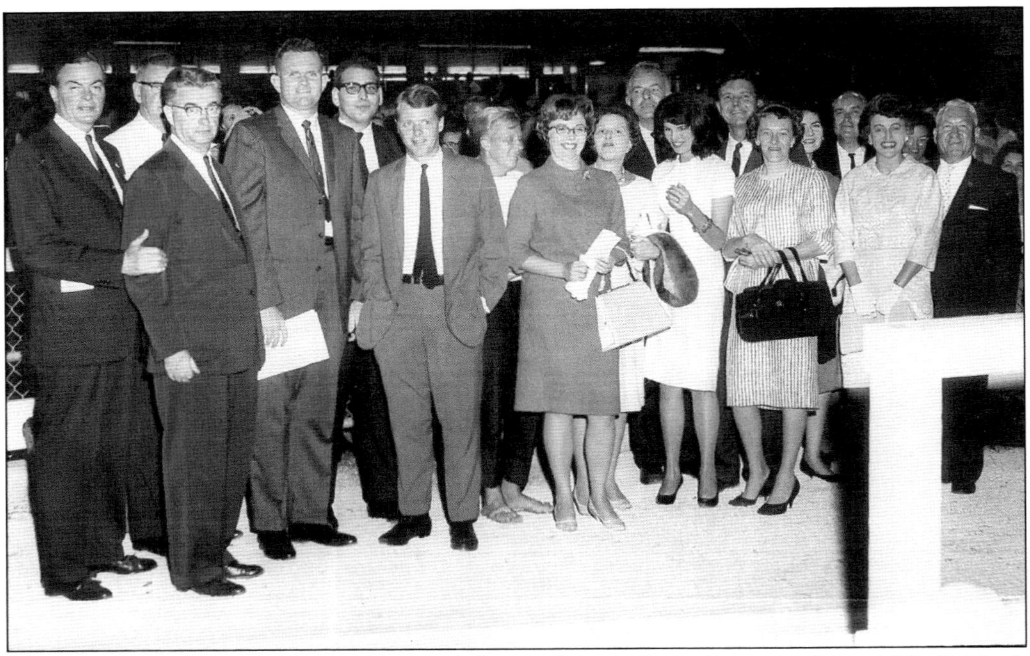

During the first season of racing, Frederick L. van Lennep hosted many influential individuals and groups to promote harness racing in Florida. Van Lennep, at left, posed with a smiling group of South Florida sports editors and extended his gratitude for their support.

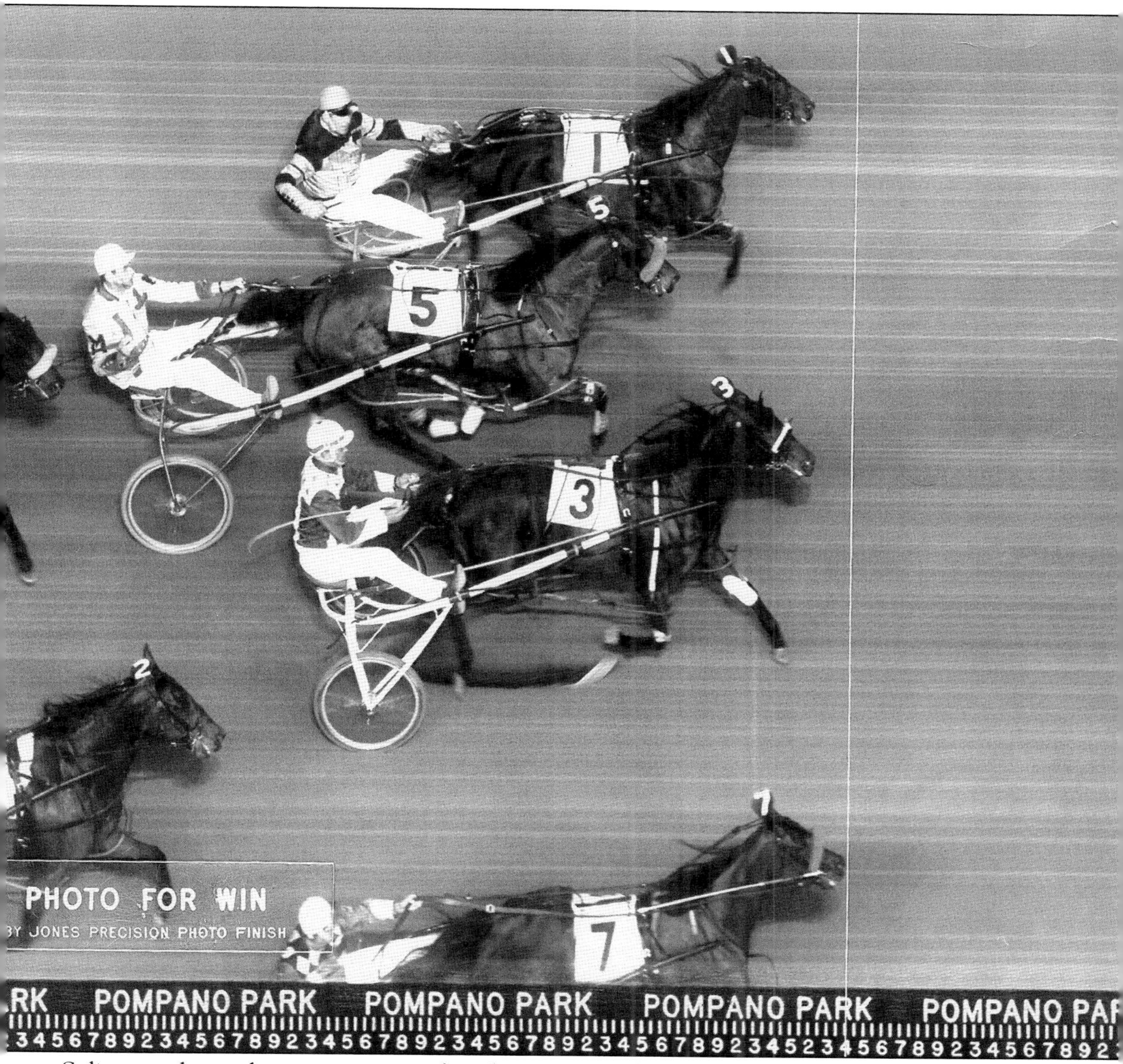

Split seconds can determine winners from losers in Standardbred racing, making it a challenge to the fan attempting to handicap races. In this exciting sixth race at Pompano Park on February 22, 1969, Armbro Irma (7), driven by Billy Haughton, at bottom, is victorious by a nose. Rusty Coast (3), driven by Walter Welch, finished second, while Chautauqua (1), driven by Bob Saul, finished third. This official photo-for-win demonstrates how close the race was.

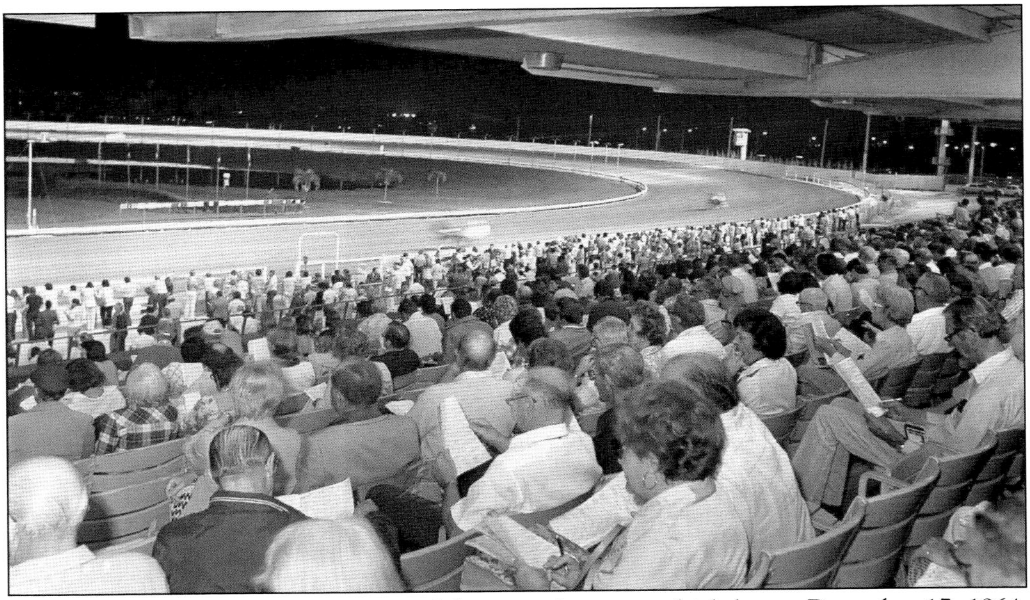

A large crowd attended the opening of the second season, which began December 17, 1964, and ran through April 6, 1965. These seats are not yet enclosed with glass. The creation of the Secretary's Series by Bill Conners was an important development. The meet's trotting division was dominated by Acs Nancy, a daughter of Hoot Mon, who left Pompano Park with a perfect 9-for-9 record in 1965 for Billy Haughton.

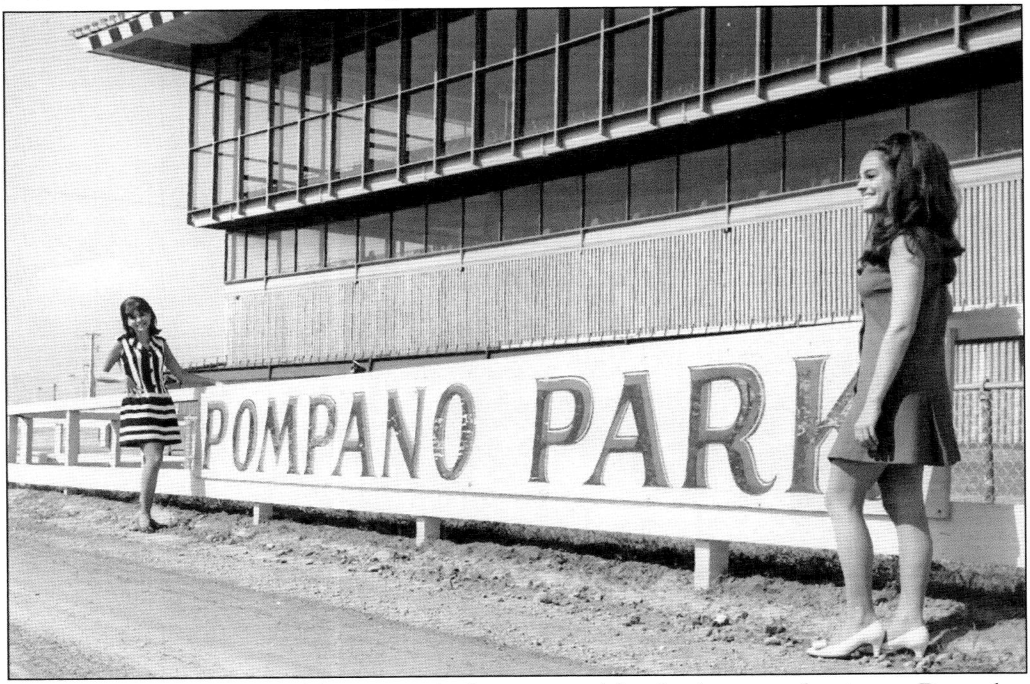

Two models pose in front of the sign at the beginning of the third season of racing on December 15, 1965. The season continued for 92 nights. The fourth-floor box seats were enclosed in plate glass so they could be cooled or heated as the weather required.

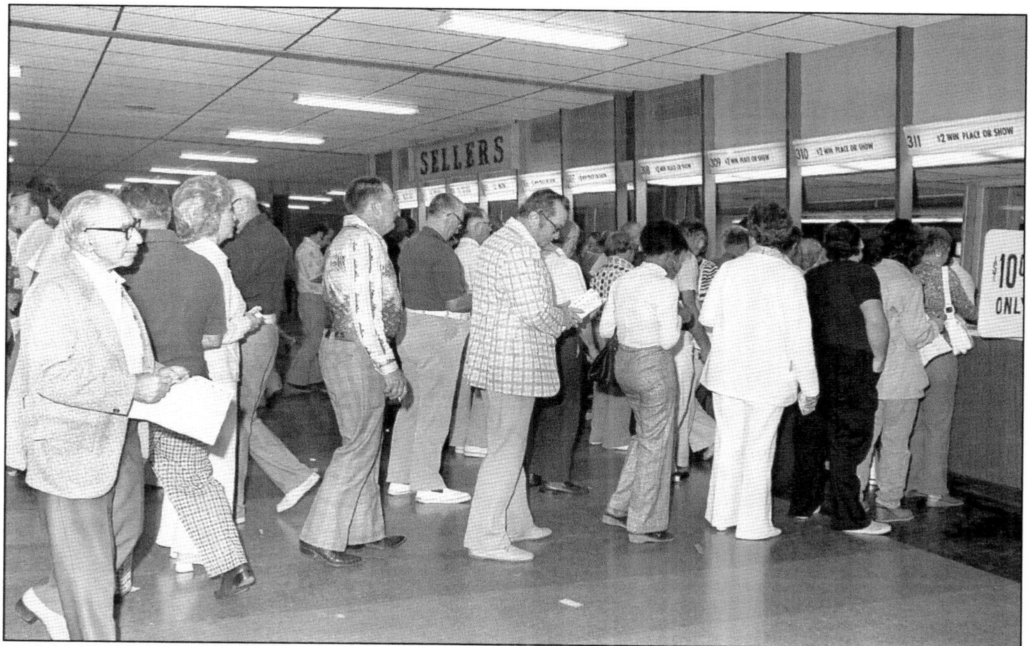

The lines were long to place a bet during the first season, which ran from February 4 through March 28, 1964. The Twin Double was instituted on March 21, and the largest payoff for the new wager was $11,669.80 just five nights later.

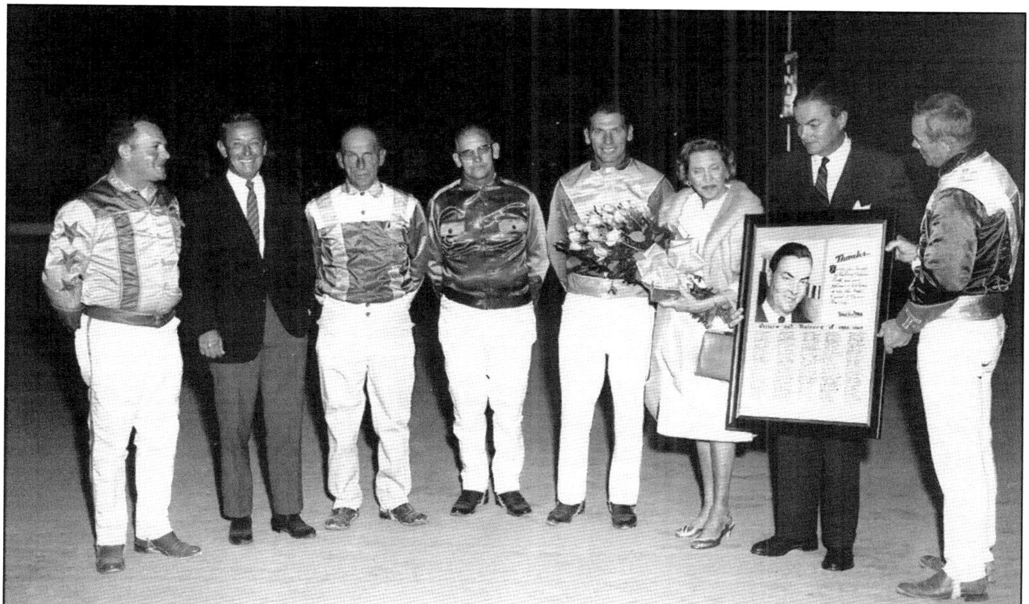

Trainers and drivers present an award to Pompano Park Harness Track Founder Frederick L. van Lennep (second from right) for his many contributions to the sport. Mrs. Frances Dodge van Lennep enjoys the event as she holds a bouquet of roses. The drivers and trainers from 1966 to 1969 signed the award containing van Lennep's picture. Second from left is Billy Haughton. At far right is Ted Taylor.

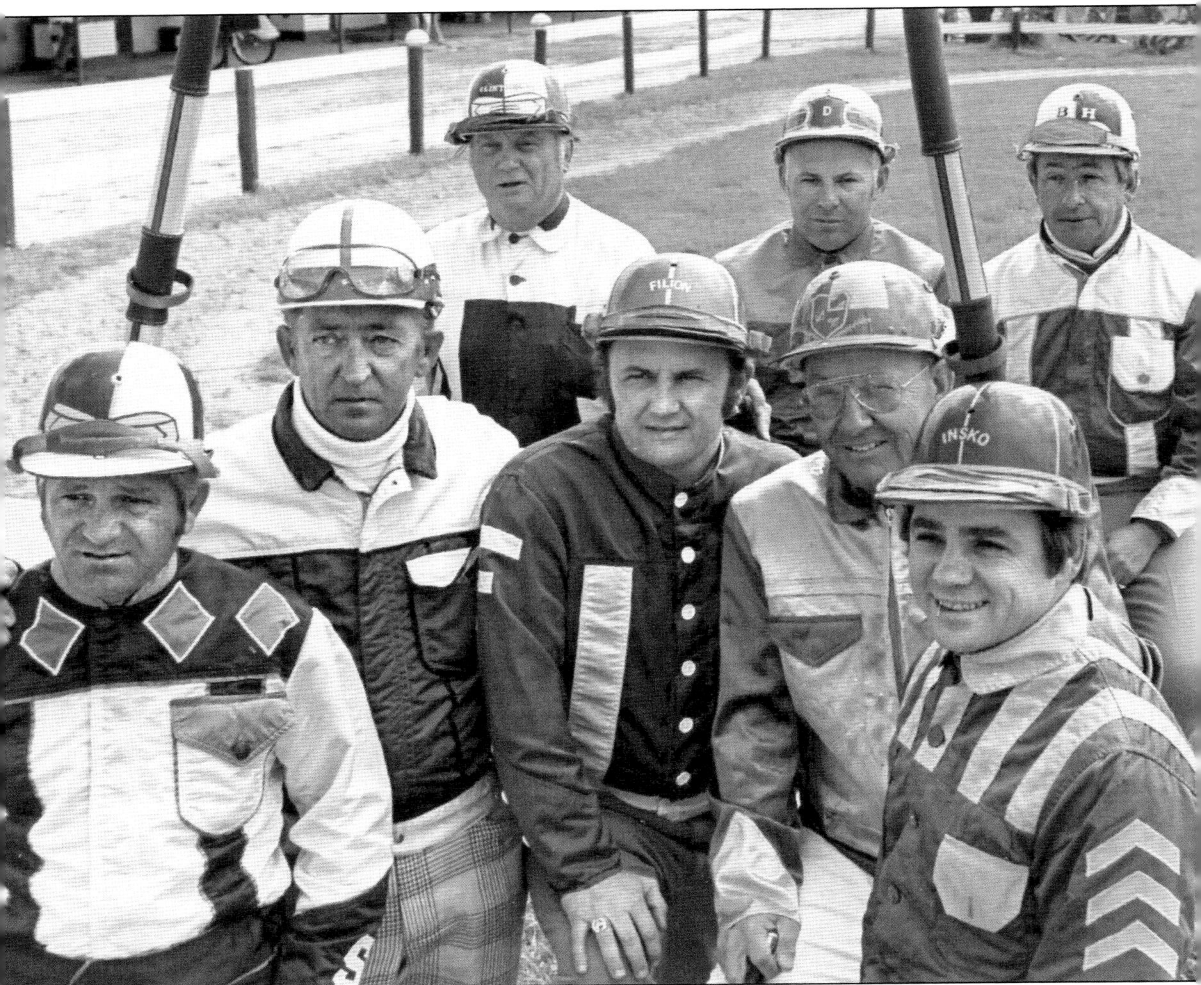

These veteran champion drivers helped to make harness racing a huge success in the early years in Florida. From left to right are (front row) George Sholty and Del Insko; (middle row) John Chapman, Herve Filion, and Del Miller; (back row) Clint Hodgins, Stanley Dancer, and Billy Haughton.

Two

GROWING

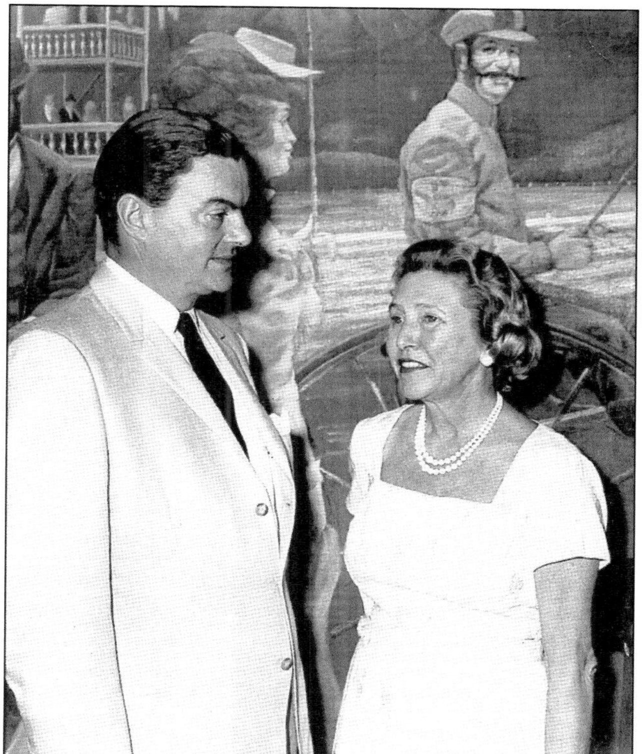

Frederick L. van Lennep and his wife, Francis Dodge van Lennep, enjoy a moment of relaxation. They wintered in South Florida while they trained and raced their horses at their own Pompano Park. They added an 18-hole golf course, a horse clinic, and an equine swimming pool, and established an entire program of Florida Standardbred breeding.

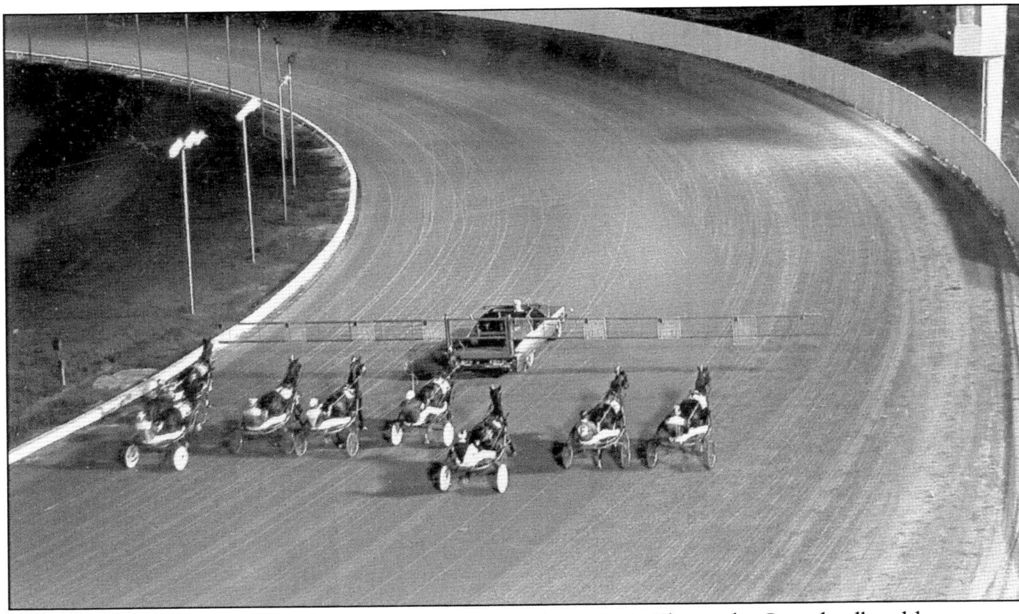

This is a familiar scene of a harness race, on April 4, 1975. The eight Standardbred horses and drivers line up behind the moving gate driven by an automobile, which will open the gate at the start. A Standardbred is a breed of horse developed for trotting and pacing competition in harness racing.

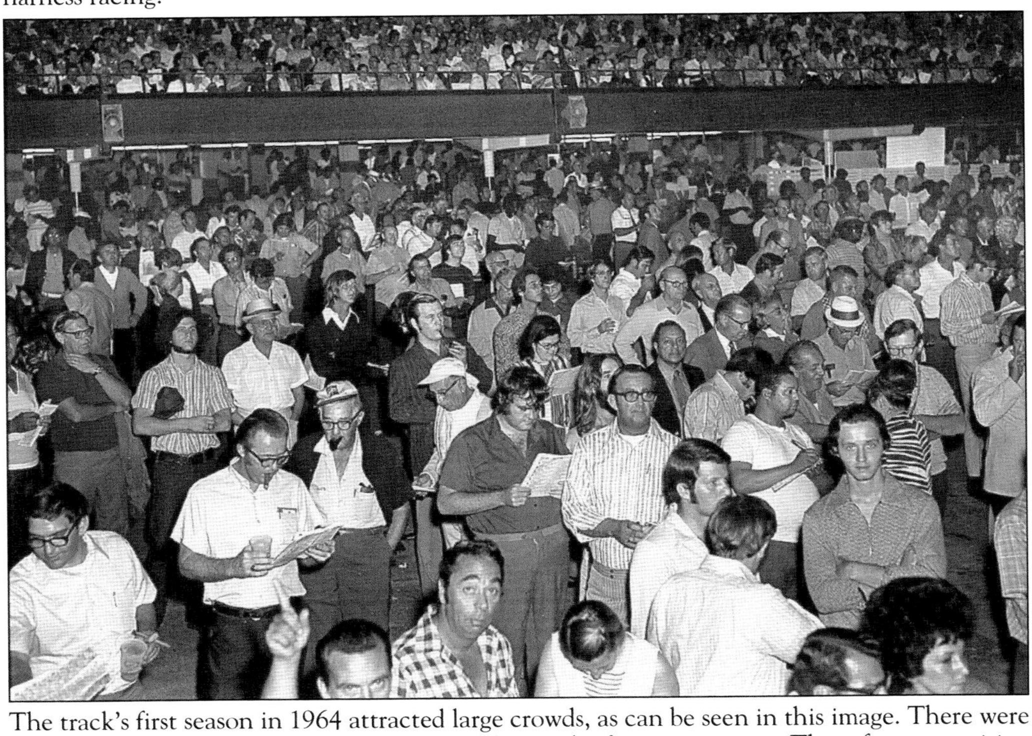

The track's first season in 1964 attracted large crowds, as can be seen in this image. There were no glass panels on the fourth-floor box seats during the first two seasons. These fans are waiting for the start of a race.

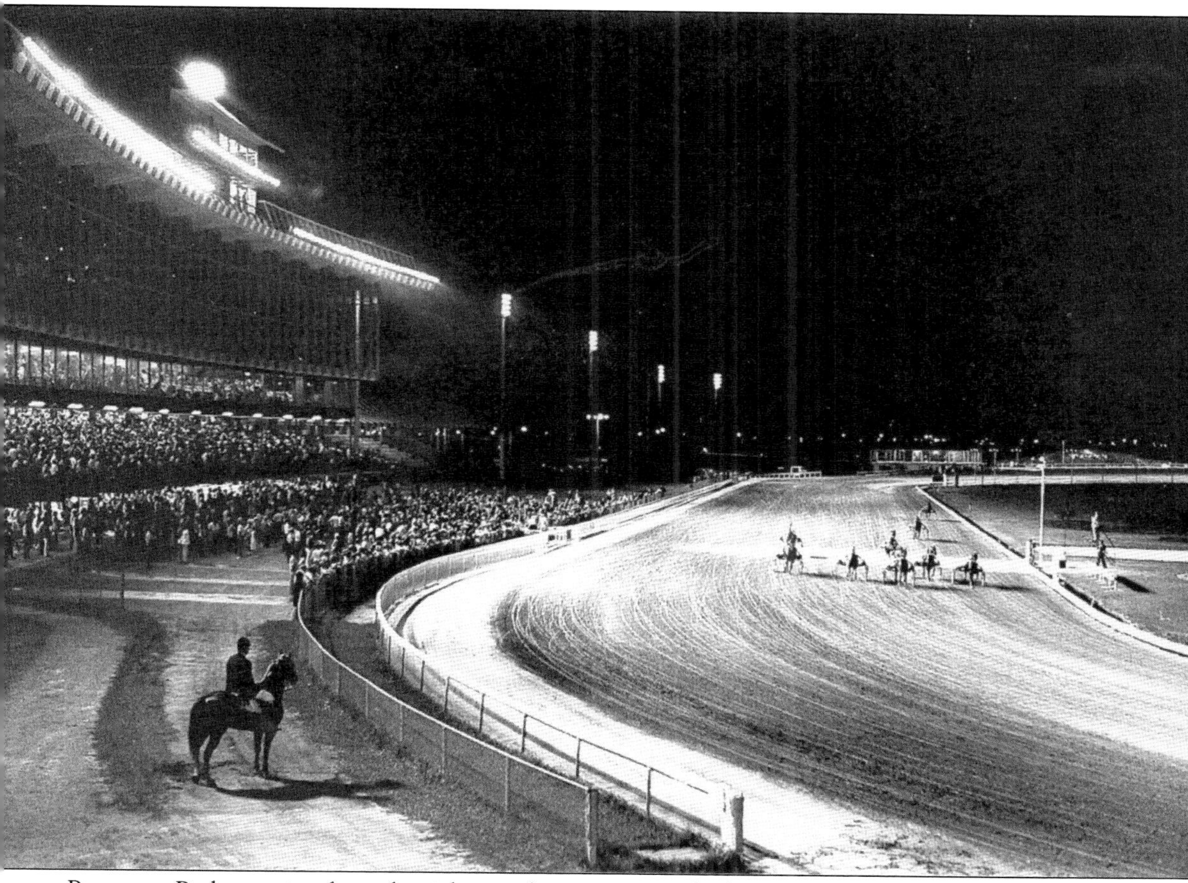

Pompano Park remains the only nighttime harness racing facility in Florida. This image records another close finish in front of a large crowd. Harness horses are more consistent and more durable than other racehorses.

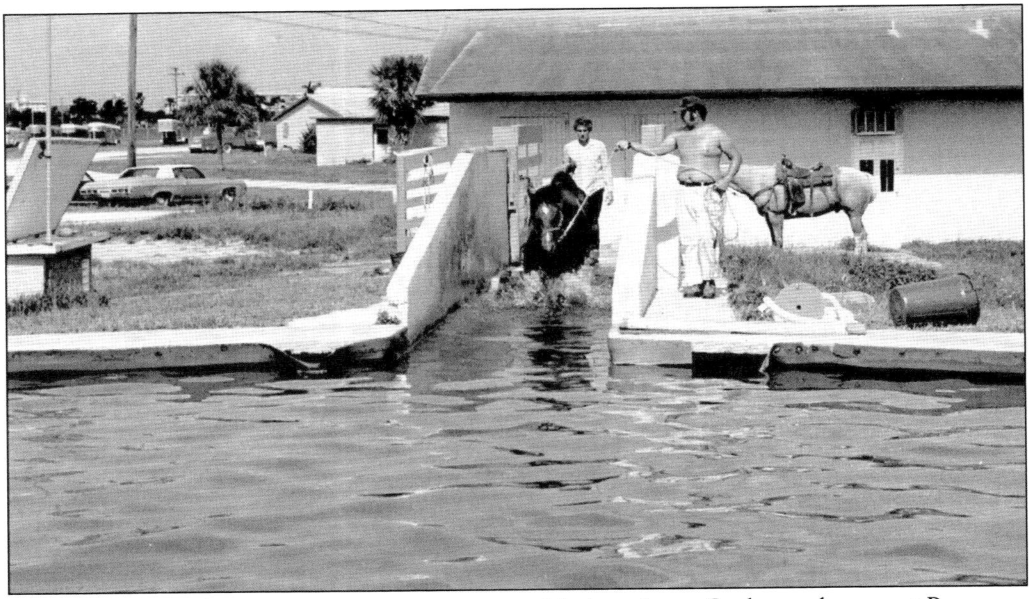

Conditioning racehorses is a very important part of their regimen. Such was the case at Pompano Park, where an equine swimming pool was factored into the conditioning of harness horses. In this scene, handlers are leading this horse into the pool for exercise.

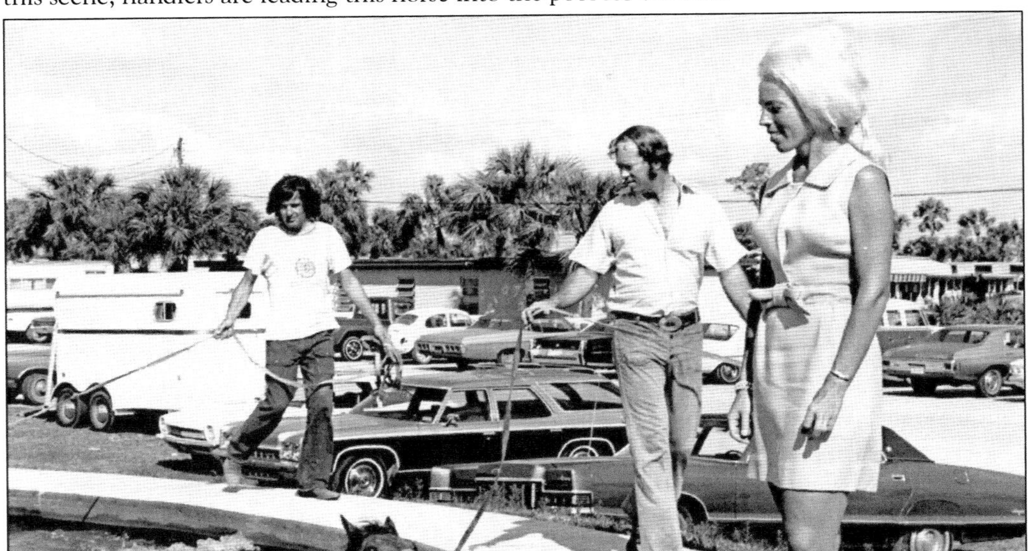

In races, horses' legs take a pounding, and that pounding may eventually affect their racing performance. Water therapy in the pool helps to cure aches, lameness, and other ailments. This horse is being handled gently by his groom, who leads the horse around the pool for exercise while the owner watches.

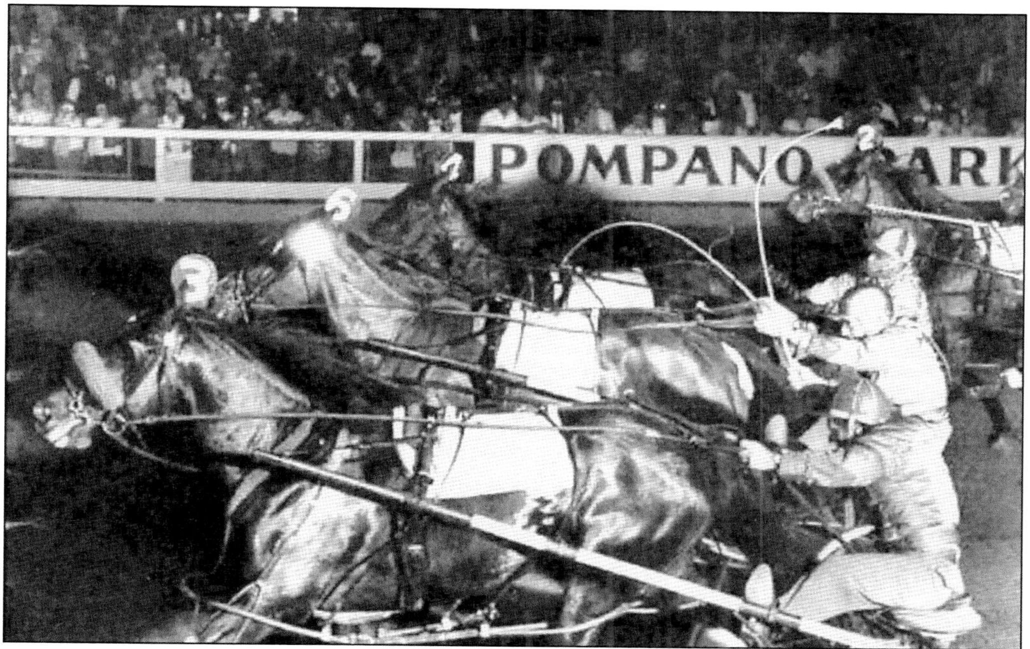

With a large crowd viewing the race on December 28, 1966, during the beginning of the third season, Crystal Spur (3), driven by Lou Rapone, finishes out his three-year-old form undefeated, as he defeats Jet Dell (6), driven by Wilfred Chicoyne. Tiny's Sparkle (4), driven by Clarence Martin, finished third.

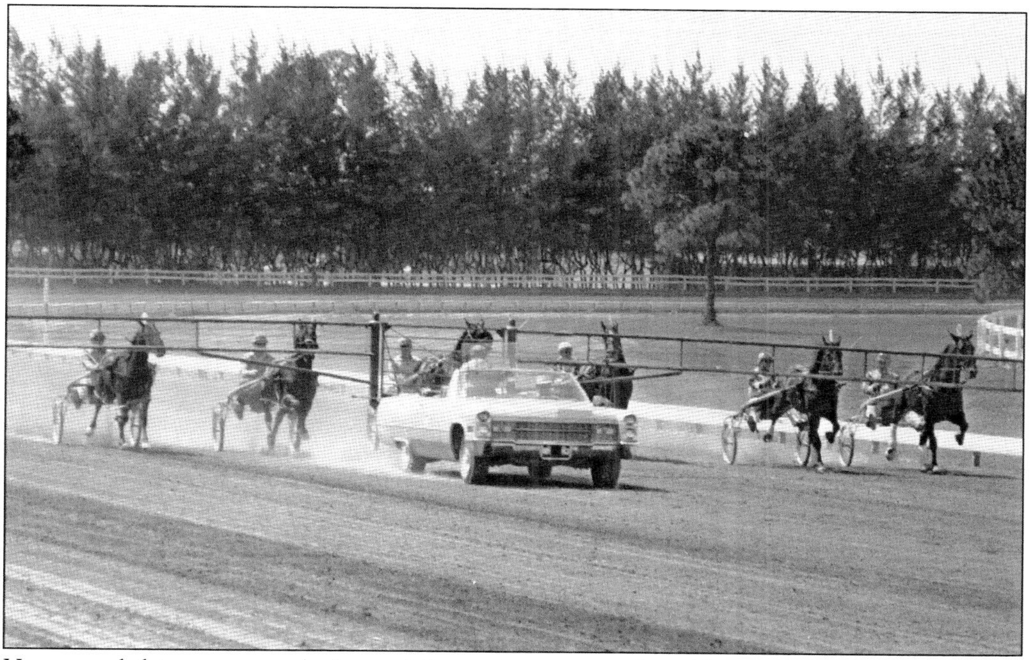

Horses and drivers approach the mobile starting gate at the old training track, north of the present Park. These horses are racing in the morning to qualify for competition. They qualify by achieving a certain time while maintaining their gait.

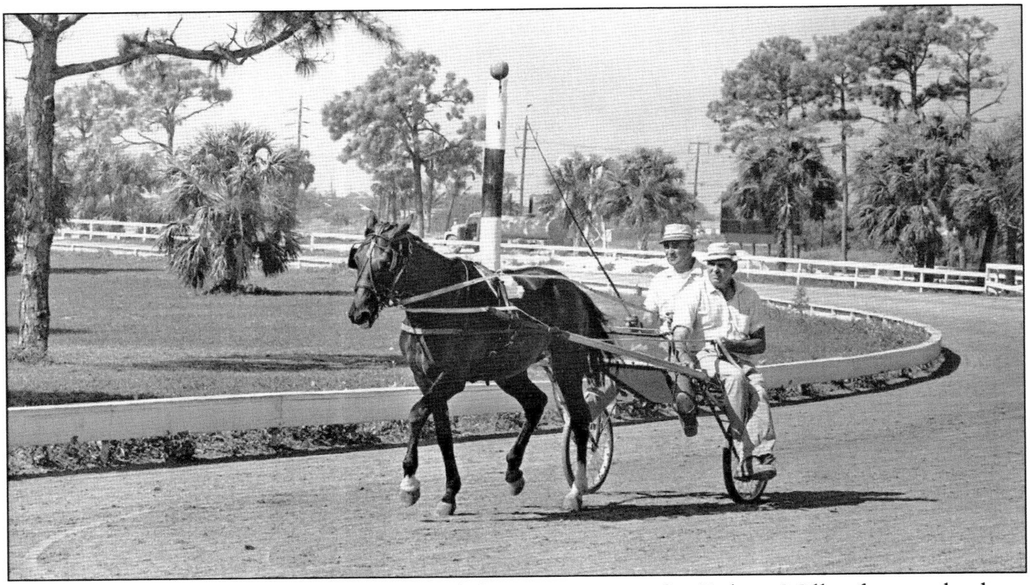

Aime Choquette, with whip in hand at left, was a trainer for Delvin Miller for nearly three decades. Assisted by a groom, at right, he is guiding a colt in a workout at the old training track north of Race Track Road (SW 3rd Street) and south of Atlantic Boulevard. The track no longer exists. The land was sold and developed into a Wal-Mart Super Center and other businesses.

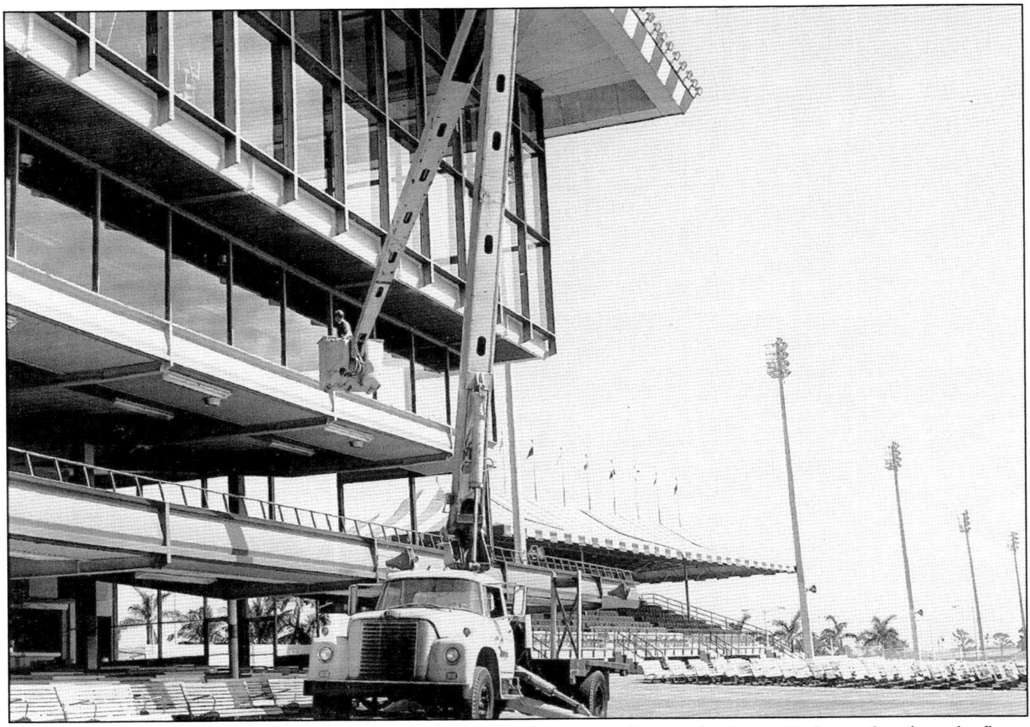

A workman, with the assist of a lift, inspects windows on the sixth floor. Below, the fourth-floor box seats will soon be enclosed with plate glass for the beginning of the third season, which began on December 15, 1965. The Sulky Room Cafeteria offered an all-you-can-eat bargain for $1.95.

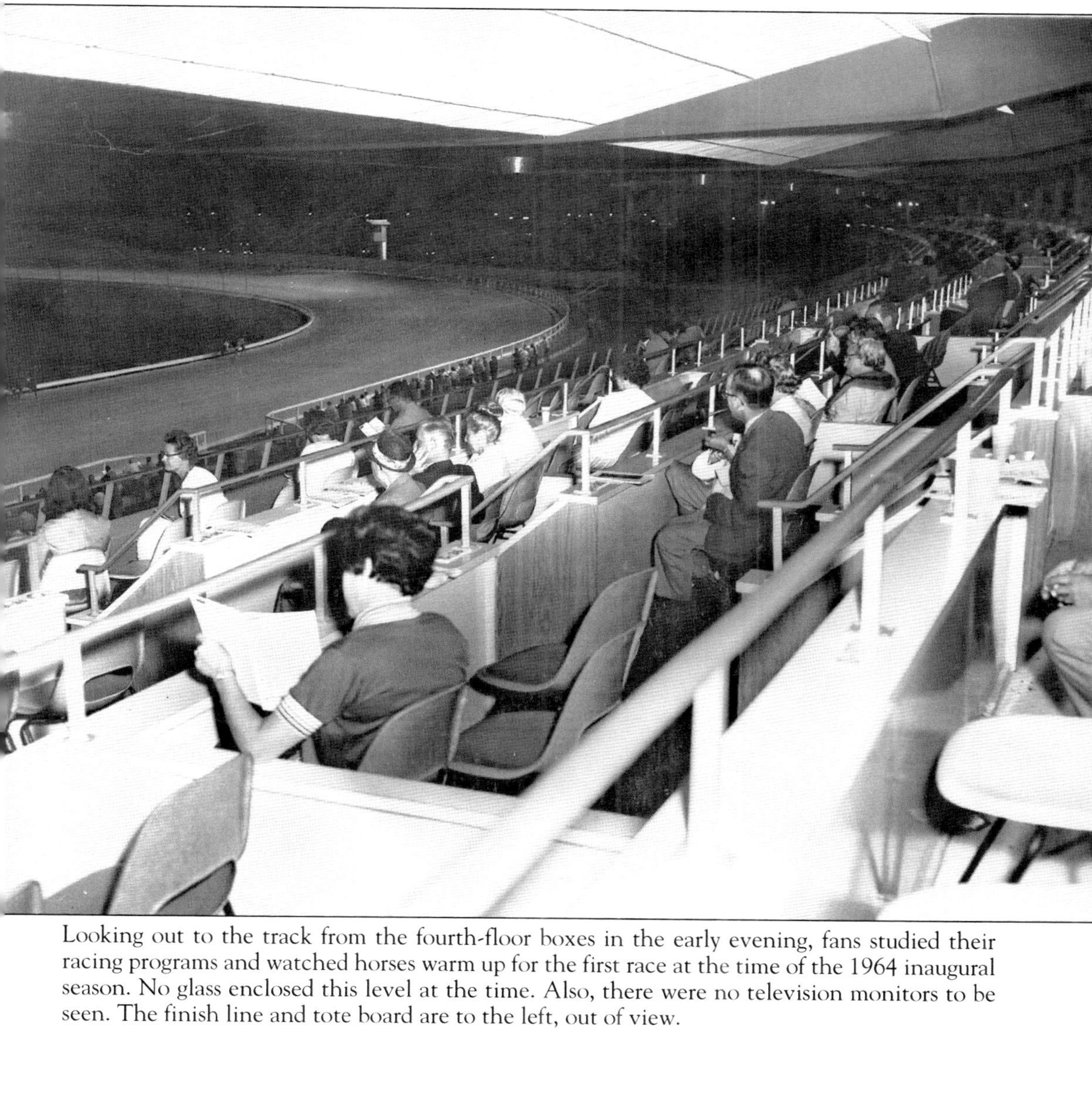

Looking out to the track from the fourth-floor boxes in the early evening, fans studied their racing programs and watched horses warm up for the first race at the time of the 1964 inaugural season. No glass enclosed this level at the time. Also, there were no television monitors to be seen. The finish line and tote board are to the left, out of view.

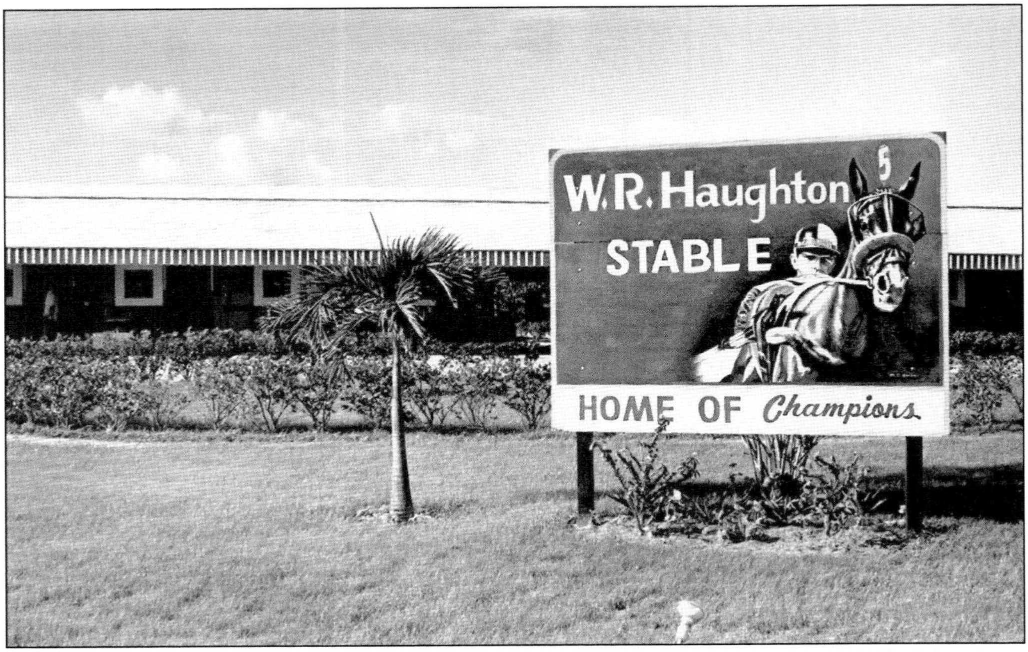

Some of the greatest trainers and drivers have stabled their horses at Pompano Park. These two signs identify the George F. Sholty Stable and the William R. Haughton Stable in April 1969. Haughton was elected to the Hall of Fame in 1968 and Sholty in 1984 by the United States Harness Writers Association. A life-like statuette of each inductee is displayed in the Hall of Fame in Goshen, New York. When a Hall of Famer dies, the statuette is transferred to the Hall of Immortals.

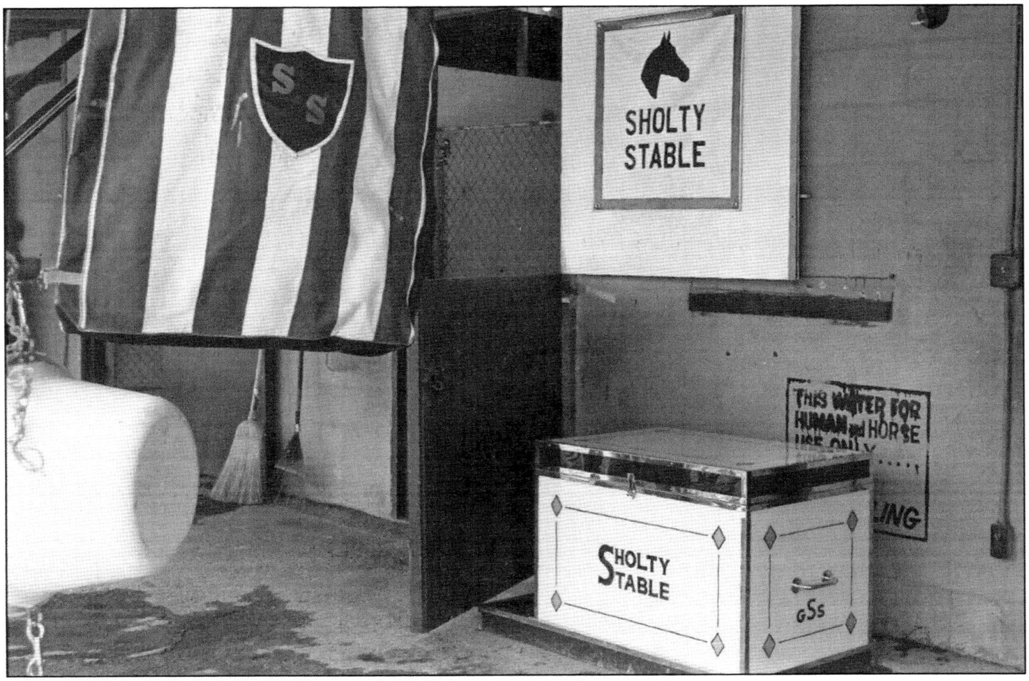

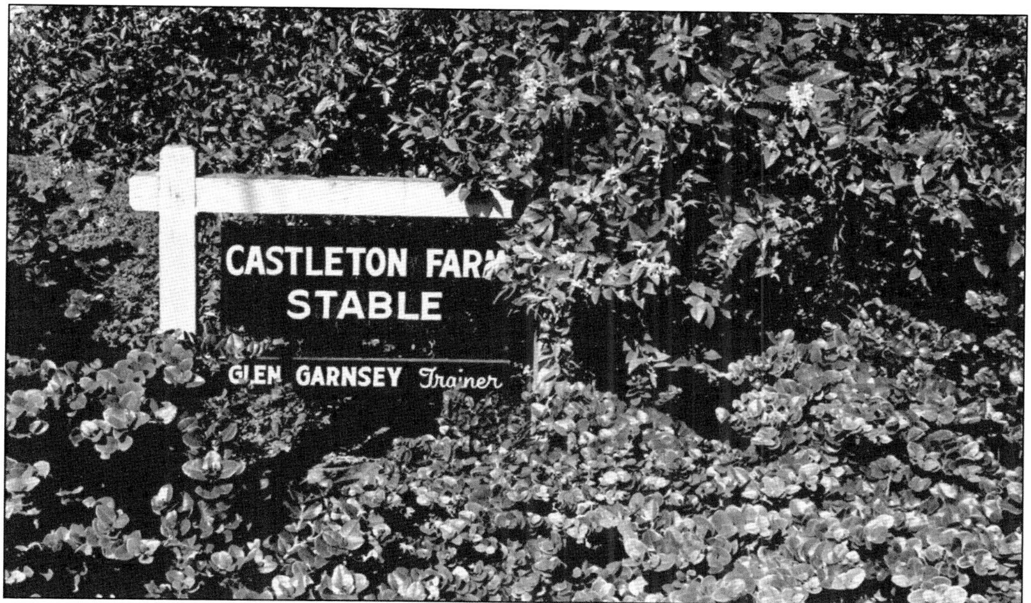

The Castleton Farm Stable at Pompano Park in April 1969 was owned by the van Lenneps. Glen Garnsey was the trainer. The stable was the first to winter-train their horses here as early as the 1950s, even before harness racing began as a pari-mutuel sport. In 1969, Castleton Farm contracted Garnsey as a private trainer to replace retiring Ralph Baldwin upon the recommendation of Baldwin and Frank Ervin.

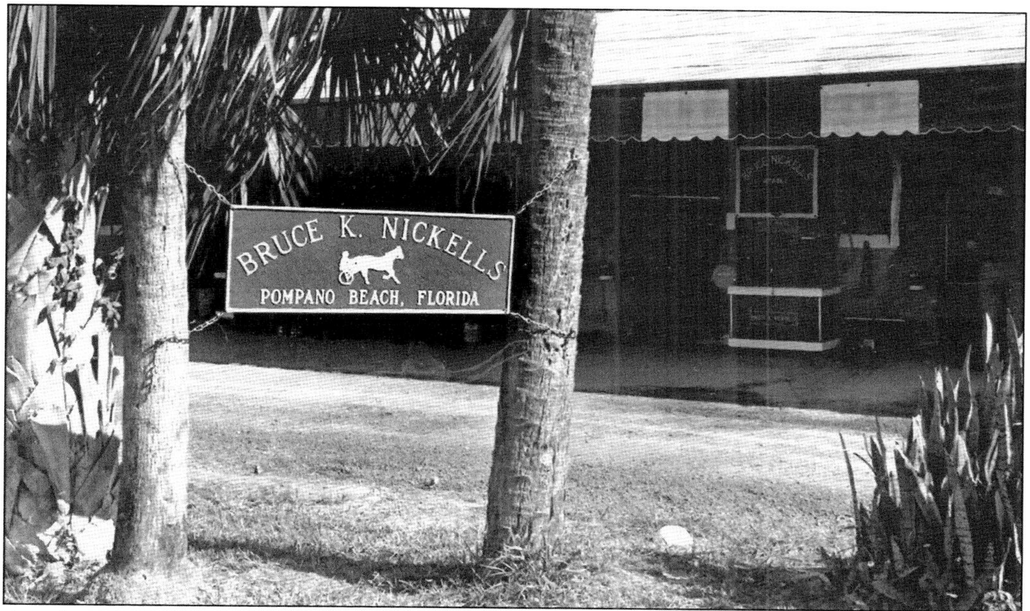

Another important part of Pompano Park was the Bruce Nickells Stable. Nickells fell in love with harness racing at an early age, and he has become an important part of the sport as driver and trainer. During the 1971–1972 season, he achieved the lone 2-minute mile on March 18, 1972, when he guided pacing colt Strike Out to victory in 1:59.4. He turned over the lines of his stable to his daughter Brooke in 1999.

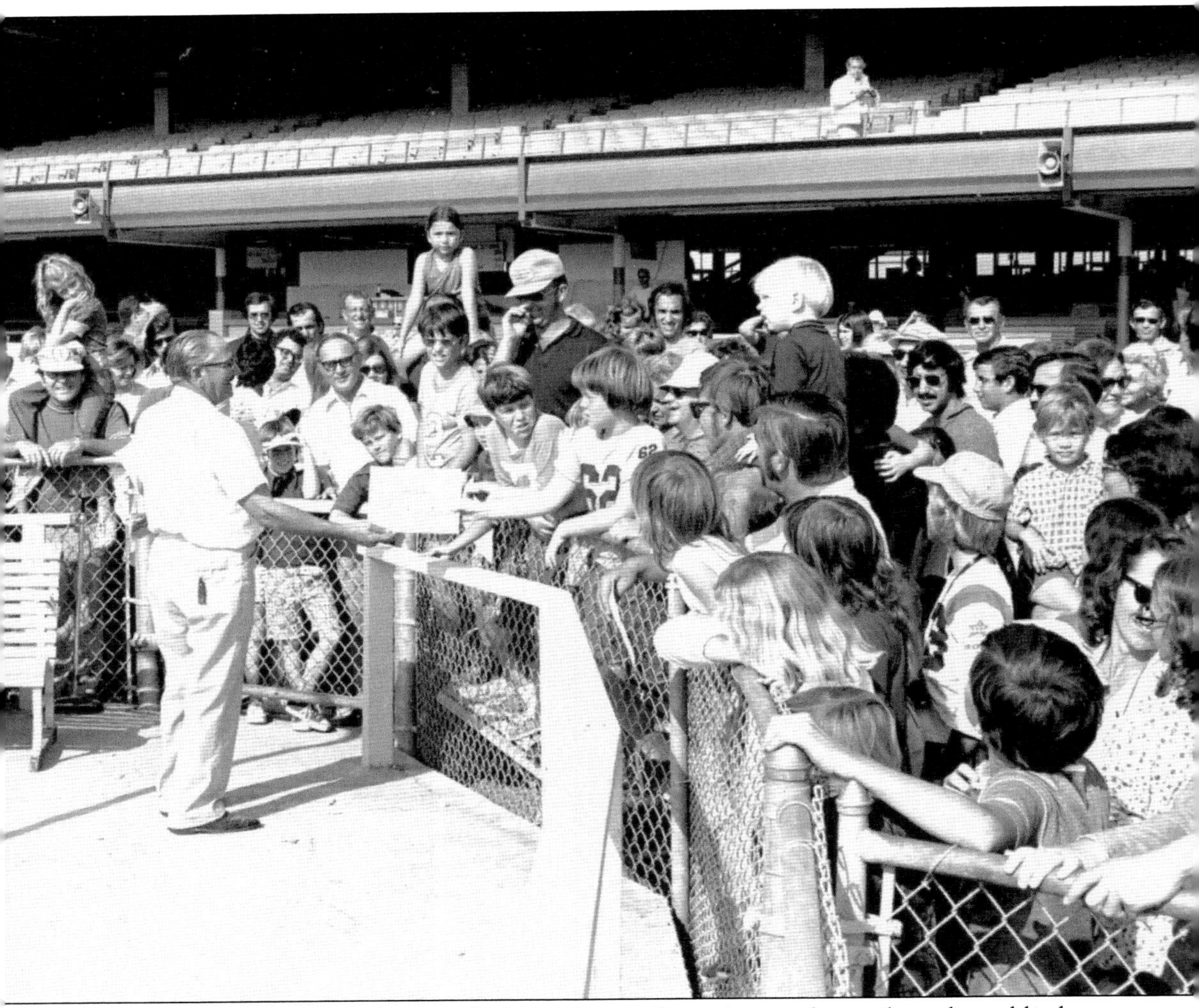

Soon after Pompano Park opened, the tradition of opening up the track to the public began. Here children are entertained and informed about harness racing. The attendant is handing a coloring book entitled "The Story of Pompano Park" to a youngster.

Frederick L. van Lennep (left) and publicist Bob Cox (right) examine a program while trying to pick a winner during the 1968–1969 winter track meet, the sixth season. The Haughton stablemates Armbro Irma and Prestwick swept the Secretary's Series. The Twin Double wager returned.

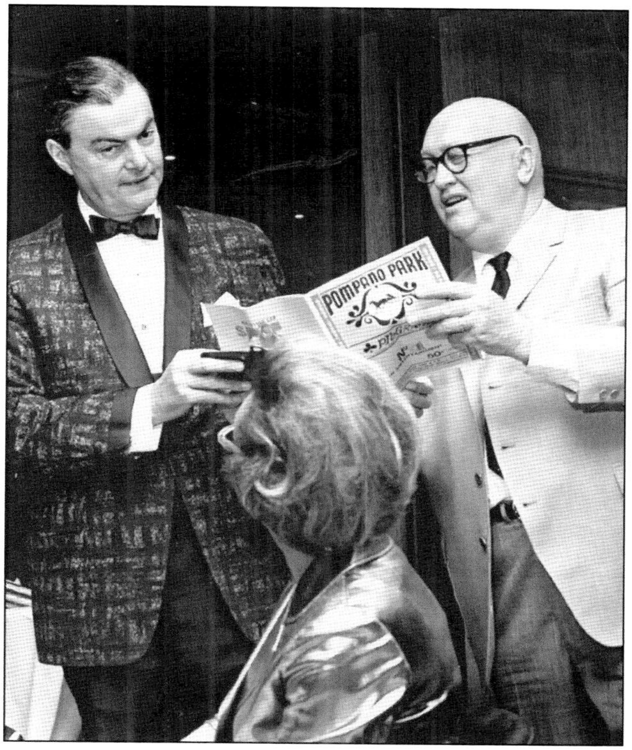

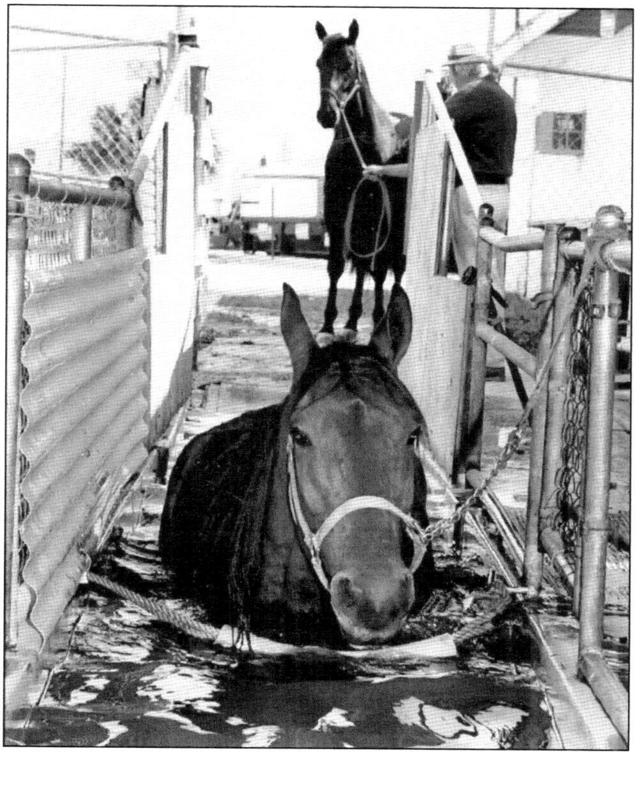

Racehorses must be carefully tended to maintain their highest level of performance. Water therapy is one way to achieve this goal. This horse is enjoying the water in the wading pool on the grounds of Pompano Park.

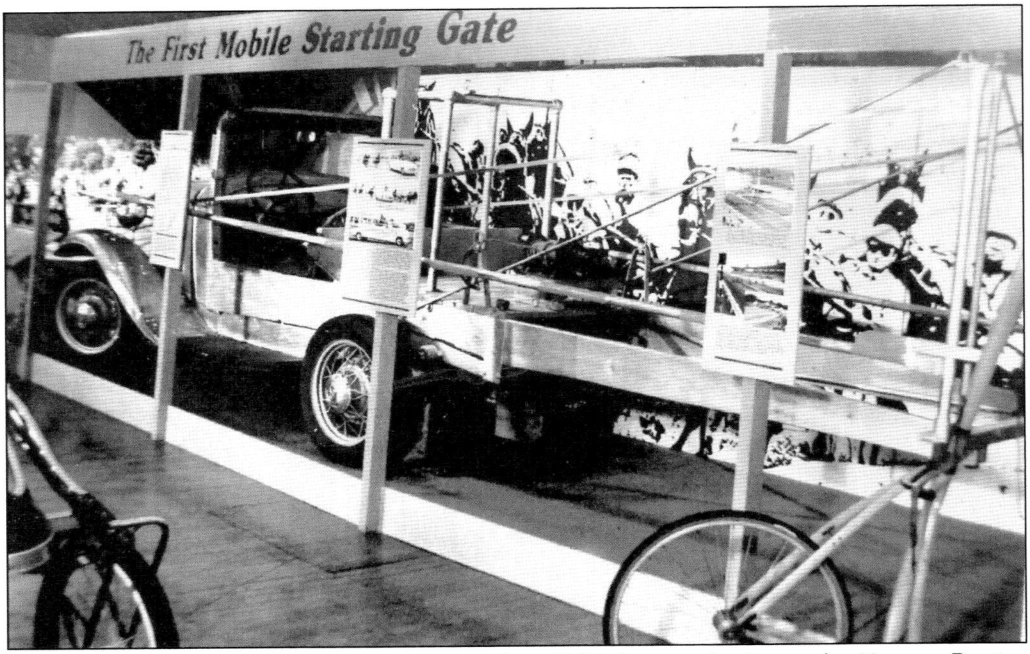

The first official mobile starting gate was used in 1937. It is on display at the Harness Racing Museum Hall of Fame at Goshen, New York. Goshen has often been called the "Cradle of Harness Racing." It is 60 miles northwest of New York City, in Orange County.

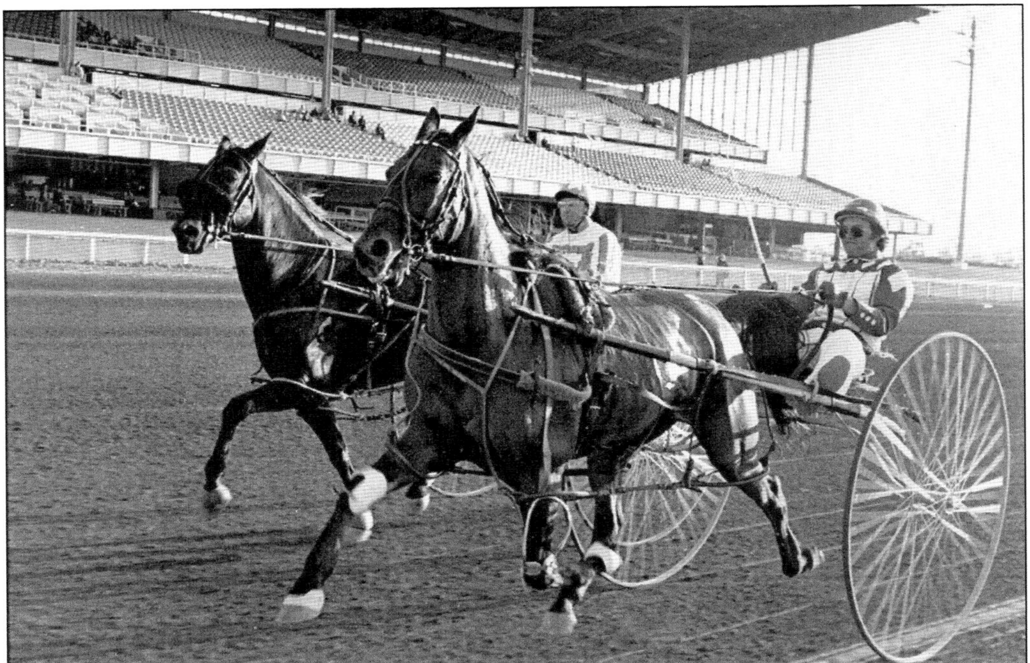

The modern sulky was introduced around 1890 and had few changes in its basic design until the 1970s, when a modified sulky was developed. These turn-of-the-century sulkies had 42-inch wheels, or high wheels. They helped to make harness racing popular to the general public.

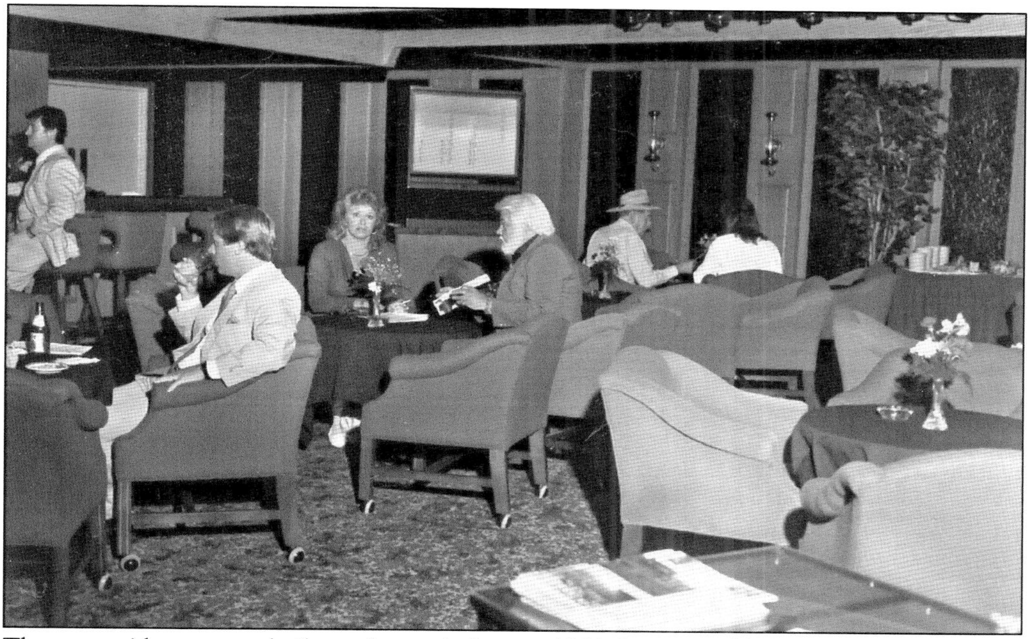

The owners' lounge was built on the sixth floor in 1988. It was established as a casual meeting place for horse owners and their guests for their comfort and convenience. Today it is named the Niatross Room.

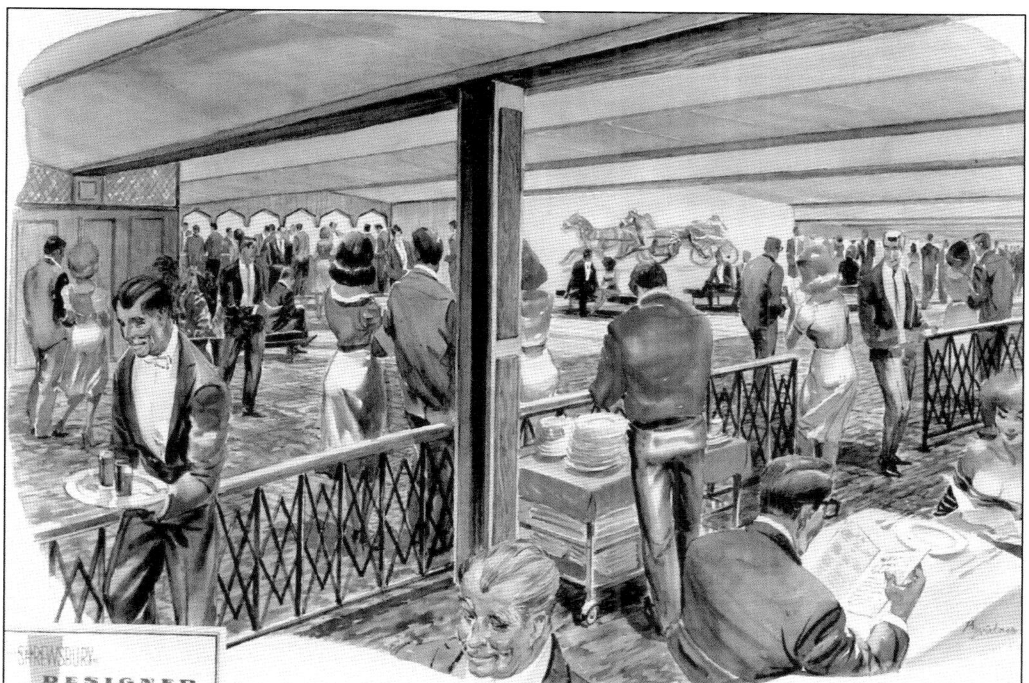

This is a designer's rendering of guests at Patten's Top of the Park Restaurant, on level six of the clubhouse, for the inaugural season in 1964. Elegance and formal attire prevail. Note the sculpture of pacers in action on the wall in the background.

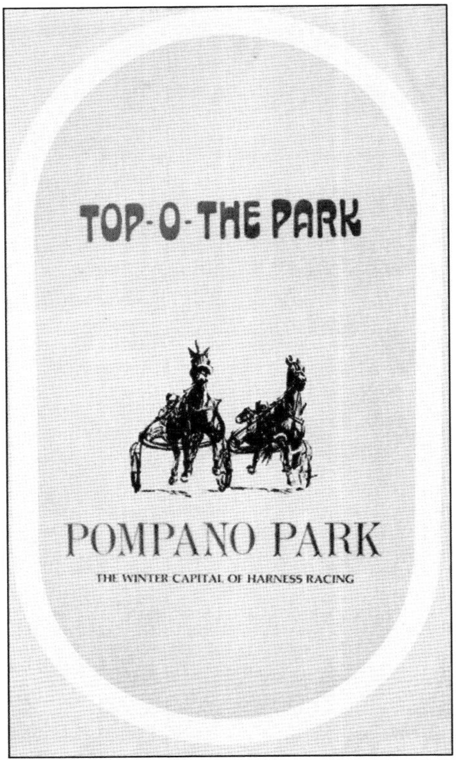

The menu cover for the Top of the Park Restaurant, as it appeared in 1973, conveyed a warm message on the reverse side: "We invite you to keep this menu as a souvenir of your visit, or, if you wish, we will mail it to a friend or relative. Just hand it to the Maitre d' with the necessary address."

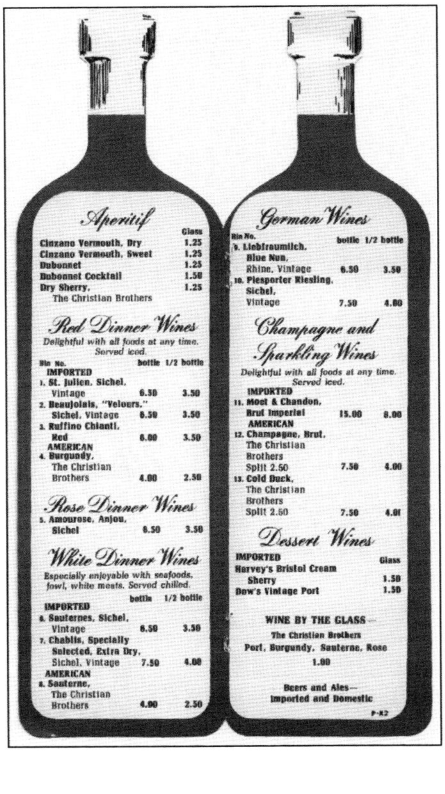

Aperitif

	Glass
Cinzano Vermouth, Dry	1.25
Cinzano Vermouth, Sweet	1.25
Dubonnet	1.25
Dubonnet Cocktail	1.50
Dry Sherry, The Christian Brothers	1.25

Red Dinner Wines

Delightful with all foods at any time. Served iced.

Bin No.	bottle	1/2 bottle
IMPORTED		
1. St. Julien, Sichel, Vintage	6.50	3.50
2. Beaujolais, "Velours," Sichel, Vintage	6.50	3.50
3. Ruffino Chianti, Red	6.00	3.50
AMERICAN		
4. Burgundy, The Christian Brothers	4.00	2.50

Rose Dinner Wines

5. Amourose, Anjou, Sichel	6.50	3.50

White Dinner Wines

Especially enjoyable with seafoods, fowl, white meats. Served chilled.

	bottle	1/2 bottle
IMPORTED		
6. Sauternes, Sichel, Vintage	6.50	3.50
7. Chablis, Specially Selected, Extra Dry, Sichel, Vintage	7.50	4.00
AMERICAN		
8. Sauterne, The Christian Brothers	4.00	2.50

German Wines

Bin No.	bottle	1/2 bottle
9. Liebfraumilch, Blue Nun, Rhine, Vintage	6.50	3.50
10. Piesporter Riesling, Sichel, Vintage	7.50	4.00

Champagne and Sparkling Wines

Delightful with all foods at any time. Served iced.

IMPORTED		
11. Moet & Chandon, Brut Imperial	15.00	8.00
AMERICAN		
12. Champagne, Brut, The Christian Brothers Split 2.50	7.50	4.00
13. Cold Duck, The Christian Brothers Split 2.50	7.50	4.0[illegible]

Dessert Wines

IMPORTED	Glass
Harvey's Bristol Cream Sherry	1.50
Dow's Vintage Port	1.50

WINE BY THE GLASS—
The Christian Brothers
Port, Burgundy, Sauterne, Rose
1.00

Beers and Ales—
Imported and Domestic

P-K2

A selection of fine American and imported wines was offered to dining guests at the Top of the Park Restaurant, which was catered by the Harry M. Stevens Company in 1973. Note the choices and prices. Guests also could select from a choice of beers and ales.

This half of the menu offered some very good bargains. It lists the light fare and desserts. Pompano Park also offered a choice of several plans designed to fit the needs of groups from 35 to 500. All plans featured special tickets, a race named for the group, and a photo in the winner's circle.

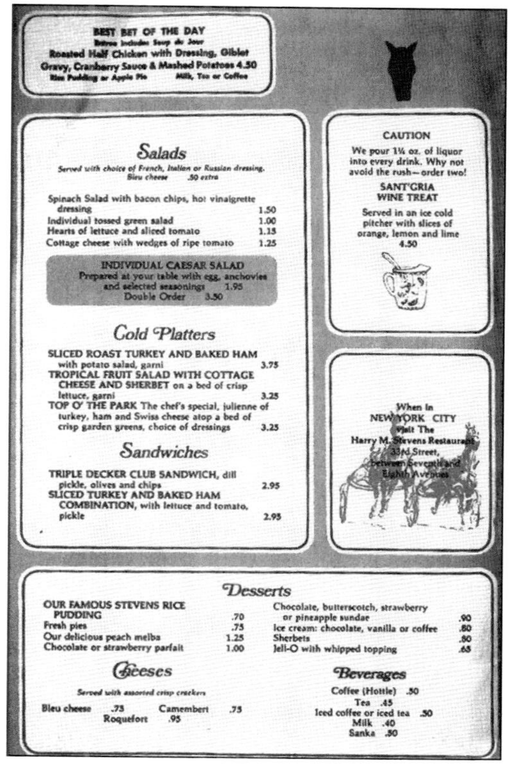

BEST BET OF THE DAY
Roasted Half Chicken with Dressing, Giblet Gravy, Cranberry Sauce & Mashed Potatoes 4.50
Milk, Tea or Coffee

Salads

Served with choice of French, Italian or Russian dressing. Bleu cheese .50 extra

Spinach Salad with bacon chips, hot vinaigrette dressing	1.50
Individual tossed green salad	1.00
Hearts of lettuce and sliced tomato	1.15
Cottage cheese with wedges of ripe tomato	1.25

INDIVIDUAL CAESAR SALAD
Prepared at your table with egg, anchovies and selected seasonings 1.95
Double Order 3.50

Cold Platters

SLICED ROAST TURKEY AND BAKED HAM with potato salad, garni	3.75
TROPICAL FRUIT SALAD WITH COTTAGE CHEESE AND SHERBET on a bed of crisp lettuce, garni	3.25
TOP O' THE PARK The chef's special, julienne of turkey, ham and Swiss cheese atop a bed of crisp garden greens, choice of dressings	3.25

Sandwiches

TRIPLE DECKER CLUB SANDWICH, dill pickle, olives and chips	2.95
SLICED TURKEY AND BAKED HAM COMBINATION, with lettuce and tomato, pickle	2.95

CAUTION
We pour 1¼ oz. of liquor into every drink. Why not avoid the rush—order two!
SANT'GRIA WINE TREAT
Served in an ice cold pitcher with slices of orange, lemon and lime
4.50

When in NEW YORK CITY
Visit The Harry M. Stevens Restaurant
33rd Street, between Seventh and Eighth Avenues

Desserts

OUR FAMOUS STEVENS RICE PUDDING	.70
Fresh pies	.75
Our delicious peach melba	1.25
Chocolate or strawberry parfait	1.00
Chocolate, butterscotch, strawberry or pineapple sundae	.90
Ice cream: chocolate, vanilla or coffee	.80
Sherbets	.80
Jell-O with whipped topping	.65

Cheeses

Served with assorted crisp crackers

Bleu cheese .75 Camembert .75 Roquefort .95

Beverages

Coffee (Hottle) .50
Tea .45
Iced coffee or iced tea .50
Milk .40
Sanka .50

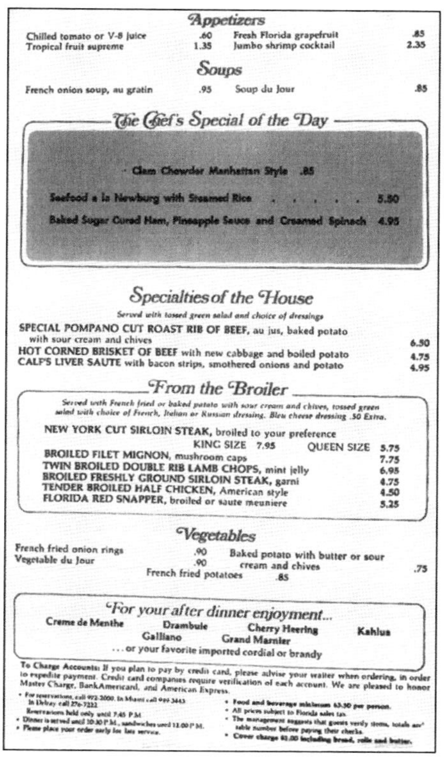

Appetizers

Chilled tomato or V-8 juice	.60	Fresh Florida grapefruit	.85
Tropical fruit supreme	1.35	Jumbo shrimp cocktail	2.35

Soups

French onion soup, au gratin	.95	Soup du Jour	.85

The Chef's Special of the Day

Clam Chowder Manhattan Style .85
Seafood a la Newburg with Steamed Rice 5.50
Baked Sugar Cured Ham, Pineapple Sauce and Creamed Spinach 4.95

Specialties of the House

Served with tossed green salad and choice of dressings

SPECIAL POMPANO CUT ROAST RIB OF BEEF, au jus, baked potato with sour cream and chives	6.50
HOT CORNED BRISKET OF BEEF with new cabbage and boiled potato	4.75
CALF'S LIVER SAUTE with bacon strips, smothered onions and potato	4.95

From the Broiler

Served with French fried or baked potato with sour cream and chives, tossed green salad with choice of French, Italian or Russian dressing. Bleu cheese dressing .50 Extra.

NEW YORK CUT SIRLOIN STEAK, broiled to your preference KING SIZE 7.95 QUEEN SIZE	5.75
BROILED FILET MIGNON, mushroom caps	7.75
TWIN BROILED DOUBLE RIB LAMB CHOPS, mint jelly	6.95
BROILED FRESHLY GROUND SIRLOIN STEAK, garni	4.75
TENDER BROILED HALF CHICKEN, American style	4.50
FLORIDA RED SNAPPER, broiled or saute meuniere	5.25

Vegetables

French fried onion rings	.90
Vegetable du Jour	.90
French fried potatoes	.85
Baked potato with butter or sour cream and chives	.75

For your after dinner enjoyment...
Creme de Menthe, Drambuie, Cherry Heering, Kahlua, Galliano, Grand Marnier
. . . or your favorite imported cordial or brandy

To Charge Accounts: If you plan to pay by credit card, please advise your waiter when ordering, in order to expedite payment. Credit card companies require verification of each account. We are pleased to honor Master Charge, BankAmericard, and American Express.

- Reservations held only until 7:45 P.M.
- Dinner is served until 10:30 P.M., sandwiches until 11:00 P.M.
- Please place your order early for fast service.
- All prices subject to Florida sales tax.
- Cover charge $1.00 including bread, rolls and butter.

The other half of the menu listed the á la carte items. Compare these prices of the 1970s with those of today, and the inflationary impact will be appreciated. The back of the menu also included information about trotters and pacers, how to bet, and the historical background of Pompano Park.

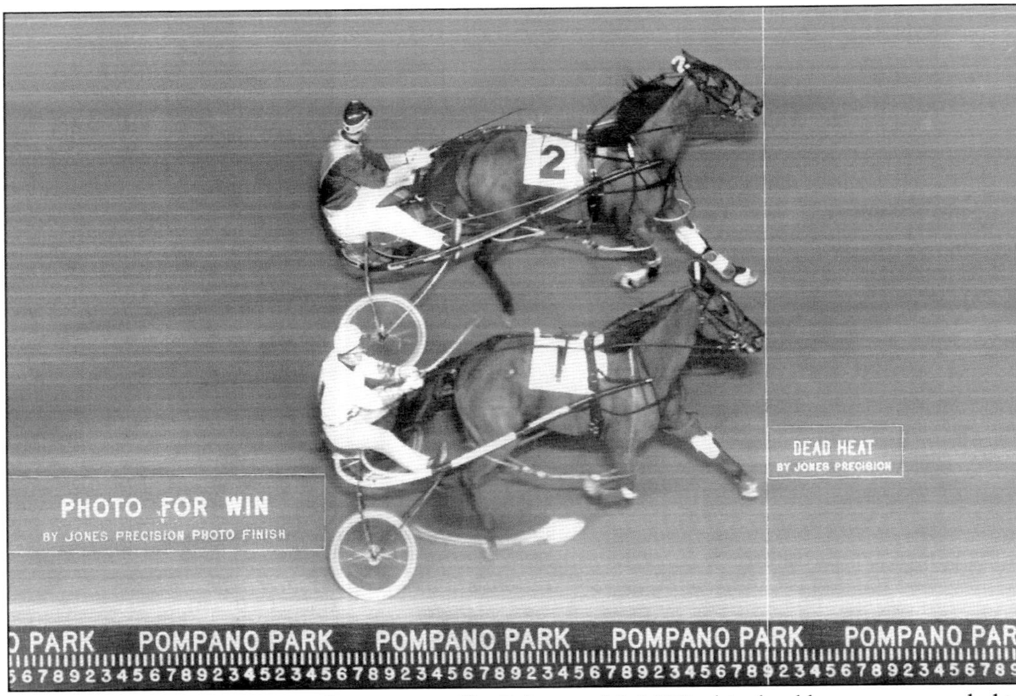

A dead heat is a rare event in horse races. On February 14, 1969, this dead heat was recorded in the eighth race for win, when the noses of the two horses touched the finish line at exactly the same time. The drivers are looking to their left at the tote board for the time of the race.

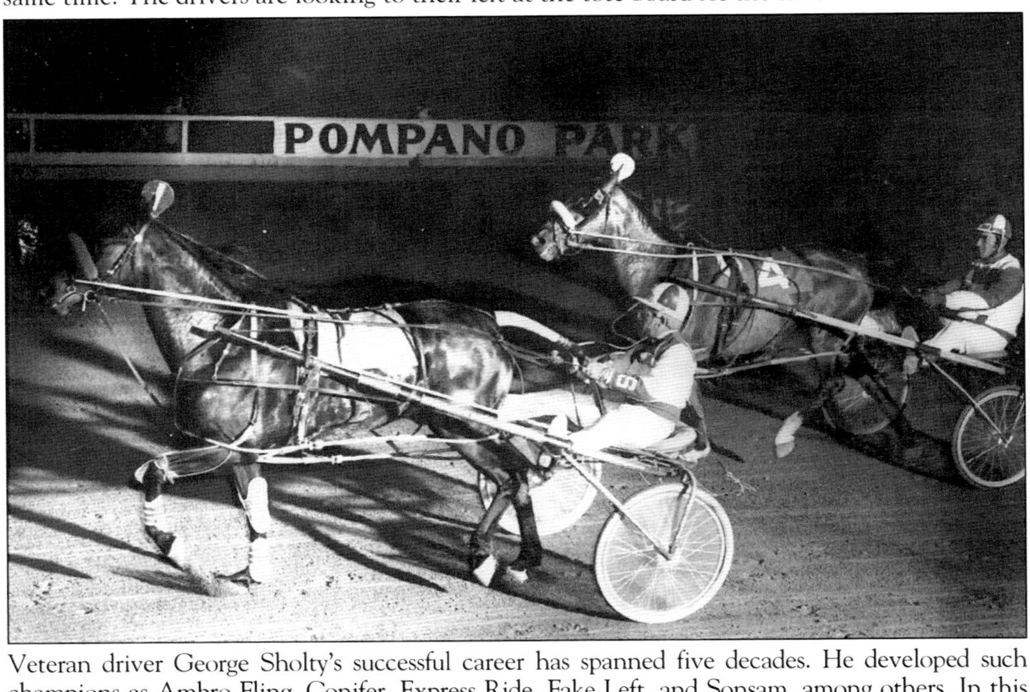

Veteran driver George Sholty's successful career has spanned five decades. He developed such champions as Ambro Fling, Conifer, Express Ride, Fake Left, and Sonsam, among others. In this race at Pompano Park on January 16, 1971, Sholty is victorious with Empire Lieutenant in 2:02.2.

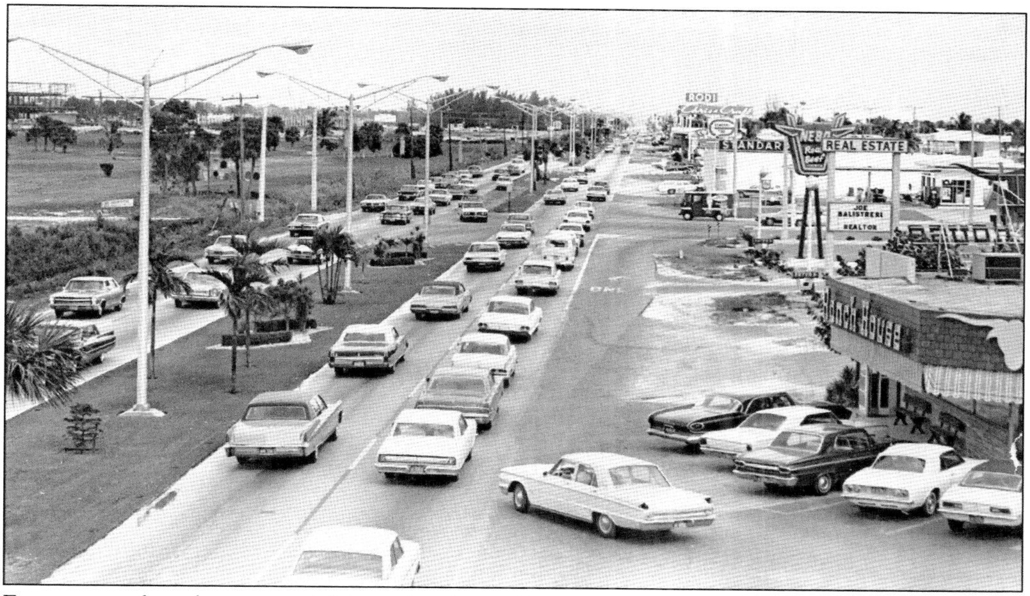

Five years after the successful introduction of harness racing to South Florida, the city of Pompano Beach experienced a period of dynamic growth. This view looking north on U.S. Highway 1 (Federal Highway) at the intersection of NE 14th Street, right, depicts heavy traffic in both directions on February 7, 1969. At the extreme left, the original Fashion Square Mall is under construction. The Joe Balistreri Real Estate office, at right, remains there today.

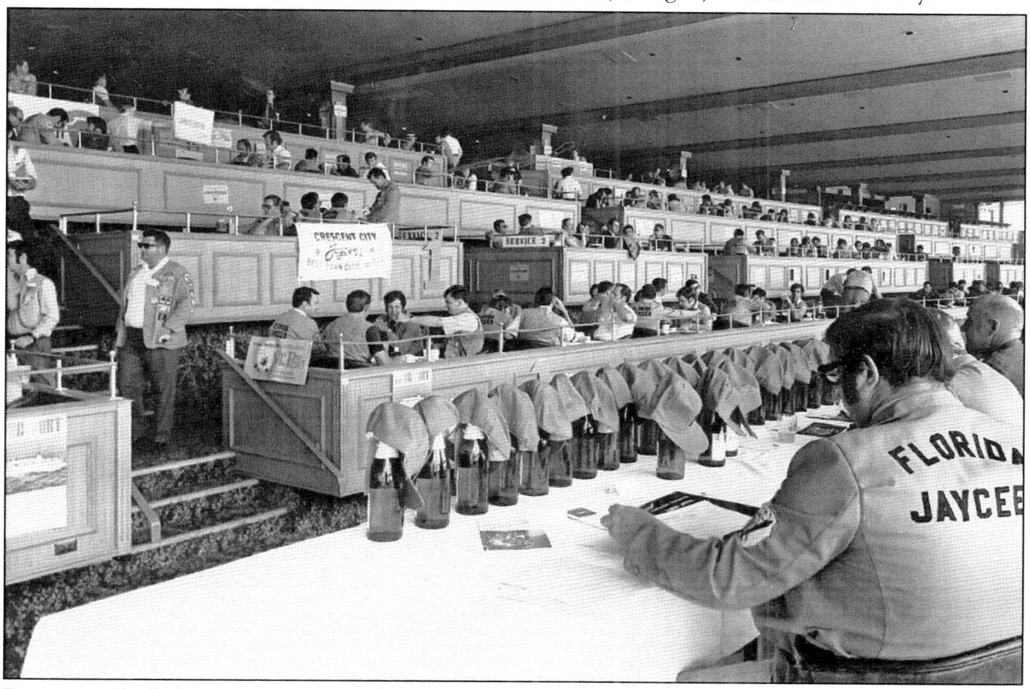

Pompano Park has accommodated numerous service organizations over the years. Here the Florida Jaycees are meeting in the clubhouse and are enjoying the amenities of harness racing in 1972. Note the champagne bottles in the foreground.

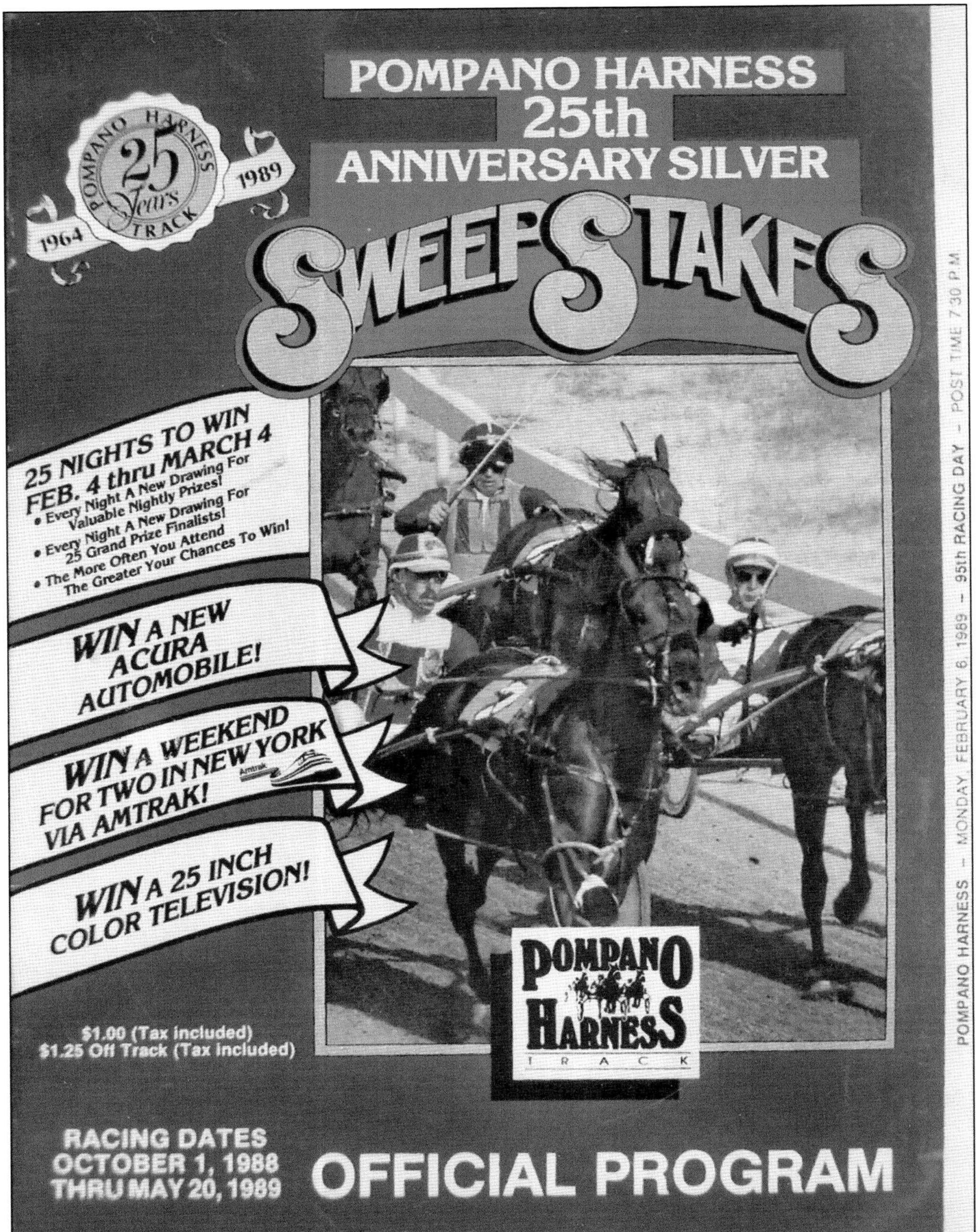

The Pompano Park Harness Track proudly announced its silver anniversary on the cover of the official program, when the racing dates began on October 1, 1988, and concluded on May 20, 1989. This 26th season witnessed Peter Wrenn achieve his third consecutive dash-winning title, driving a record 199 horses to victory, most of those for leading trainer Bob Duncan. On February 18, 1989, the swiftest night of all, 8,464 fans saw a 13-race card, in which every race was under 2 minutes, and 8 of the 13 races went in 1 minute, 56 seconds or less.

Three

THE DRIVERS

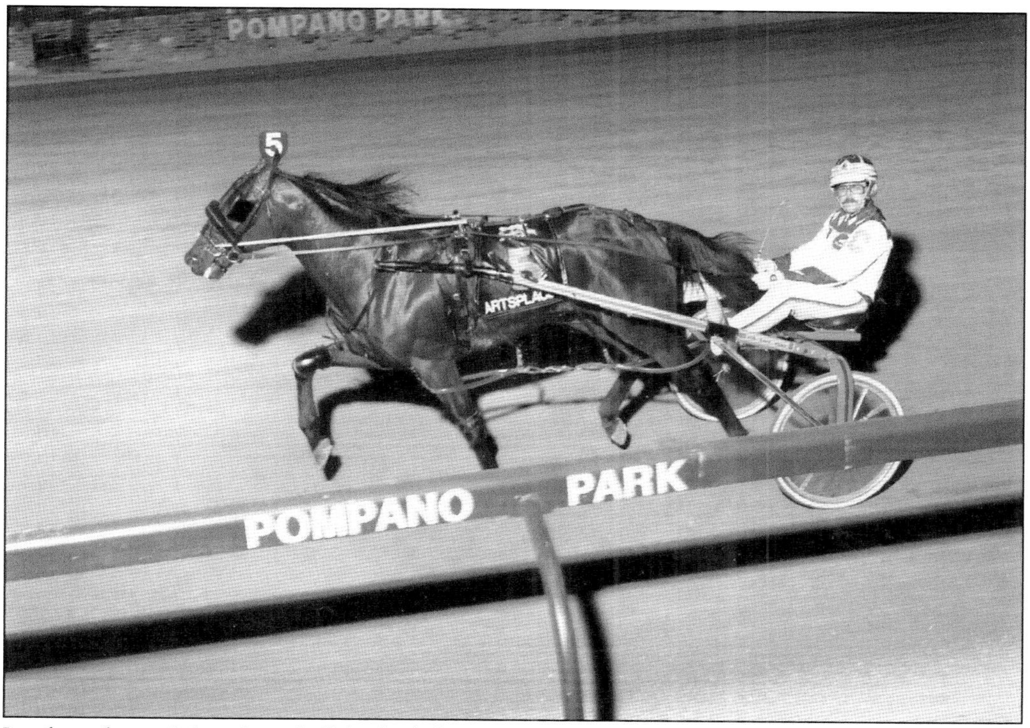

Leading driver John Campbell looks left to check his winning time on the scoreboard as he guides pacer Artsplace to victory in the Breeders Crown on November 30, 1990, setting a 1:51.1 world record. Several years earlier at Pompano, in 1988, he drove Peace Corps to a world record for a freshman filly trotter in 1:57.1. Campbell was elected by the United States Harness Writers Association to the Hall of Fame at age 35 in 1990, the youngest person to be so honored.

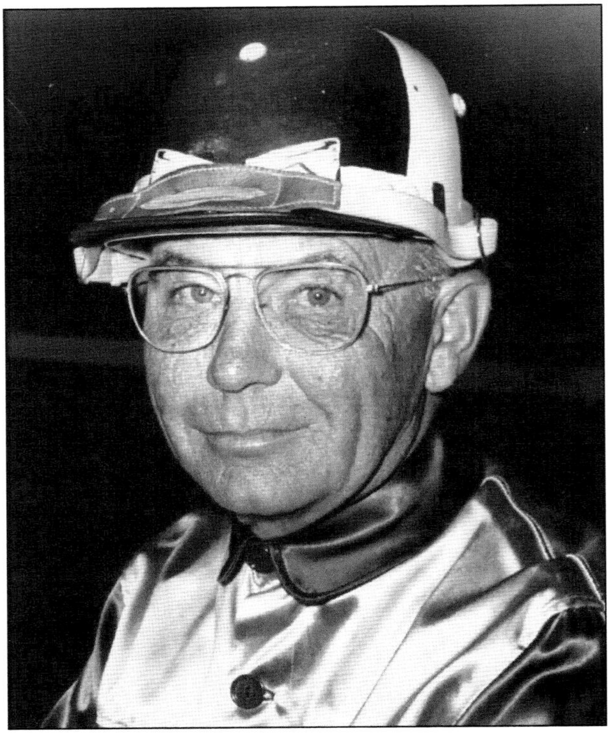

Ralph Baldwin, 1963 Horseman of the Year, was one of the best drivers who performed weekly at Pompano Park. In 1960, he became head trainer for Castleton Farm Stable, and in 1971, he assumed the same position at Arden Homestead Stable. He developed Hambletonian champion Speedy Scot. In 1973, he won the Hambletonian with Flirth. A Hall of Famer in 1971, he winter-trained at Pompano Park.

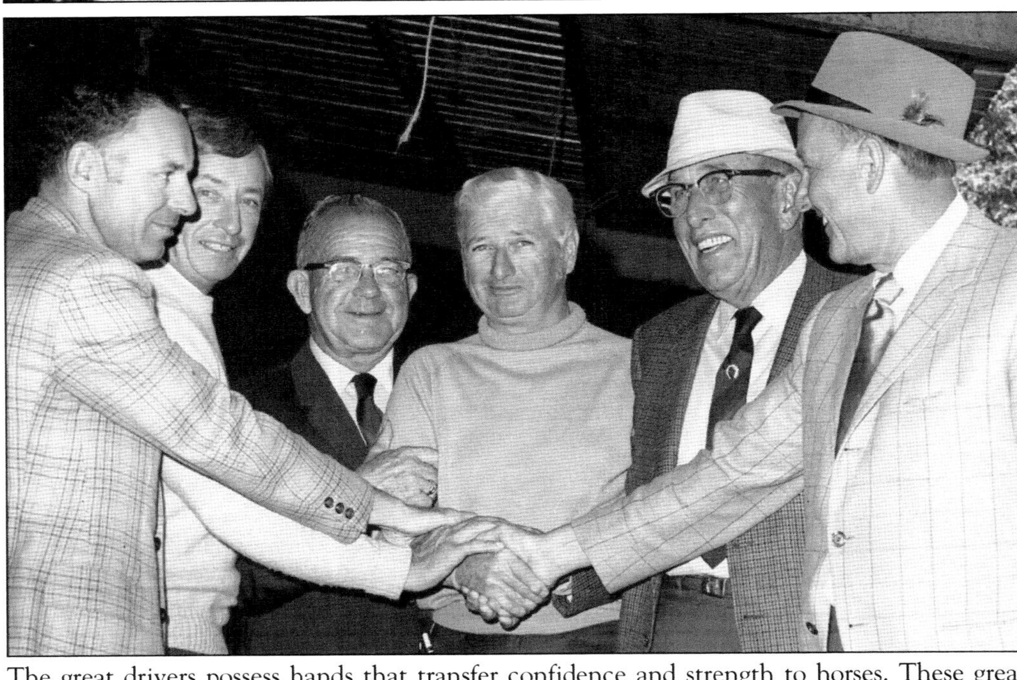

The great drivers possess hands that transfer confidence and strength to horses. These great drivers exhibited that skill. They joined their hands together at a reunion in the 1970s. From left to right are Stanley Dancer, Billy Haughton, Curly Smart, Joe O'Brien, Frank Ervin, and Delvin Miller.

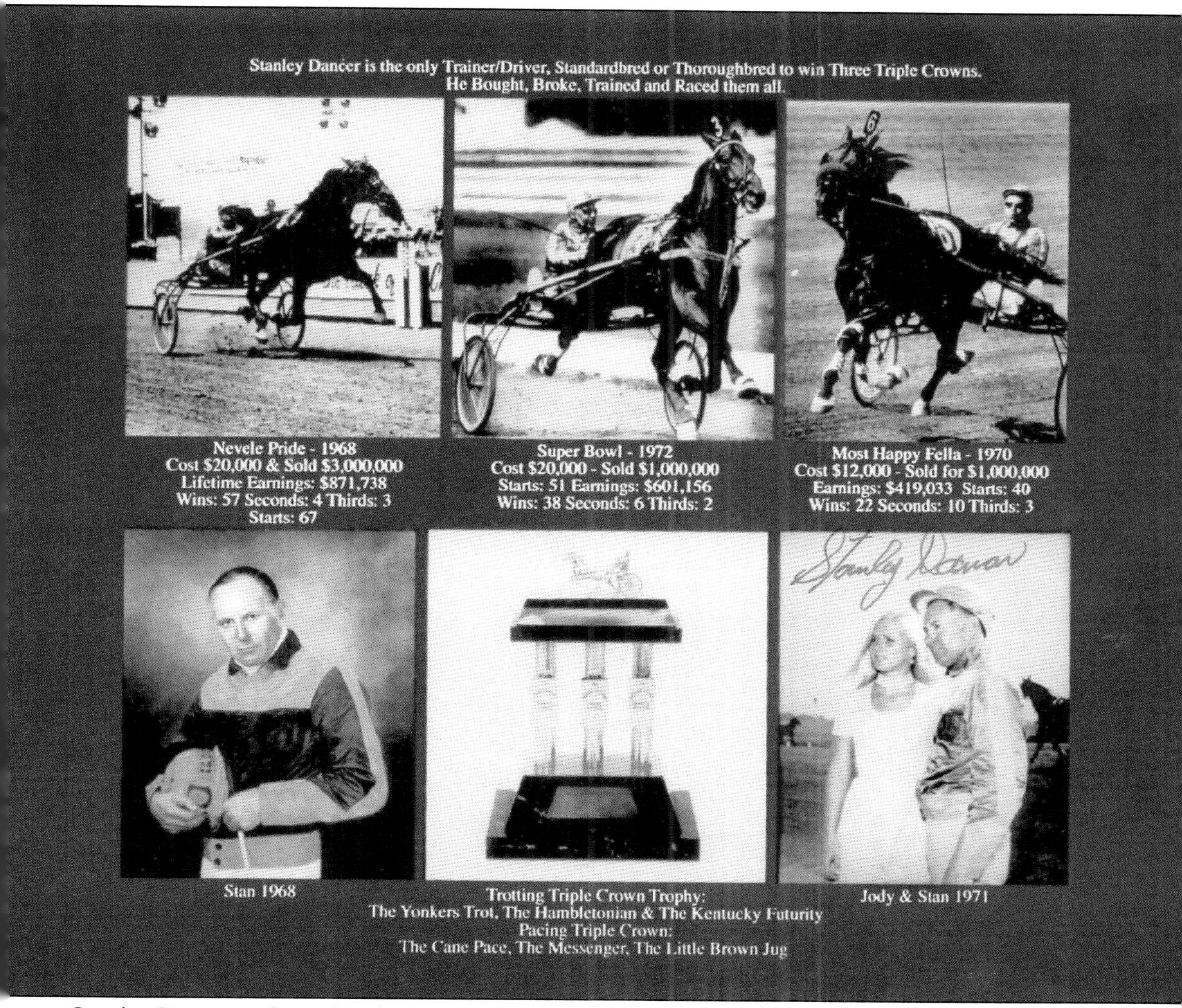

Stanley Dancer, a legend in his own time, is one of the best-known drivers in harness racing. He was elected by the United States Harness Writers Association to the Hall of Fame in 1969. Dancer was a United States Trotting Association director from New Jersey, where he was born, but he now makes his home in Pompano Beach. This composite of images depicts some his major achievements.

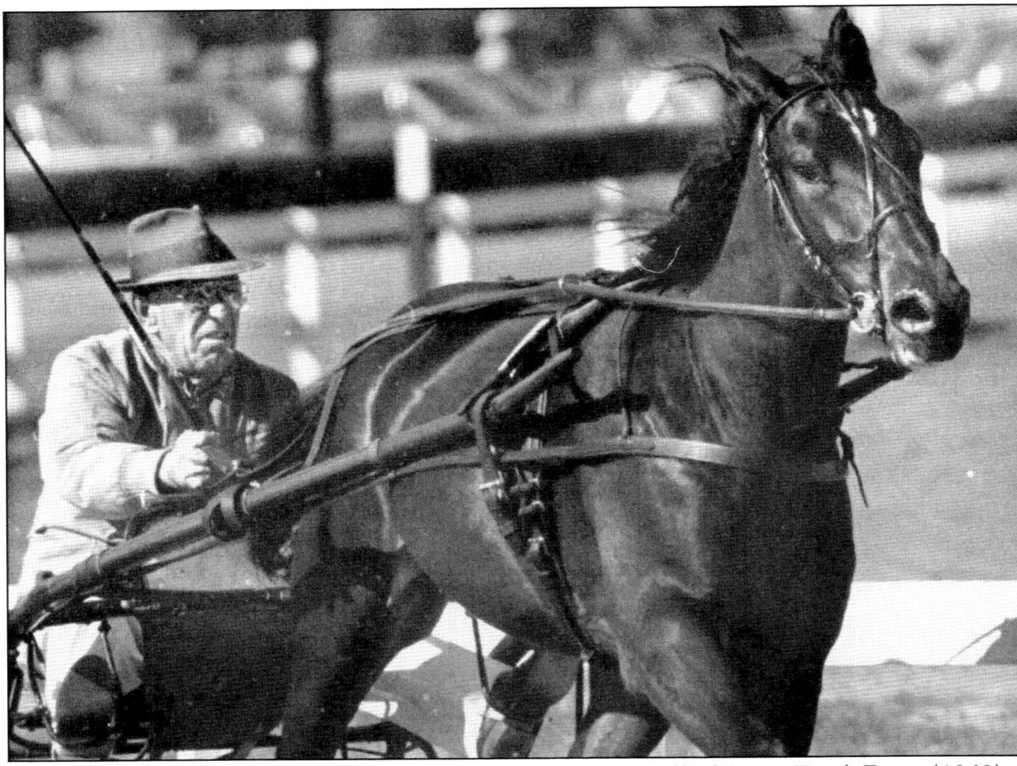

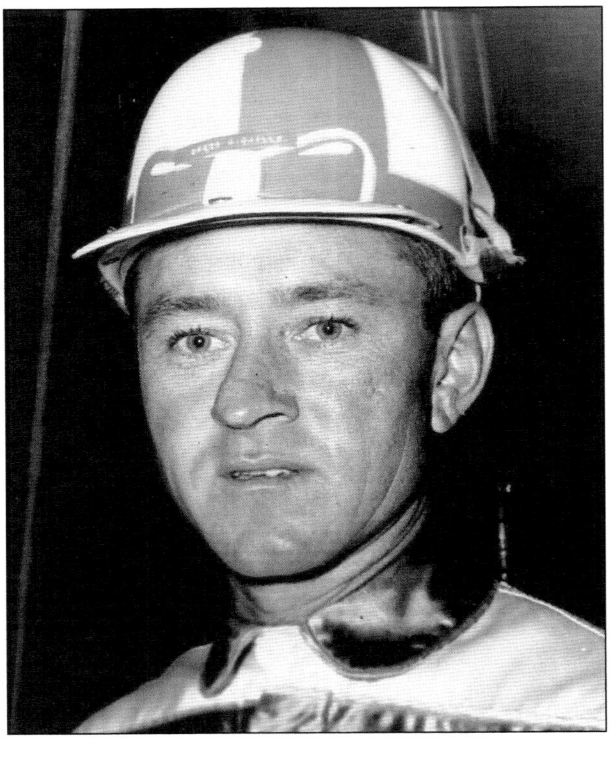

Hall of Famer Frank Ervin (1968) helped to make harness racing the success it is today. He had victories in both the Hambletonian and the Little Brown Jug. Here he is driving Miss Bluegrass. He trained and drove Bret Hanover, who ranked with Nevele Pride as the only horses to win Horse of the Year laurels for three years.

Bruce Nickells operated a racing stable at Pompano Beach for owners from a dozen states. He trained a large crop of two-year-old trotters and pacers each winter. Six times, a Nickells-trained filly earned freshman divisional honors: Follow My Star (1985); Central Park West (1988); Miss Easy (1990); Hazelton Kay (1991); Immortality (1992); and Freedom's Friend (1993).

Howard Beissinger, shown with Helena Hanover, was elected to the Hall of Fame in 1974. In his early career, he developed Hambletonian winners Lindy's Pride (1969) and Speedy Crown (1971); world-champion pacing filly Tarport Lib; and the 1971 two-year-old record holder Entrepreneur. As a resident of Pompano Beach, each winter Beissinger hosted a "rodeo party" for trainers and their families at his Florida ranch.

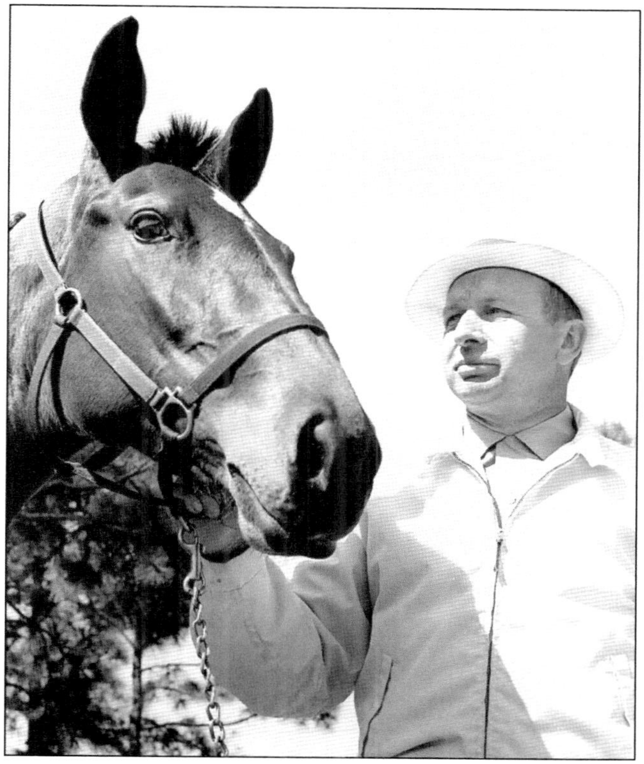

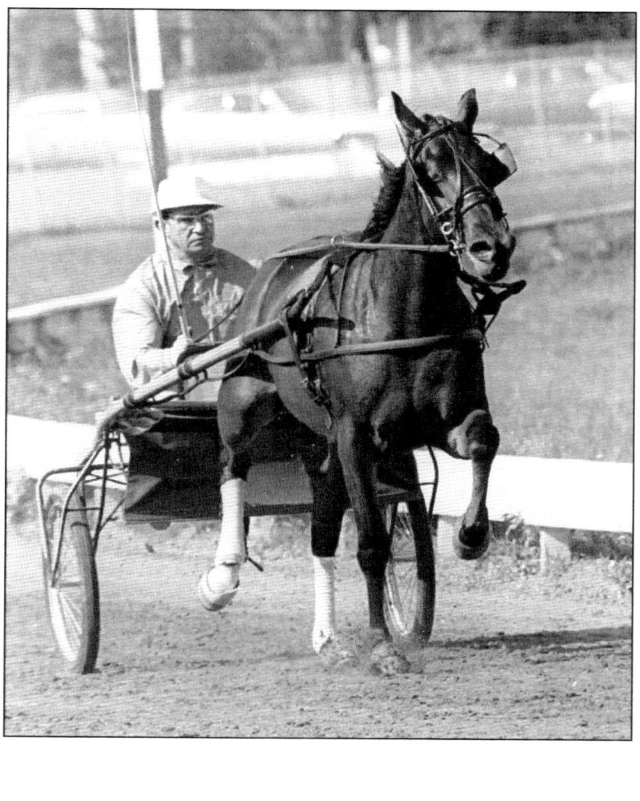

William R. (Billy) Haughton was one of the most brilliant drivers in American racing. He drove winners of more than 120 major stakes races, including four Hambletonians, five Little Brown Jugs, and six Messenger Stakes. He was elected to the Hall of Fame in 1968. Here he is driving Linda Hanover. Haughton died in a tragic racing accident at Yonkers Raceway in 1986.

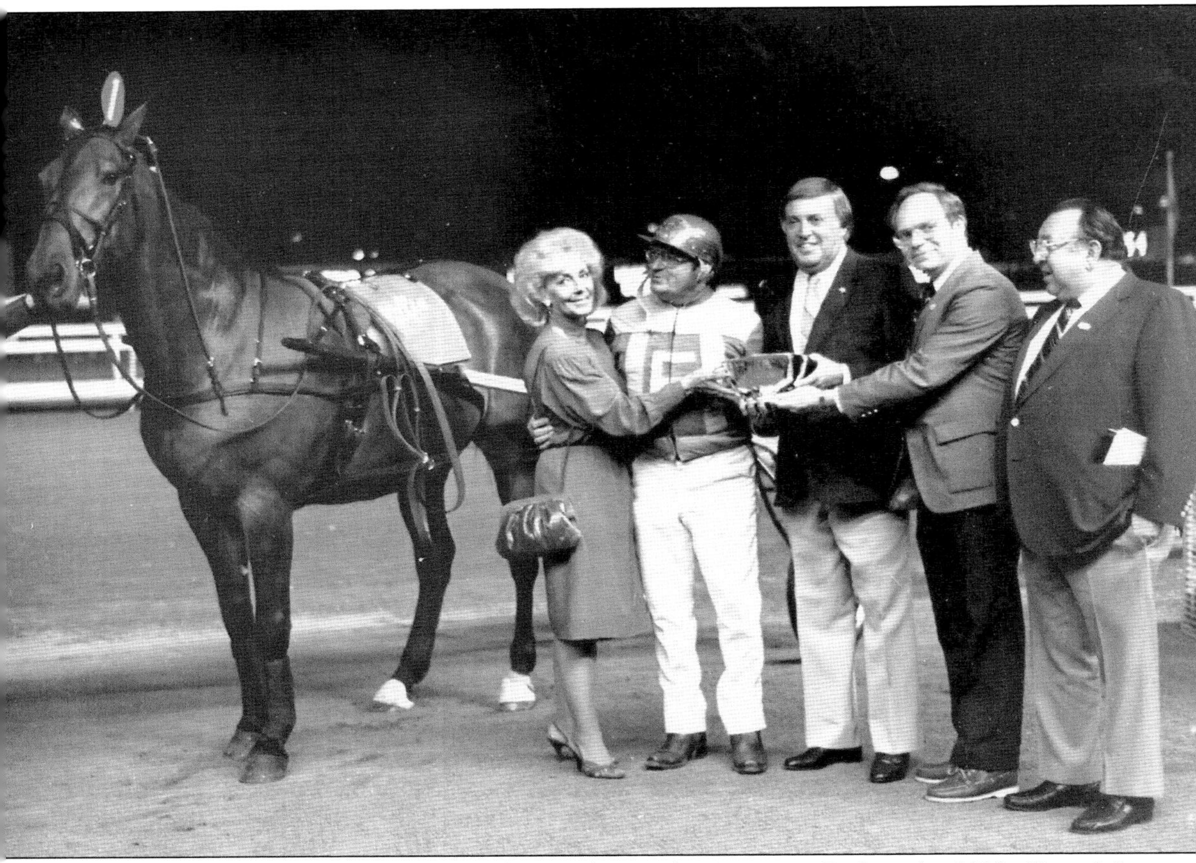

Harness racing legend Rambling Willie was honored at Pompano Park in the 1980s. From left to right are Vivian and Bob Farrington, Allen J. Finkelson, John Berry, and Harness Horsemen International president Dominic H. Frinzi.

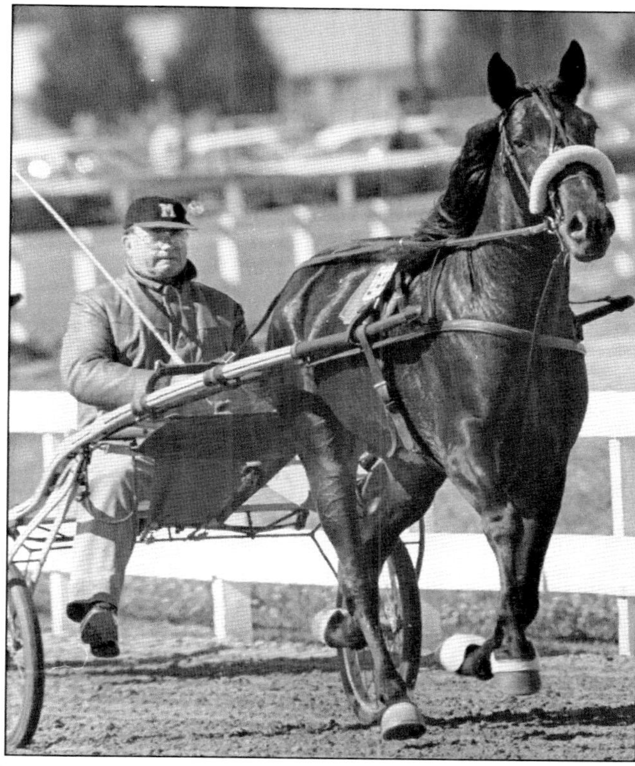

One of the top "money" drivers, Clint Hodgins raised, trained, and drove pacer Skipper Thorpe to eight stakes victories. He wintered and trained in Orlando, Florida. Hodgins was elected to the Hall of Fame by the United States Harness Writers Association in 1972. Here he is driving Bye Bye Pat.

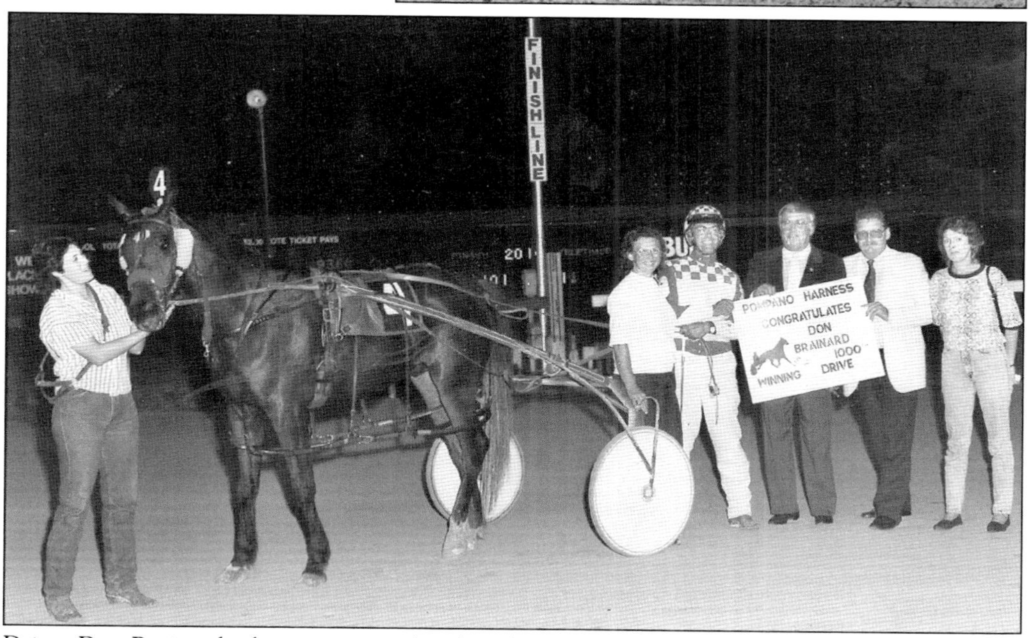

Driver Don Brainard is being congratulated in the winner's circle for a career achievement—his 1,000th victory. From left to right are daughter Michelle, Ocala Royal Dream, wife Barbara, Don Brainard, Pompano Park vice president Allen J. Finkelson, Director of Communications Joe Hartmann, and family friend Peggy Massey.

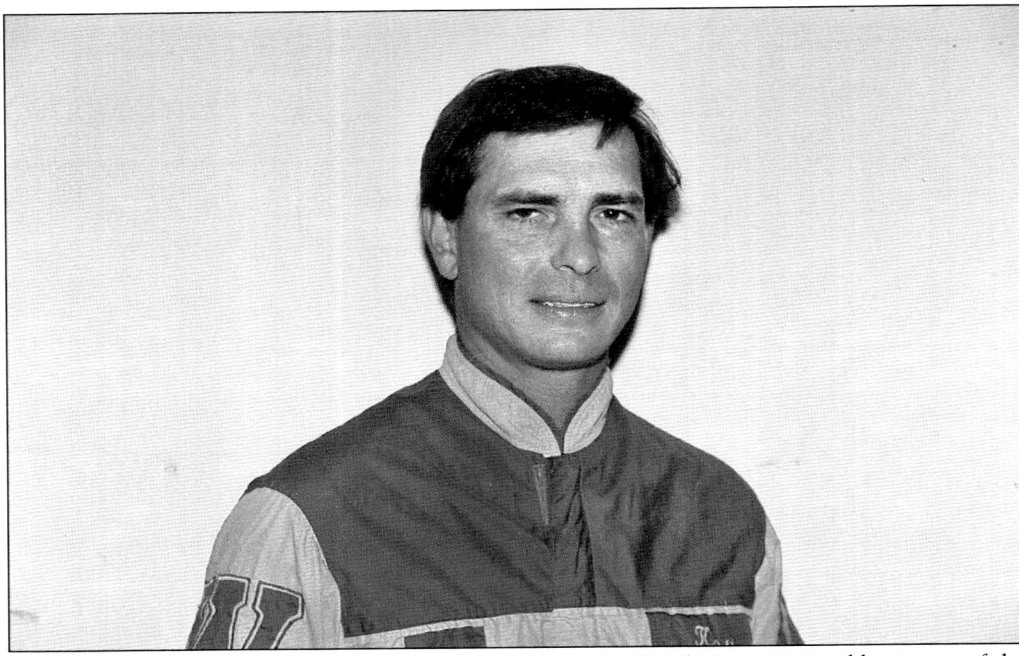

Kevin Wallis has become one of the fastest-rising stars in North America, and he is one of the most sought-after drivers. He splits his time between Pompano Park and Hazel Park. Wallis conditions a quality stable. Two of his outstanding horses have been pacing gelding Robitaille and top-class trotter Beemers Taylor T.

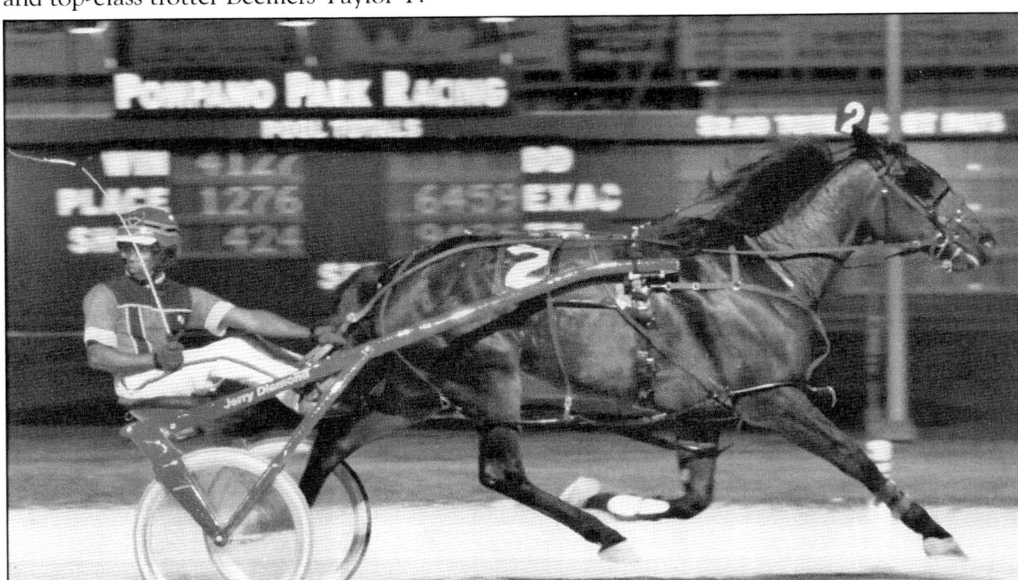

Allan Johnson looks back at the competition as he sweeps to victory with Supreme Confidence in August 1998. Johnson participated in the first Martin Luther King Race in January 2001 honoring the civil rights leader.

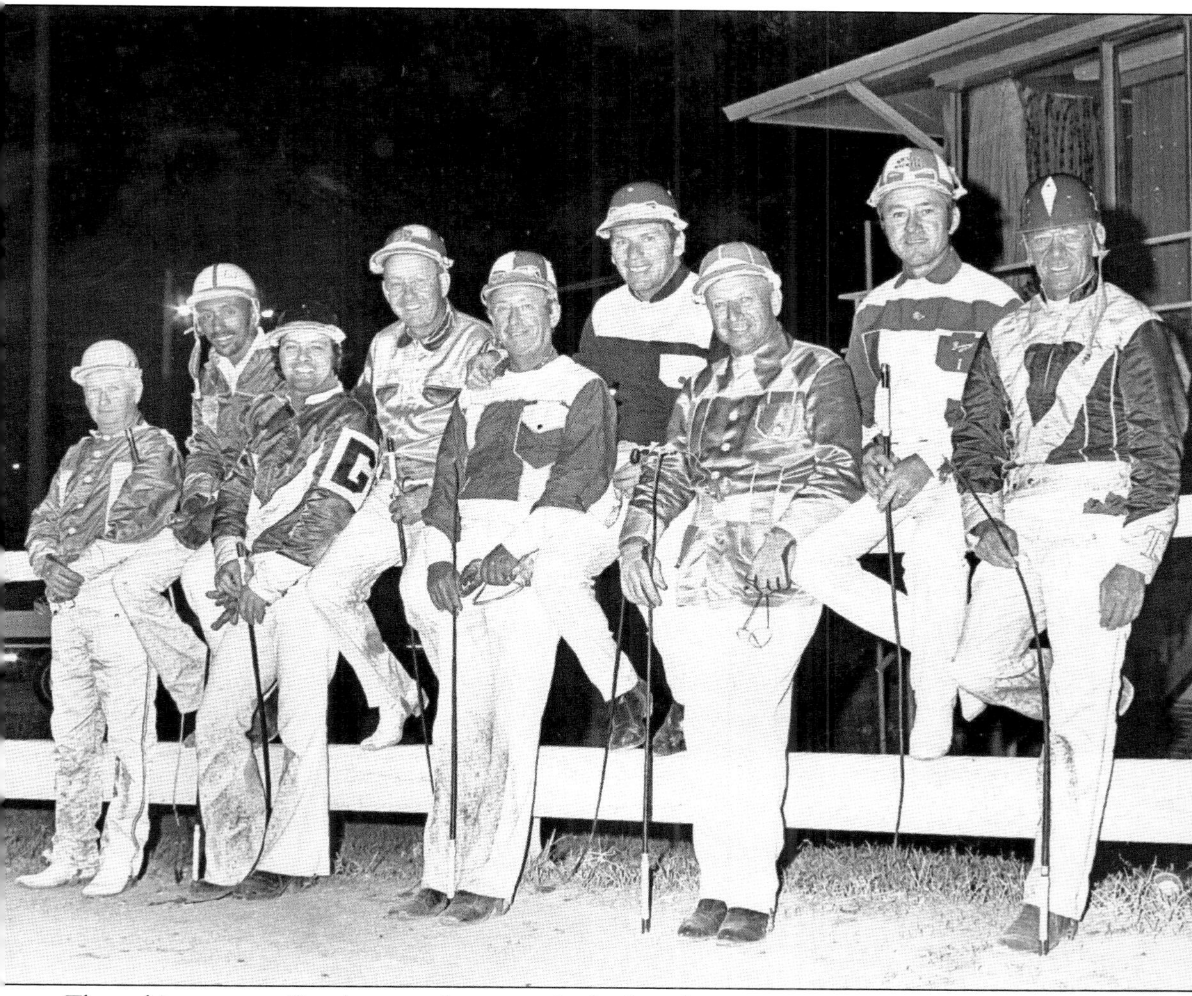

These drivers are smiling because they were the leading drivers at Pompano Park in the 1970s and 1980s. They also were noted for their achievements in North America. From left to right are Joe O'Brien, Lewis Williams, Gilles Gendron, Del Miller, Billy Haughton, Glen Garnsey, Howard Beissinger, Bruce Nickells, and Ted Taylor.

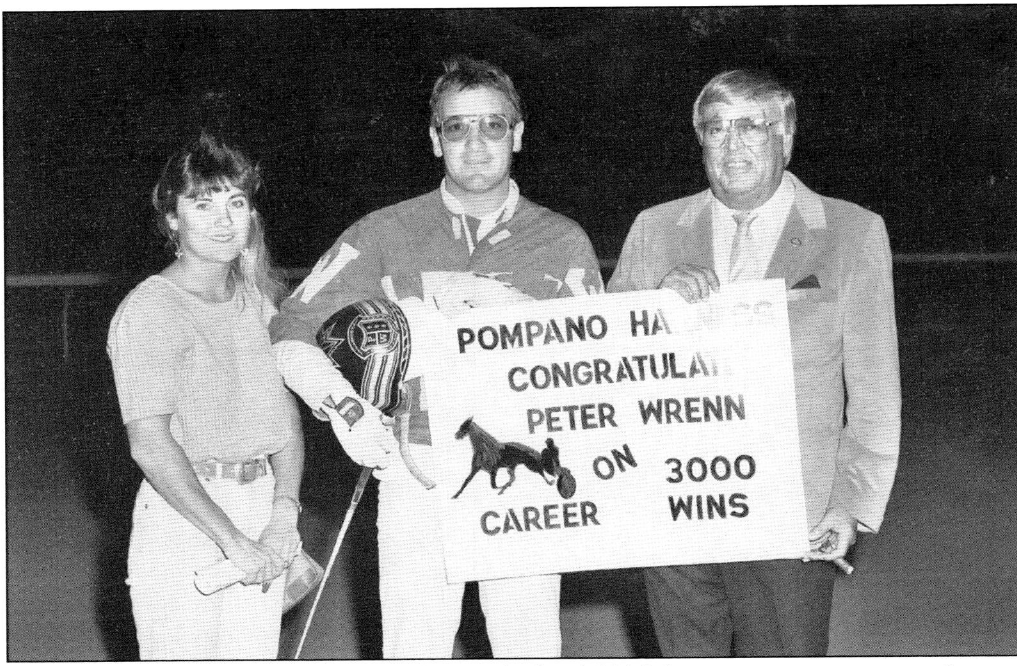

Driver Peter Wrenn receives congratulations for his 3,000th harness racing victory on January 3, 1993. From left to right are wife Melanie Wrenn, Peter Wrenn, and Pompano Park publicist Allen J. Finkelson.

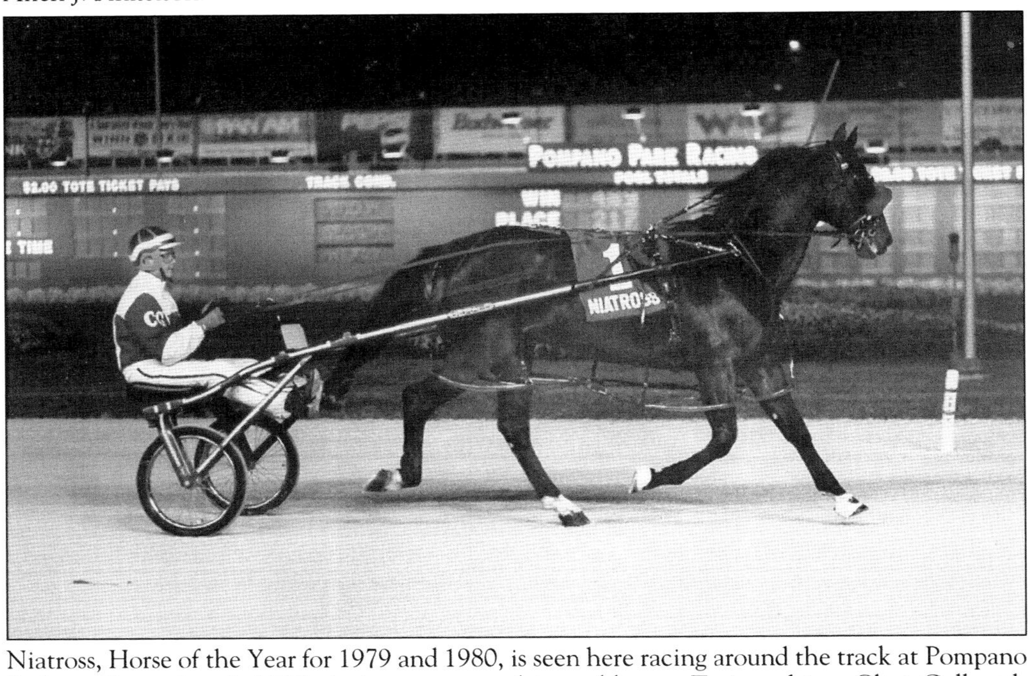

Niatross, Horse of the Year for 1979 and 1980, is seen here racing around the track at Pompano Park on December 6, 1987, during a stop on his world tour. Trainer-driver Clint Galbraith is guiding this magnificent champion. Niatross retired to stud in 1981 at Castleton Farm in Lexington, Kentucky.

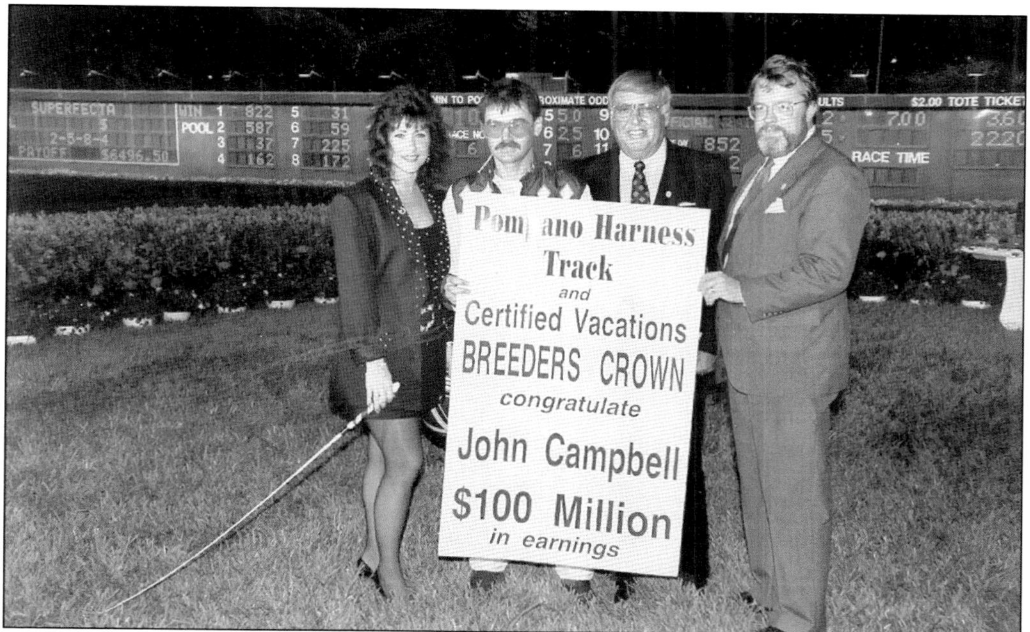

With the totalizator board in the background, John Campbell receives kudos for reaching the $100 million mark in earnings on October 25, 1991. Allen J. Finkelson is second from right, joined by representatives of Certified Vacations.

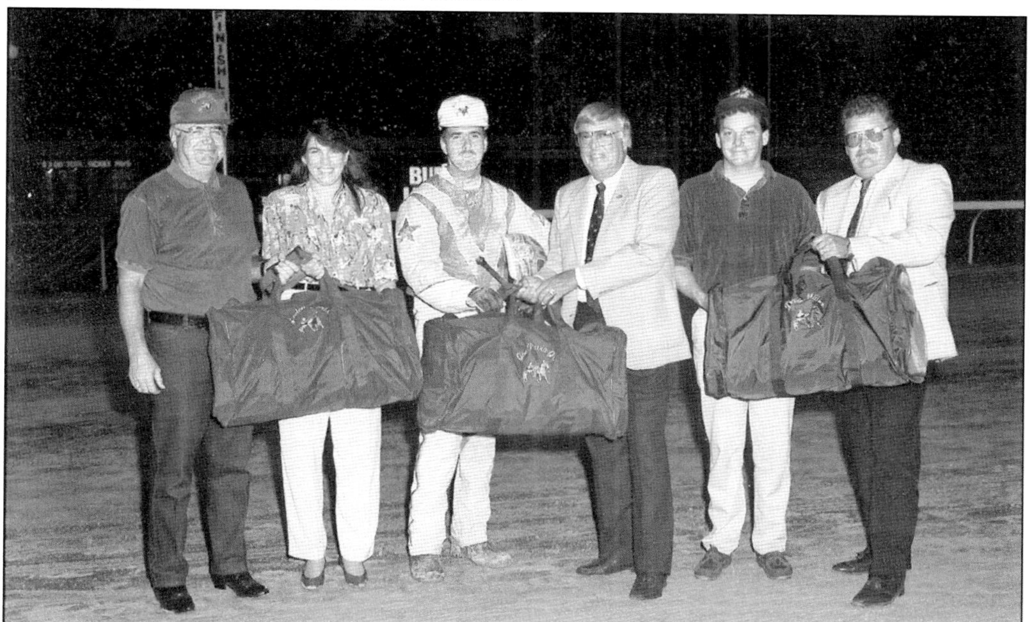

Pompano Park's top trainers and drivers for the 1991–1992 season received custom equipment bags in a ceremony conducted by the Florida chapter of the United States Harness Writers Association (USHWA). From left to right are Gordon Norris, chapter president Denise Loewe, Joe Pavia Jr., USHWA chairman Allen J. Finkelson, Don Miller (substituting for brother Doug), and Florida chapter delegate Joe Hartmann.

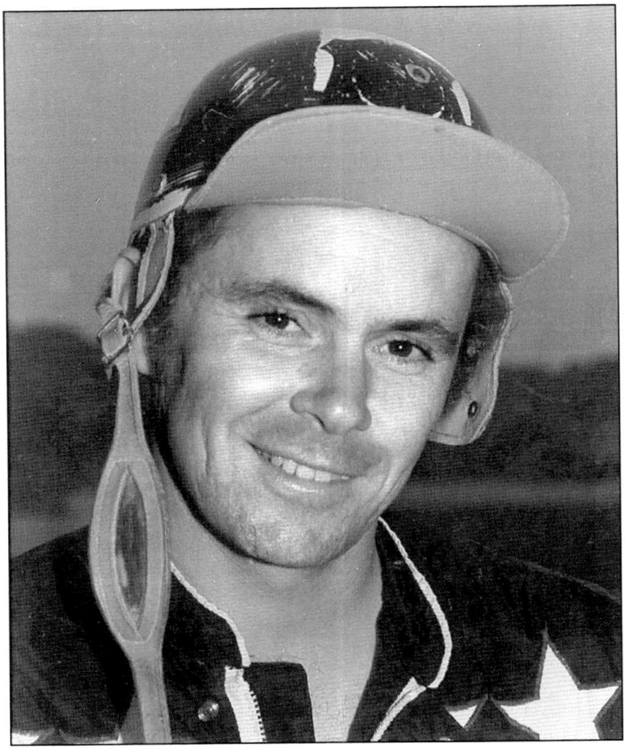

A former vendor at Yankee Stadium, Micky McNichol won his share of races at Pompano Park. He also won the 1992 Hambletonian with Alf Paloma, the Hambletonian Oaks with Jef's Spice in 1986, and the 1982 Adios with Higher Power. He recorded his 4,000th victory in 2002 and has earned more than $40 million in purse money.

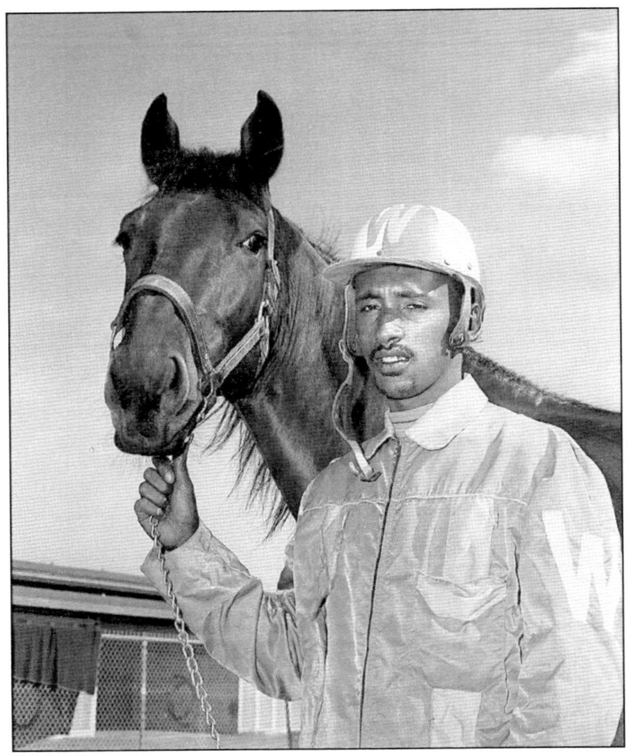

Lewis Williams (1947–1989) became the youngest driver to win 1,000 races at age 26. "Super Lew" was honored during the Pompano Park birthday celebration of Dr. Martin Luther King. In 1972, he was the leading Pompano Park driver, with 52 wins. Williams died in a tractor accident at 42 years of age.

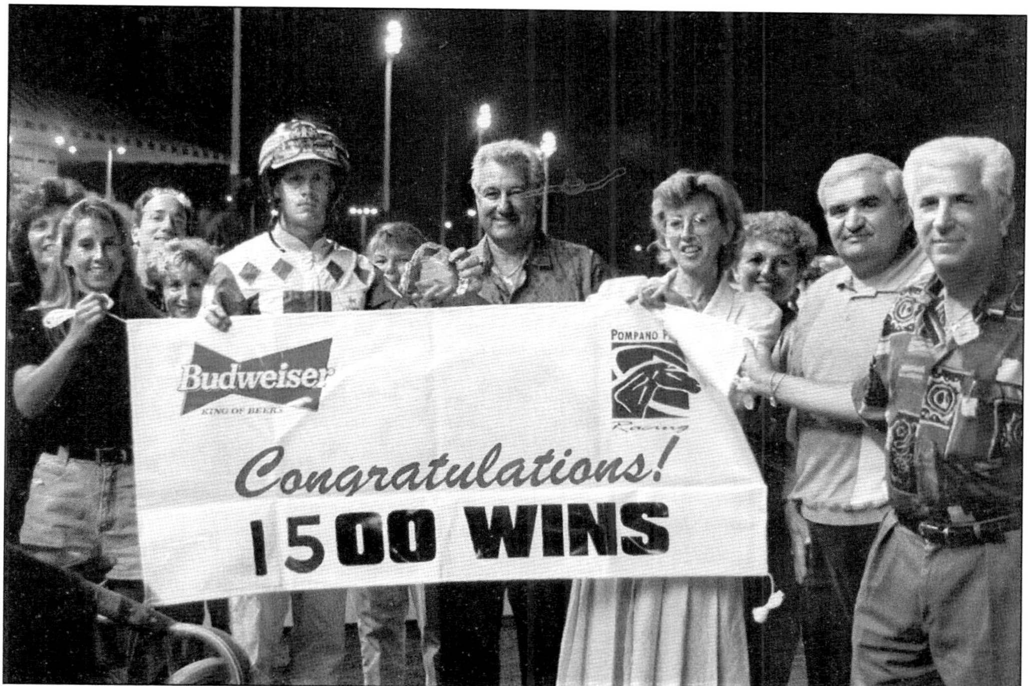

Friends and relatives join the celebration of Jeff Gregory for his gaining a milestone 1,500th win on March 6, 1997. He drove Turnpike Token to victory.

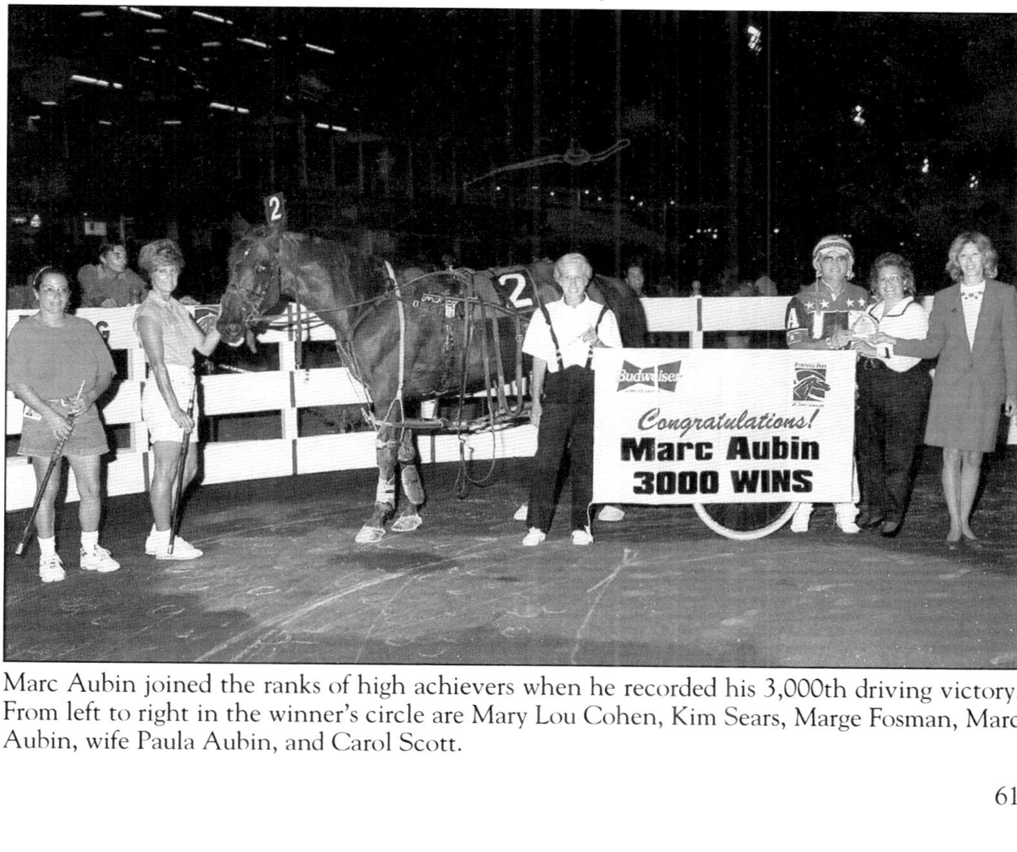

Marc Aubin joined the ranks of high achievers when he recorded his 3,000th driving victory. From left to right in the winner's circle are Mary Lou Cohen, Kim Sears, Marge Fosman, Marc Aubin, wife Paula Aubin, and Carol Scott.

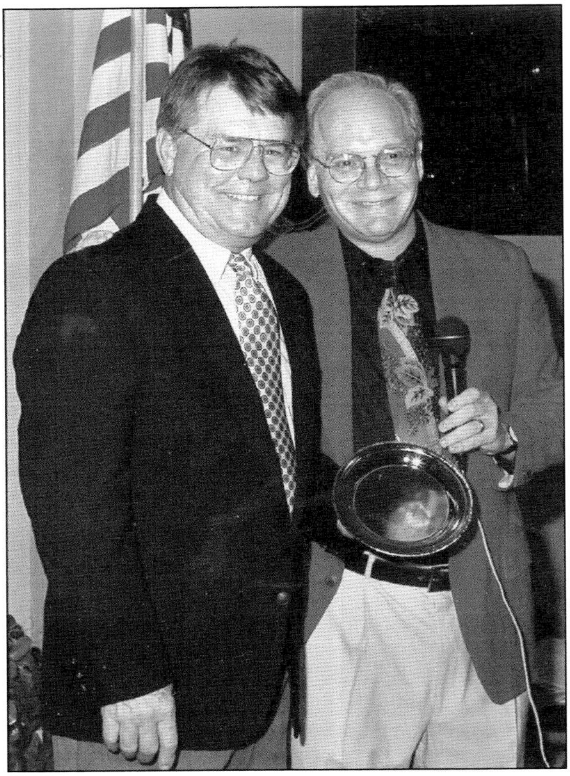

Pompano Park's John Berry (right) honors horseman Jay Sears during the Hall of Fame dinner at Palm Aire on March 31, 1998. For more than 25 years, Sears operated a stable and raced at Pompano Park and Vernon Downs. In 1992, Sears was hired as executive director of the Florida Standardbred Breeders and Owners Association, a position he held for 10 years. He is a member of the Frederick L. van Lennep Florida Racing Hall of Fame.

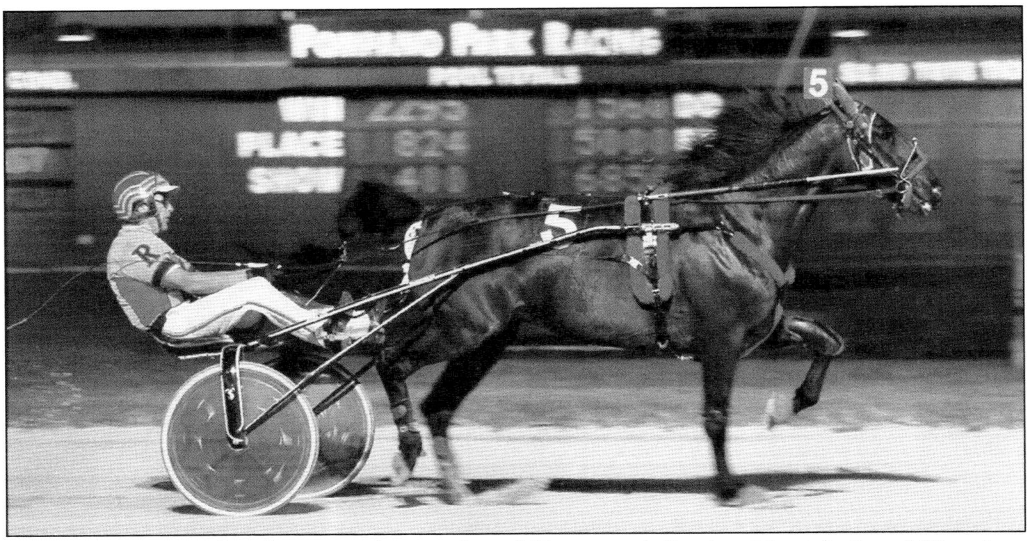

Bruce Ranger clinches his 3,600th win aboard Diane and Gordon Norris's Speed Pine in a 1:58.3 trotting mile on August 6, 1999. Jay Pocza was the trainer. By September 2004, Ranger had more than 5,700 career wins as a driver, with more than 4,000 of those victories at Pompano Park, where he has won eight driving and training titles.

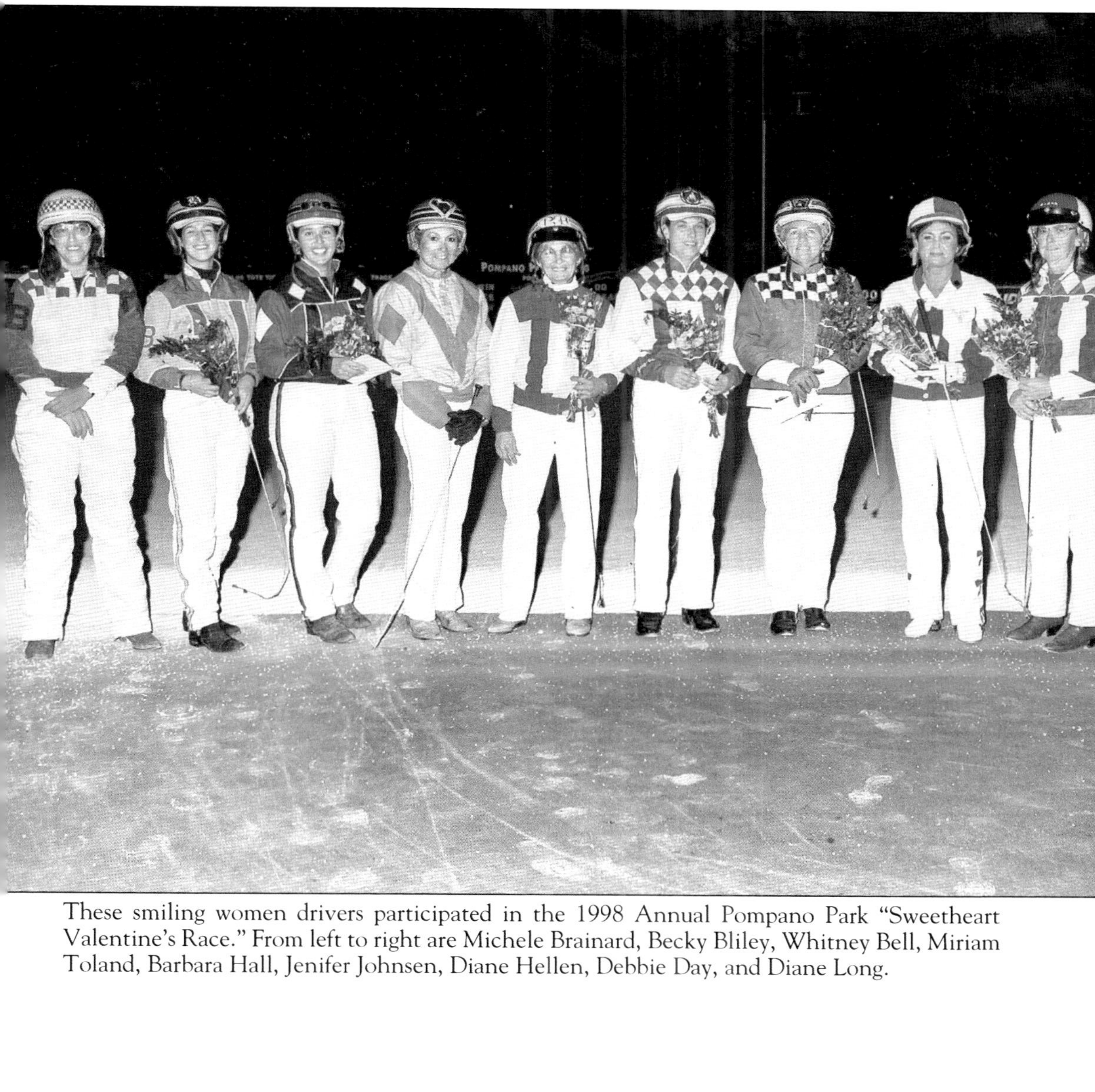

These smiling women drivers participated in the 1998 Annual Pompano Park "Sweetheart Valentine's Race." From left to right are Michele Brainard, Becky Bliley, Whitney Bell, Miriam Toland, Barbara Hall, Jenifer Johnsen, Diane Hellen, Debbie Day, and Diane Long.

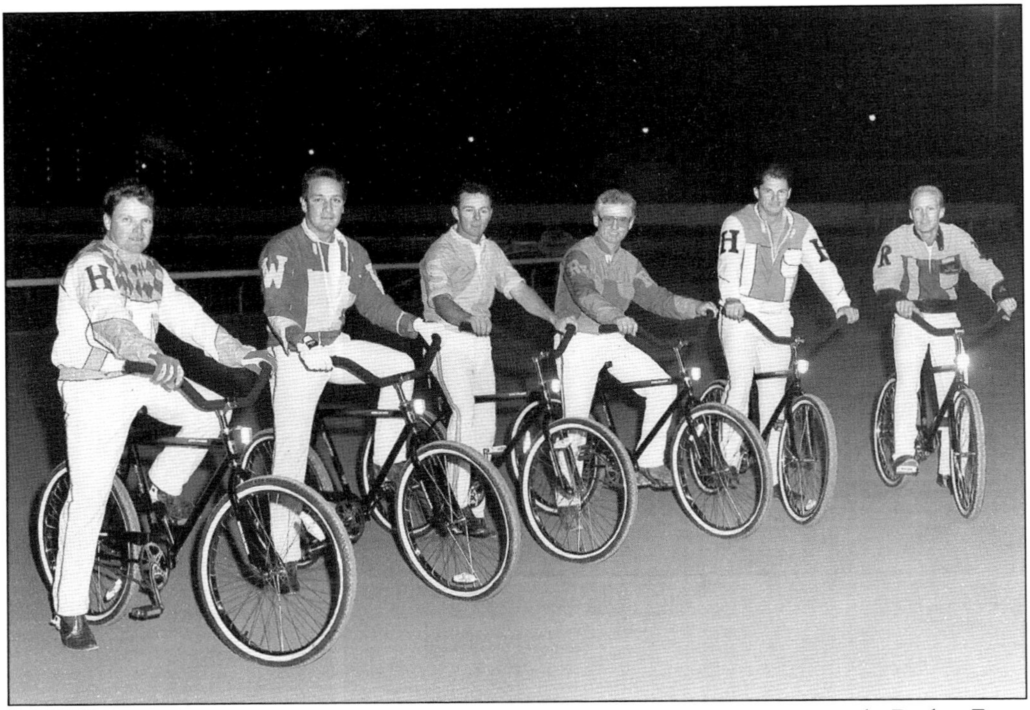

Pompano Park's top drivers line up after competing in the 1998 Drivers Bicycle Derby. From left to right are Wally Hennessey, Peter Wrenn, Kevin Sizer, Ron Waples, Don Harmon (who finished first in the eighth-of-a-mile dash), and Bruce Ranger, who was second.

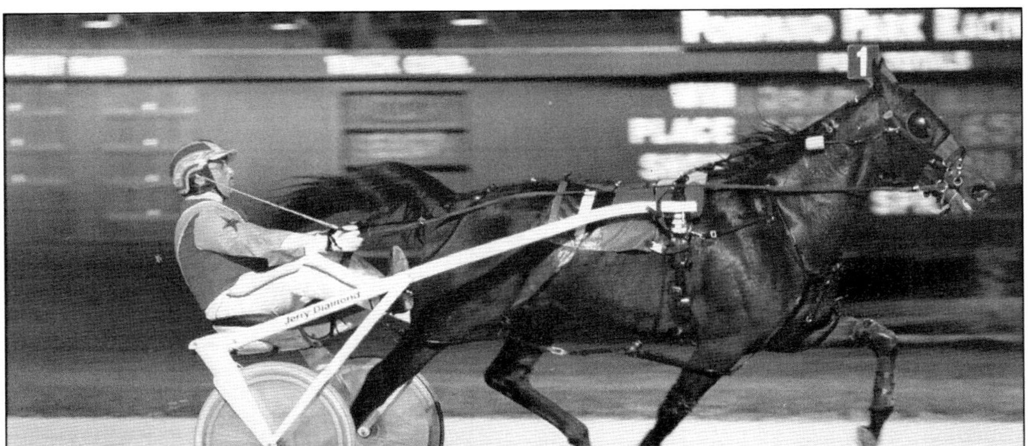

Joe Pavia Jr. has always been at the top of the standings. He adapts his driving style to the horse not vice versa. Here he drives Private Ritual to victory on November 7, 1998. Pavia got his start in harness racing at Vernon Downs with Bob McNulty and Tony Mondi.

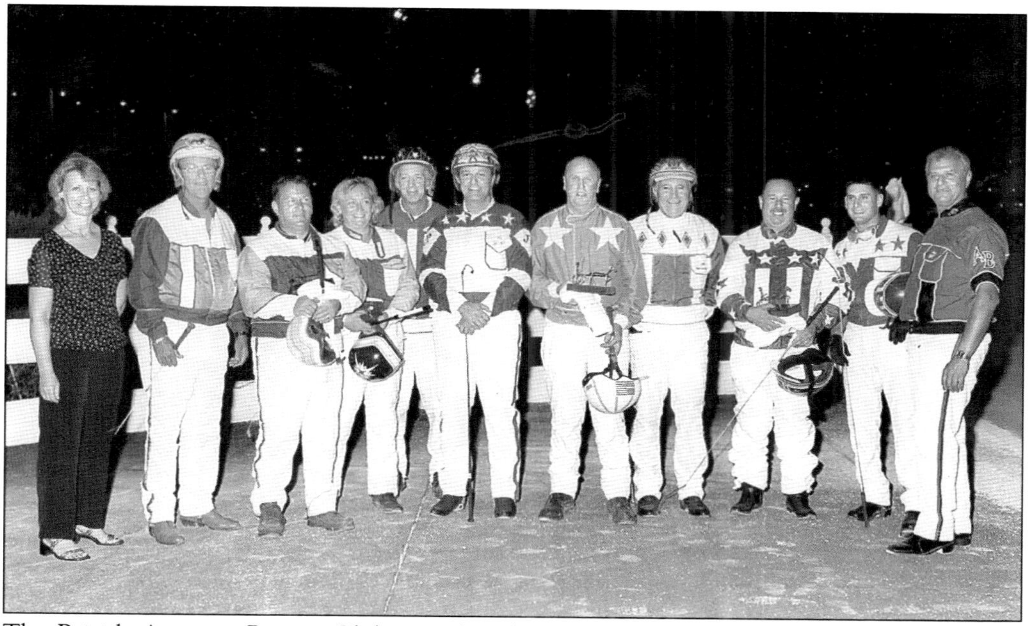

The British Amateur Racing Club joined with several Pompano Park drivers in 2001. The promotional competition was friendly between the cousins across the Atlantic. From left to right are unidentified, Bob Keeler, David Pearson, Remine Pearson, Gary Barbieri, Joe Pennacchio, Mickey Yoemans, Bud Hatfield, John Hammond, Anthony Napolitano, and Alan Benjamin.

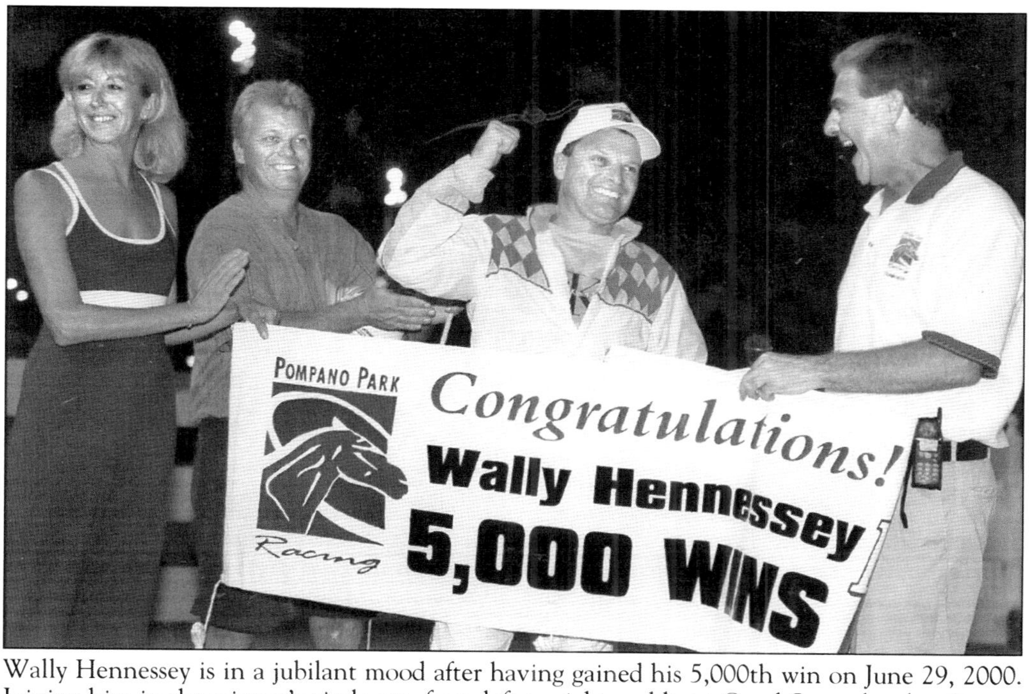

Wally Hennessey is in a jubilant mood after having gained his 5,000th win on June 29, 2000. Joining him in the winner's circle are, from left to right, publicist Carol Scott, brother Danny Hennessey, and Larry Albano.

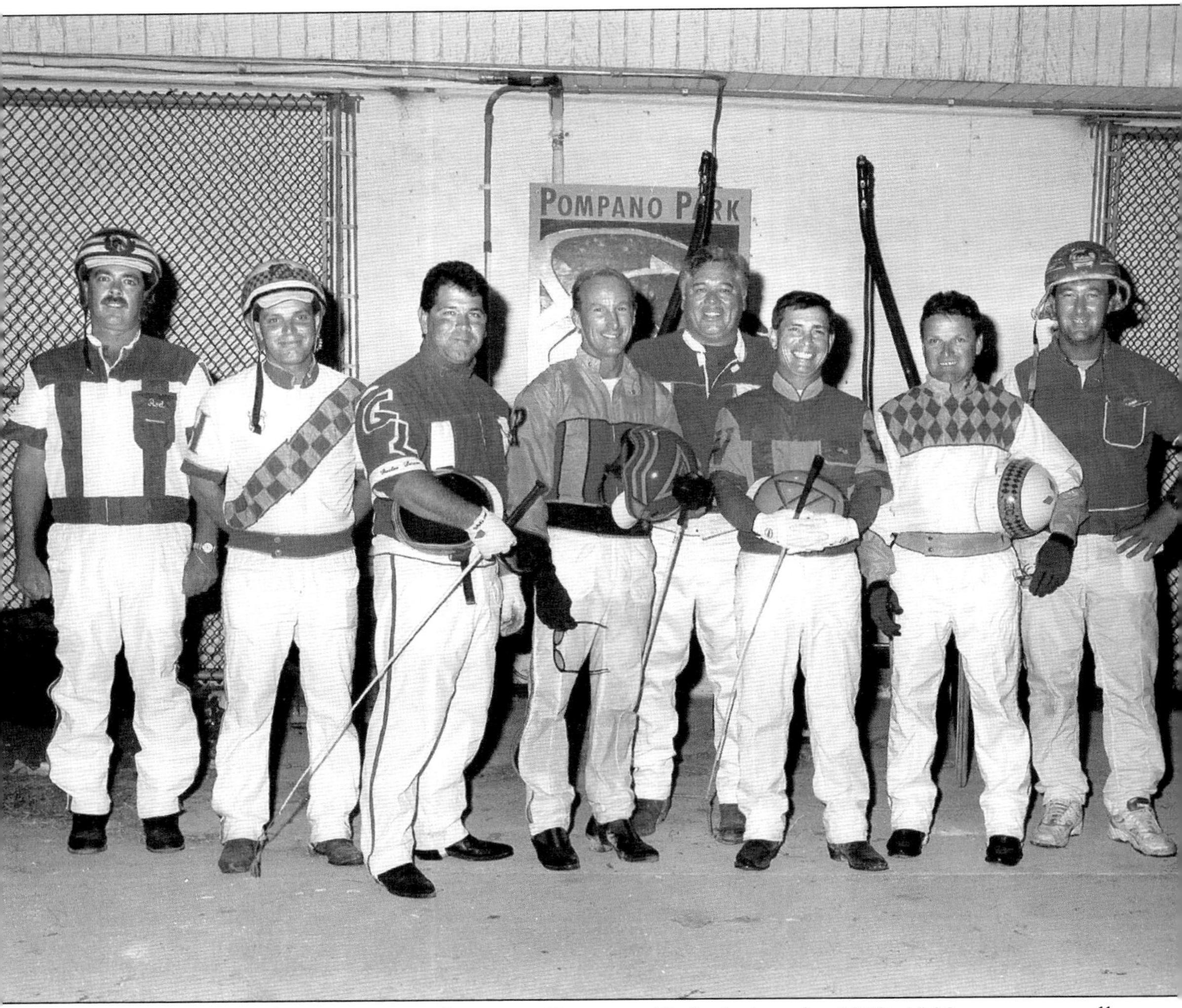

The dominant harness-racing drivers at Pompano Park during the 1997–1998 season are all smiles as they pose for this group photo. From left to right are Rod Lorenzo, John Hallett, Gaston Lareau, Bruce Ranger, John Martin, Kevin Wallis, Wally Hennessey, and Craig Mosher. Ranger established his dominance during the summer meets of the 1990s, but in the 35th season, he was dominant throughout the regular meet with 384 wins.

Four

HAPPENINGS

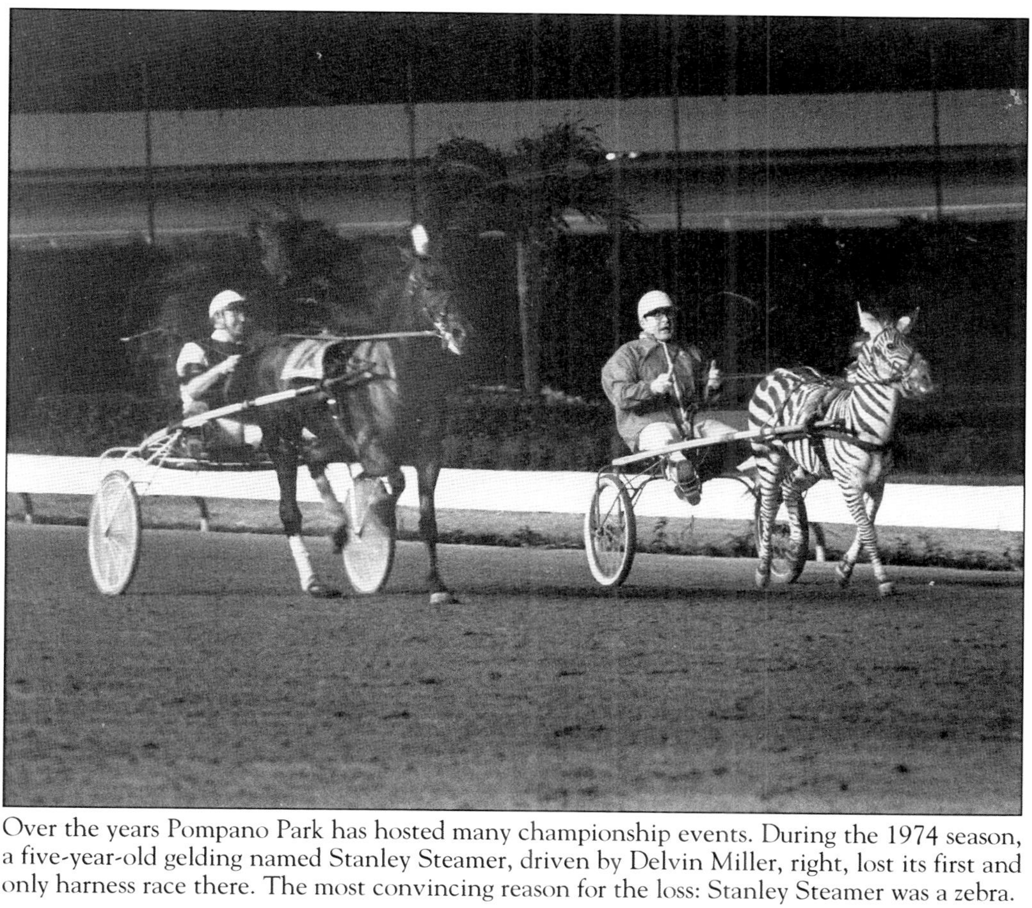

Over the years Pompano Park has hosted many championship events. During the 1974 season, a five-year-old gelding named Stanley Steamer, driven by Delvin Miller, right, lost its first and only harness race there. The most convincing reason for the loss: Stanley Steamer was a zebra.

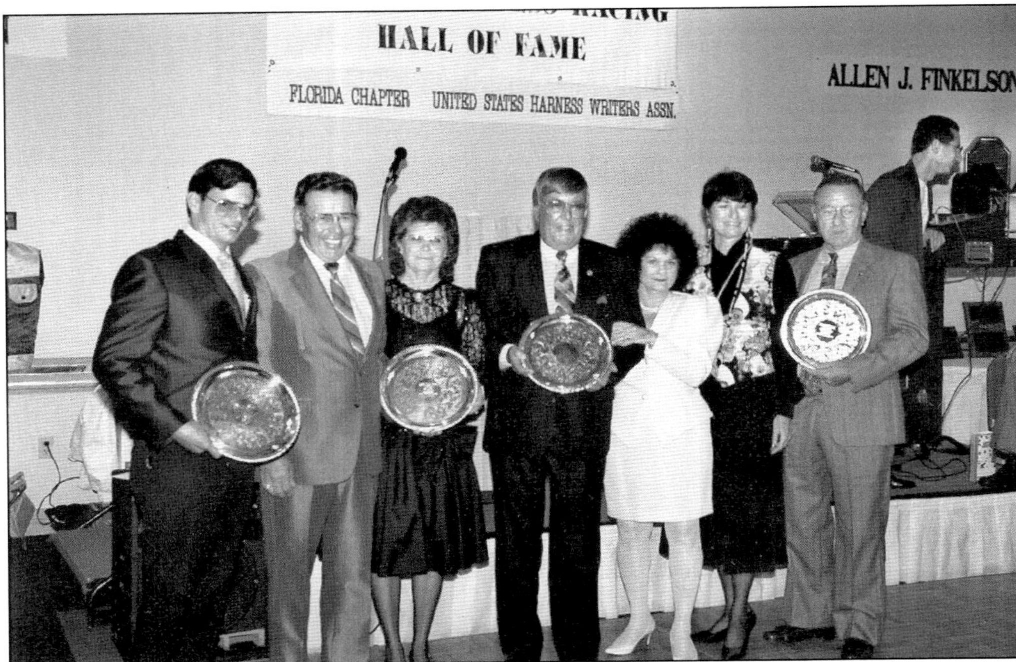

The newest inductees into the Frederick L. van Lennep Florida Harness Racing Hall of Fame display their hardware during the induction ceremonies in Fort Lauderdale on March 21, 1993. From left to right are John van Lennep representing his mother Frances, Carl and Mae Jean Allen, Allen J. and Betty Finkelson, and Joanne and Bruce Nickells.

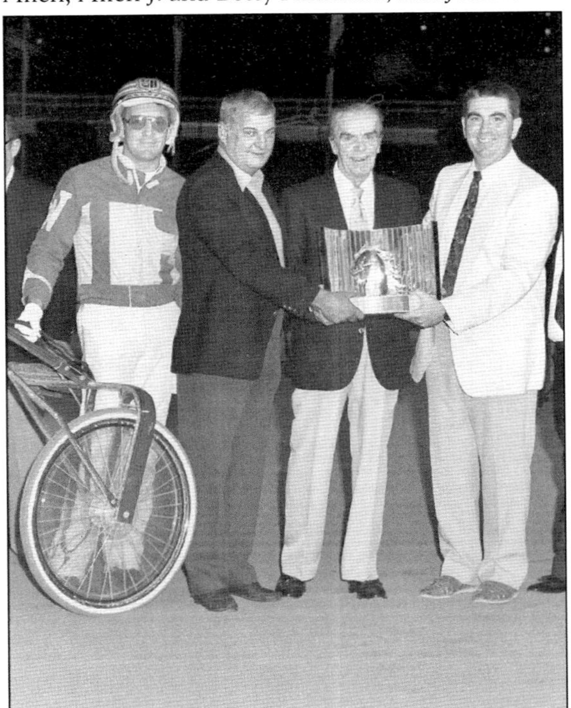

As part of the convention of the American Racing Secretaries Association, former Pompano Park director of racing Bill Connors, second from right, was honored at the track on December 4, 1992. Participating in the presentation are, from left to right, Pompano's defending driving champion Peter Wrenn, Hazel Park racing secretary Ken Marshall, Connors, and Pompano Park racing secretary Kent Williams.

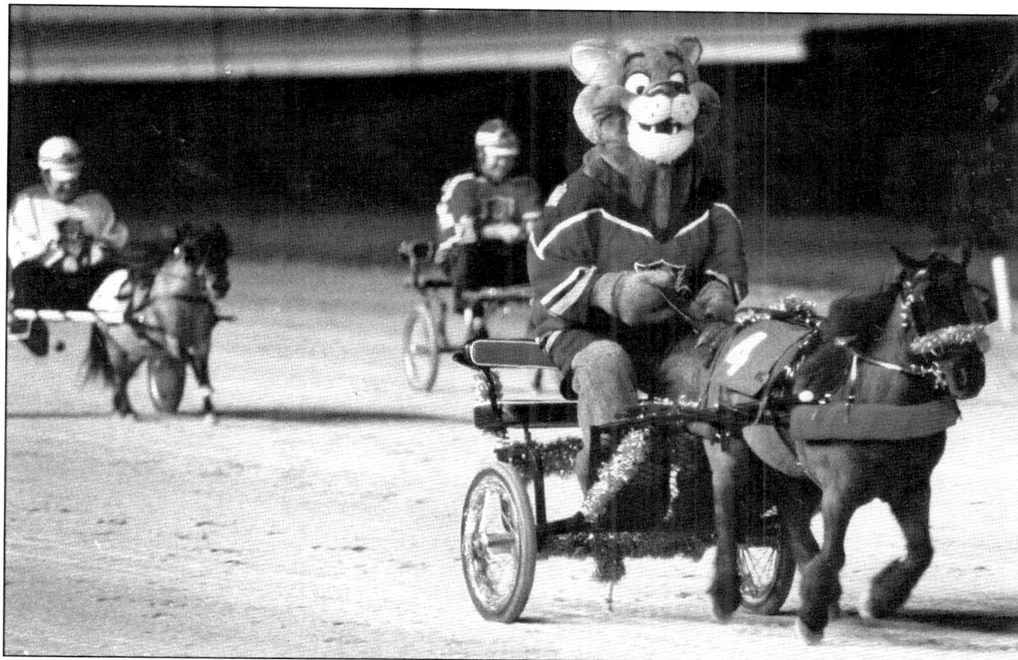

In a special promotion with the Florida Panthers hockey team, mascot "Stanley O'Panther" races to victory with his mini horse during the celebration of St. Patrick's Day in 1997. The Pompano Park Minis are a popular attraction to young and old.

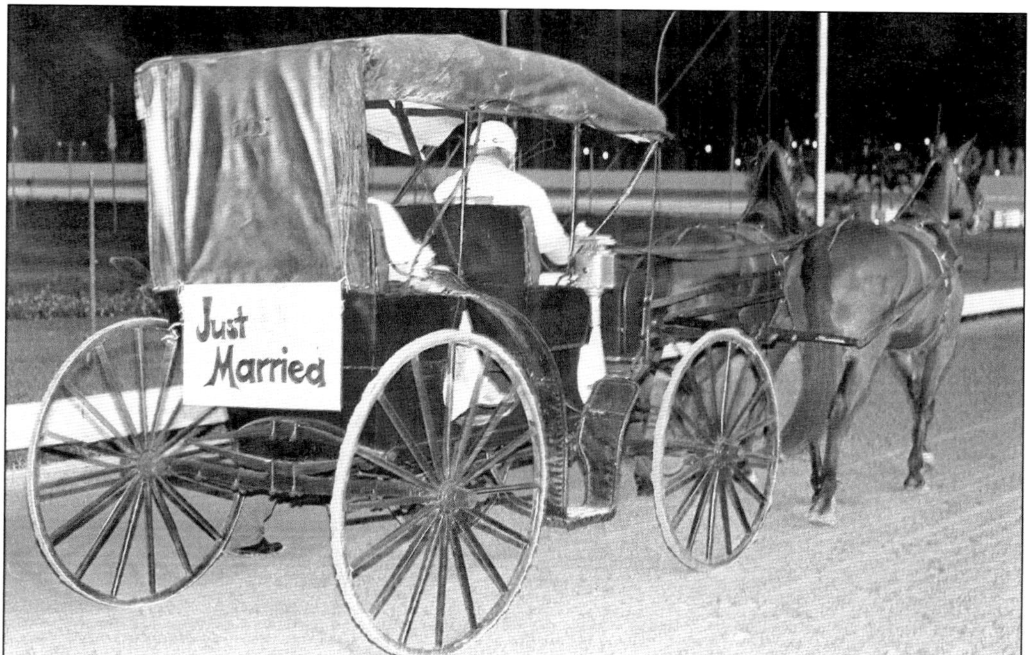

"Just Married" is what the sign says, but "Love and marriage go together like a horse and carriage" is the appropriate lyric for this newly married couple. They are being driven around the track before the evening racing card started.

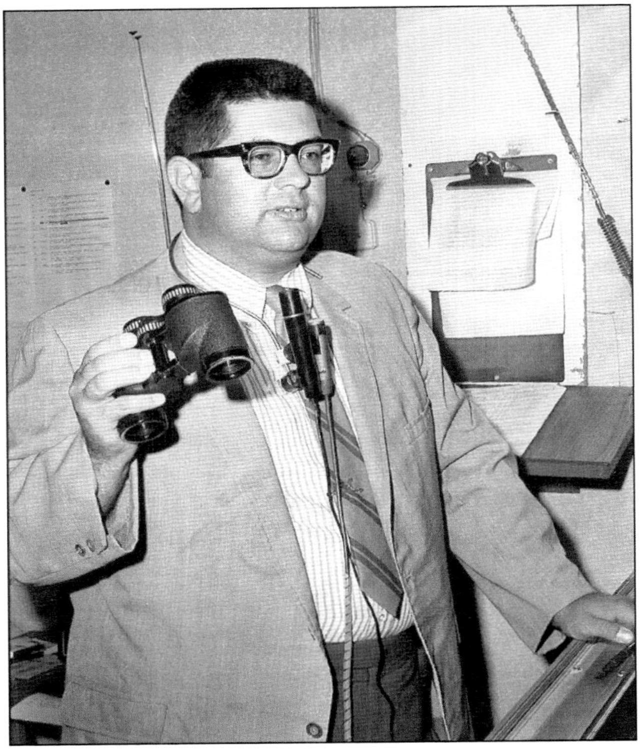

Roger Huston, one of the few track announcers elected to the Writer's Corner of the Hall of Fame, was the Pompano Park track announcer in the 1970s. Today, Huston is known as the "Voice of the Little Brown Jug." He began announcing races in 1960.

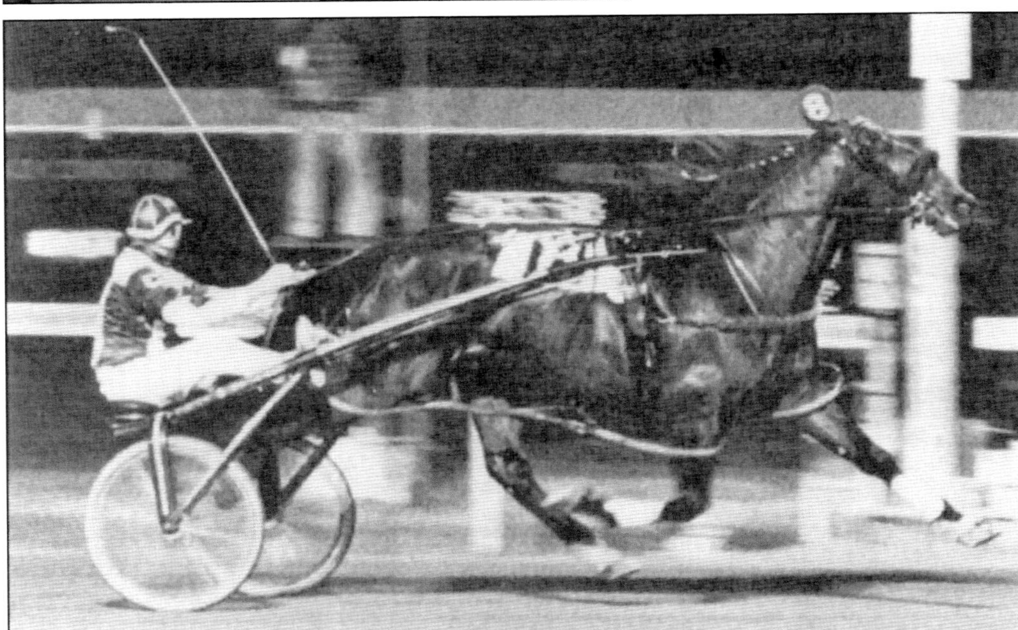

Clint Galbraith drives Niatross to a fifteen-length victory in the $35,000 Invitational Pace and the mile in 1:54.3—the fastest ever at the Pompano Park five-eighths mile strip—on December 27, 1980, before a record crowd. Niatross won 37 of 39 career starts and was timed faster than 2 minutes in 34 of them. (Courtesy of *The Horseman and Fair World* magazine.)

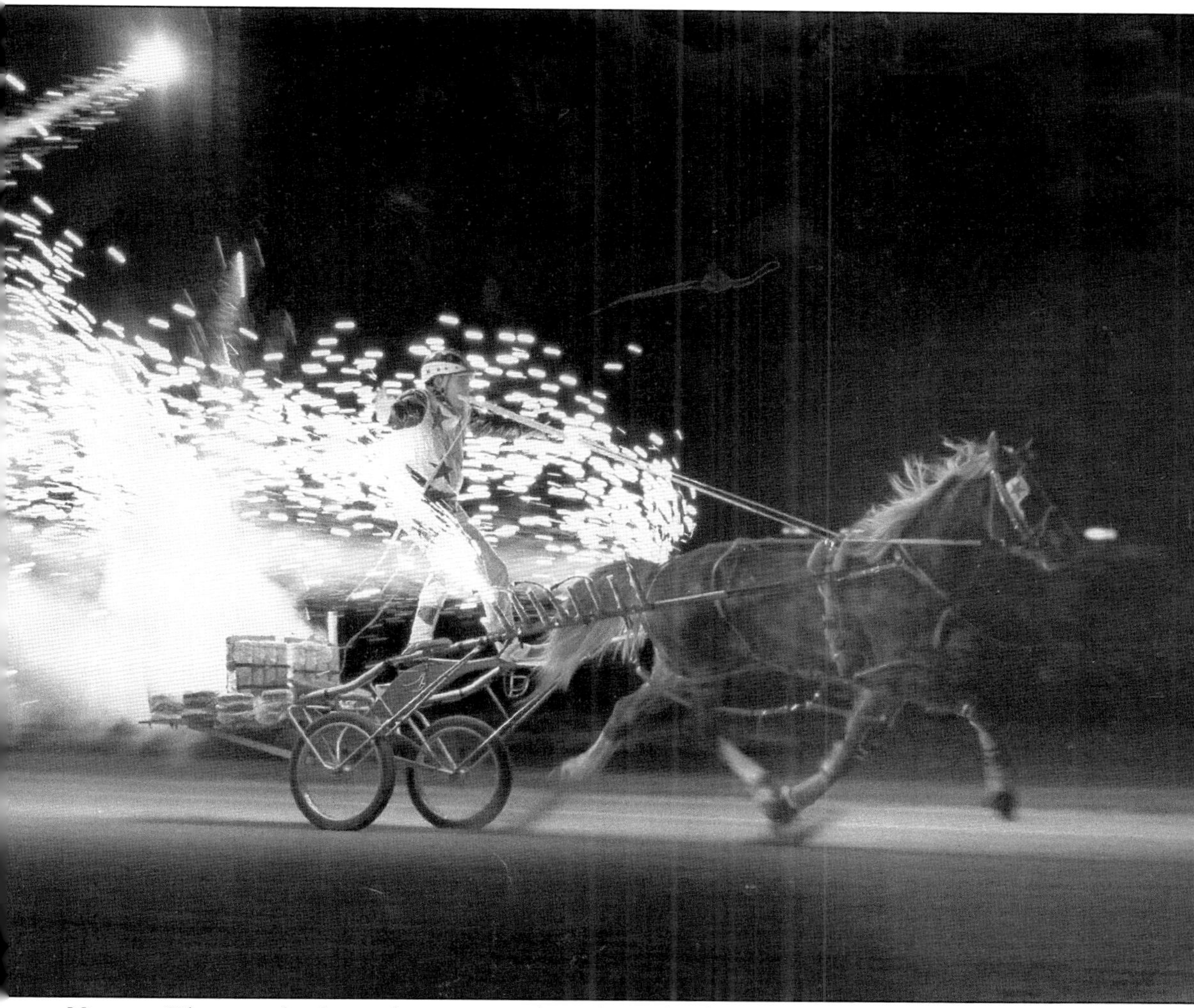

Vincent Silvestro, the fireworks stuntman from Australia, has thrilled Pompano fans with his stunning "Hot to Trot" performance. Standing on the shafts of a harness racing bike, he grasps the lines in his teeth, holds 15,000–candle-power marine flares in his hands, and shoots off massive rounds of fireworks—more than 2,000 explosions. At the same time, his horse, Hand Me Silver, speeds around the darkened track at 25 miles an hour.

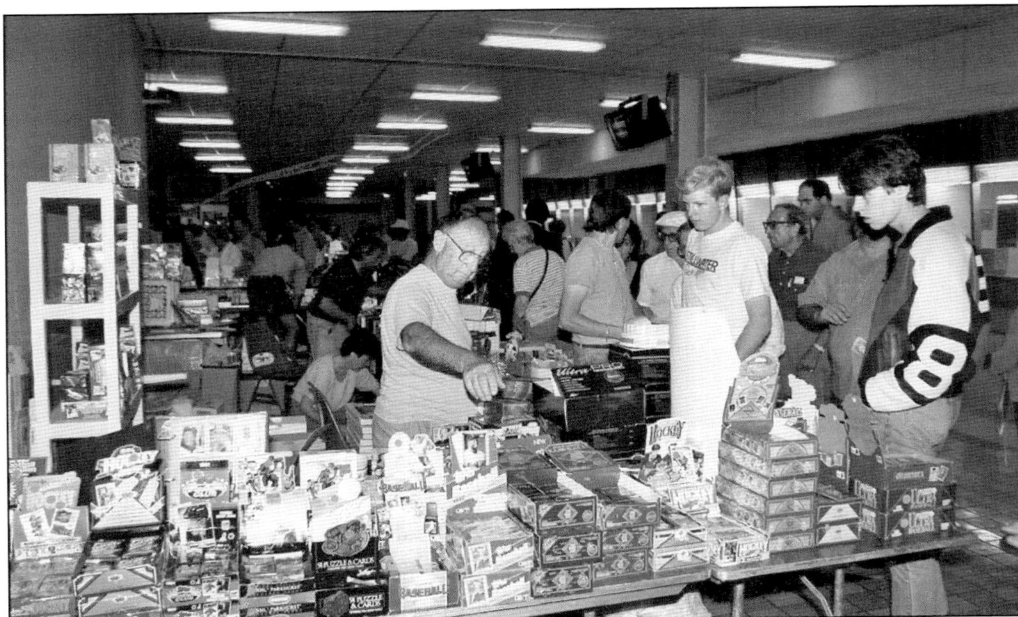

As part of the 29th season in 1991–1992, Pompano Park hosted a card show. Collectors and other interested people showed up to examine the displays and to purchase memorabilia. There were 178 racing nights that season, the most at the time. Trainer Gordon Norris sent out a record 119 winners from his barn to take his sixth straight title, propelling Peter Wrenn to the top of the drivers' standings for the fourth time overall.

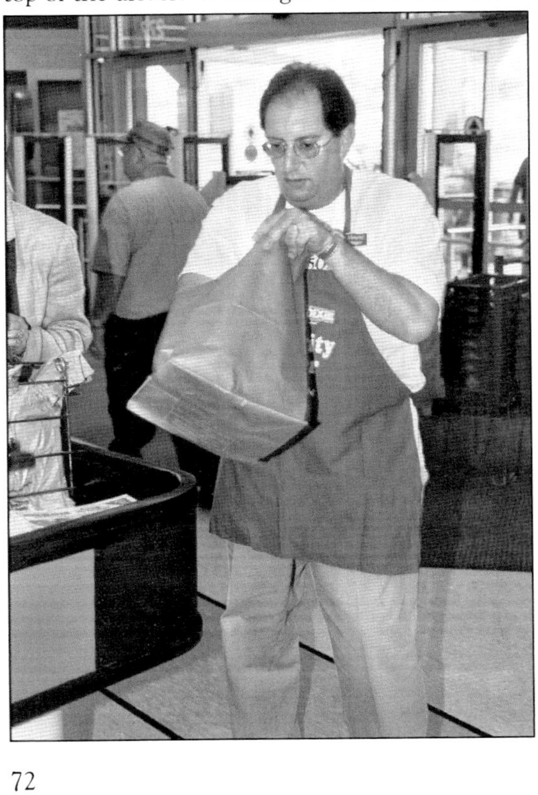

Steve Wolf, director of marketing and communications, bags food at a local Winn-Dixie supermarket during a major fund-raising event in 2001. Pompano Park employees, trainers, and drivers all contributed their time and effort to raise money for the American Cancer Society.

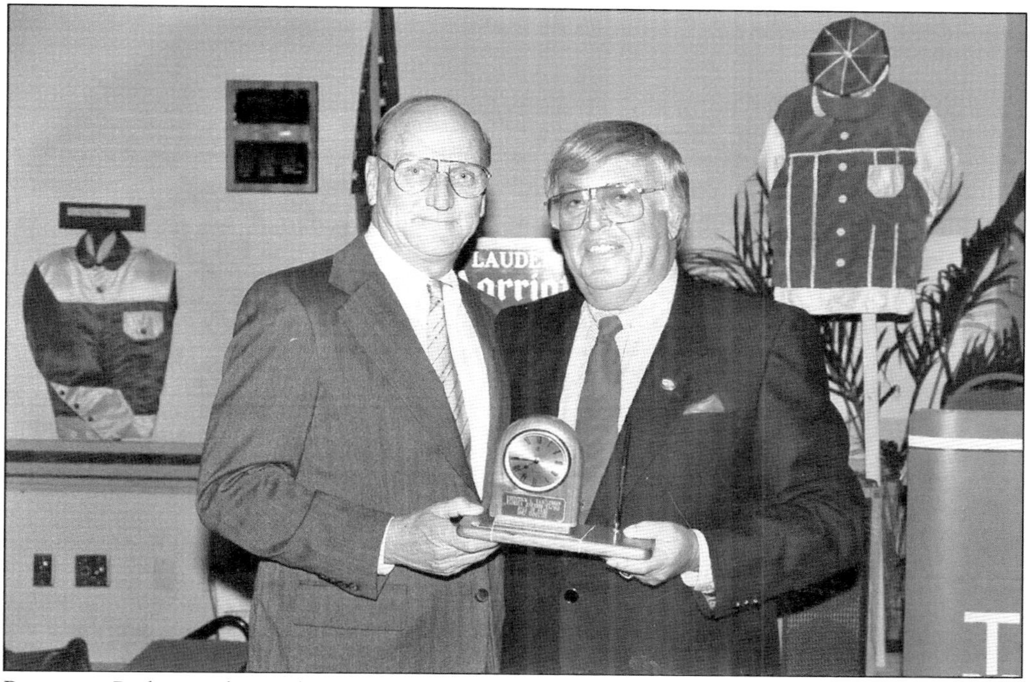

Pompano Park president John Cashman Jr. receives an award for his contribution to the sport from Allan J. Finkelson on Cashman's induction to the Florida Harness Racing Hall of Fame. The ceremony was part of the annual awards dinner held at the Fort Lauderdale Marriott in 1992.

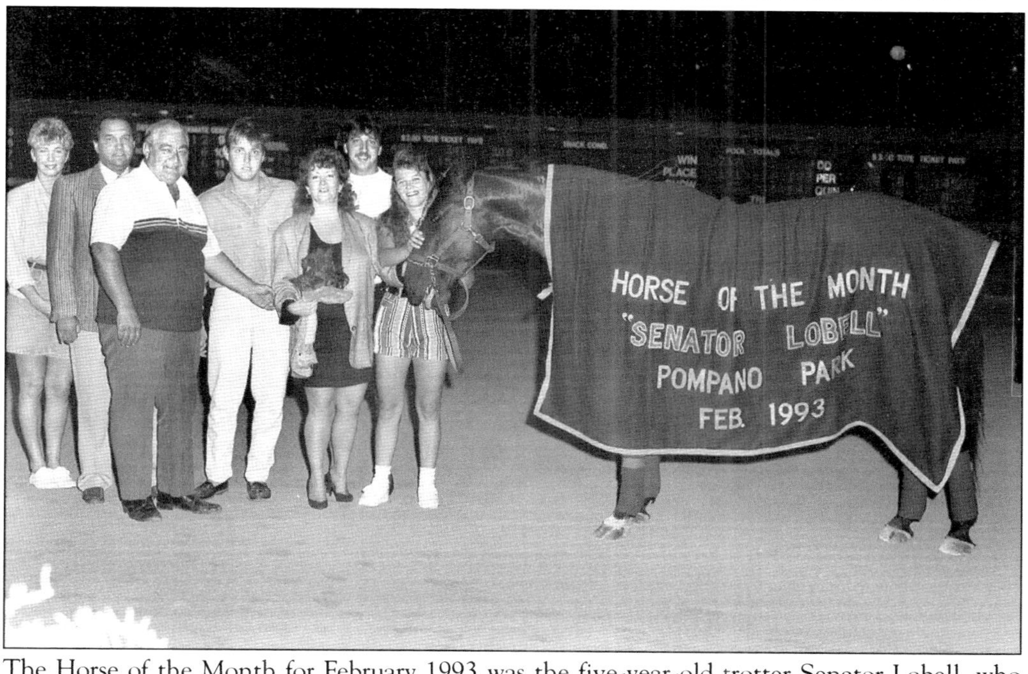

The Horse of the Month for February 1993 was the five-year-old trotter Senator Lobell, who swept through five consecutive starts without a defeat. The presentation was made by Mike Perry, second from left, of the Florida chapter of the United States Harness Writers Association.

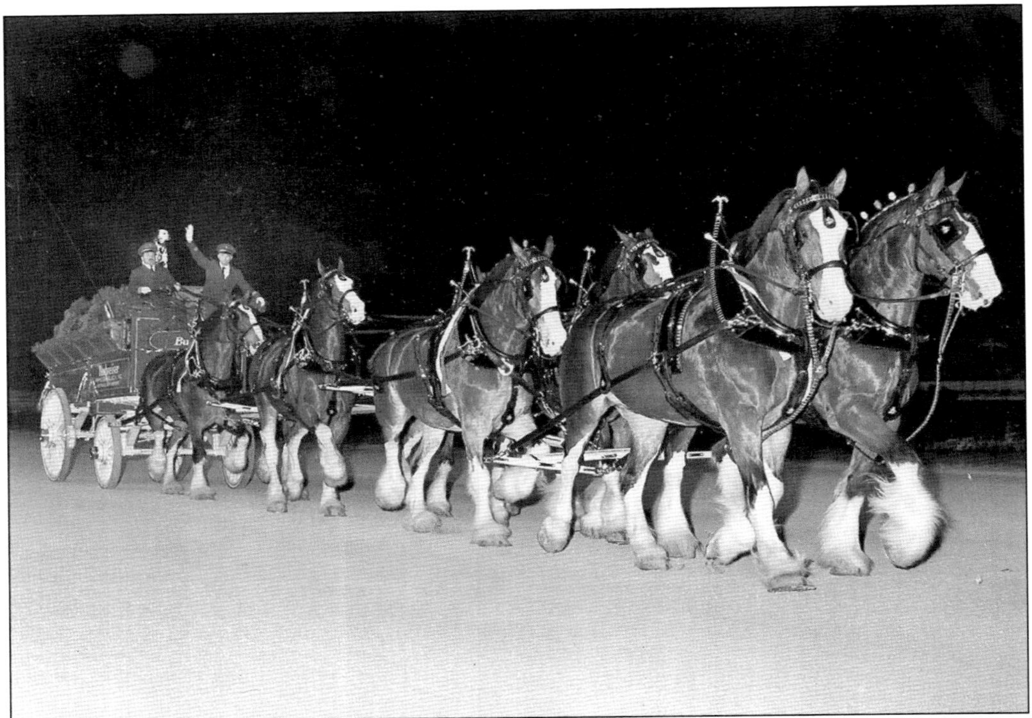

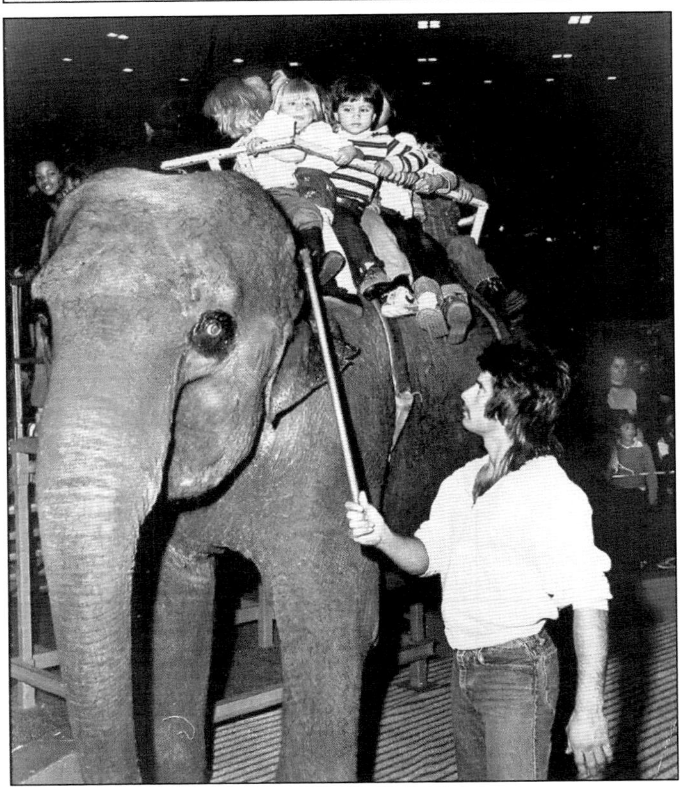

In this image, the popular Budweiser Clydesdale horses are parading around the track during a recent Christmas event. The Budweiser Corporation has been a strong supporter of harness racing in Florida, and Budweiser has presented a visible presence at the park.

The Royal Hanneford Circus has performed at Pompano Park to the delight of all. Here a handler is guiding Tina the Elephant as children enjoy a ride in the play area at the track.

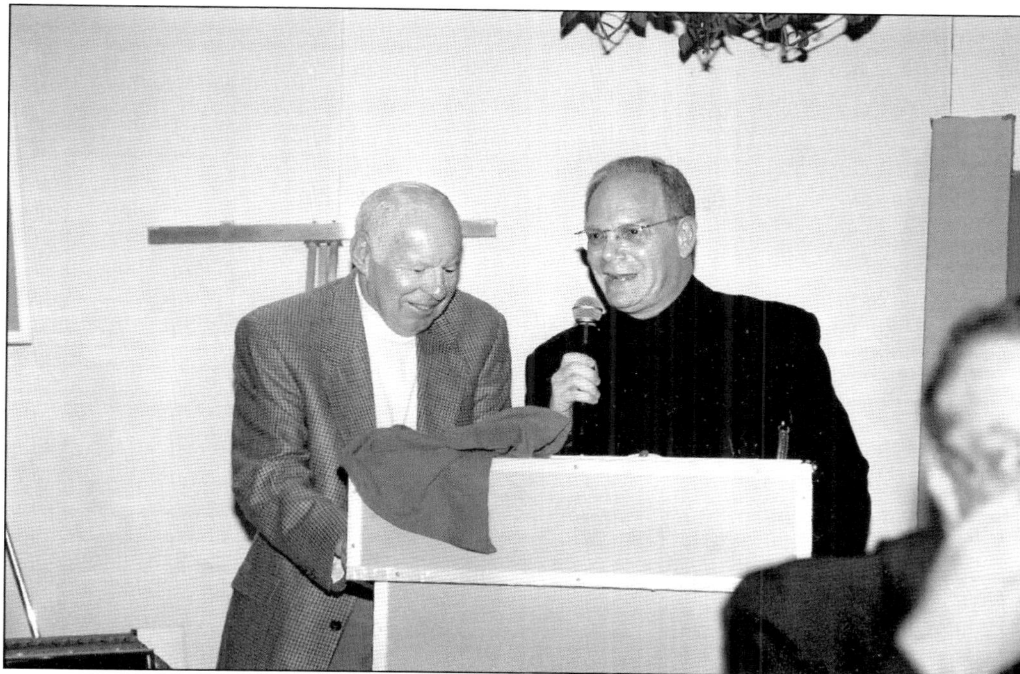

John Berry, right, served as master of ceremonies at the United States Harness Writers Association Hall of Fame Dinner in the spring of 2002. Here he presents an award to Stanley Dancer, a legend of harness racing and a member of the Hall of Fame.

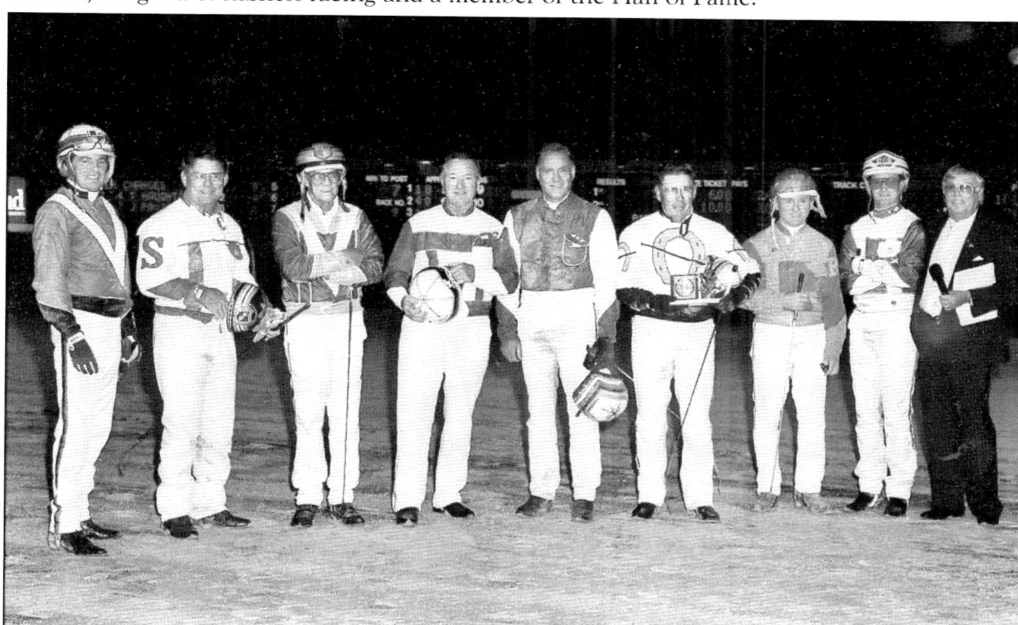

The March 20, 1995 card at Pompano was highlighted by a Hall of Fame Drivers Race, held in conjunction with the Frederick L. van Lennep Florida Harness Racing Hall of Fame induction dinner on March 21. From left to right are John Hogan, Jay Sears, Ted Taylor, Bruce Nickells, Bill Popfinger, race winner Carl Allen, Ron Waples, Tom Haughton, and Allen J. Finkelson.

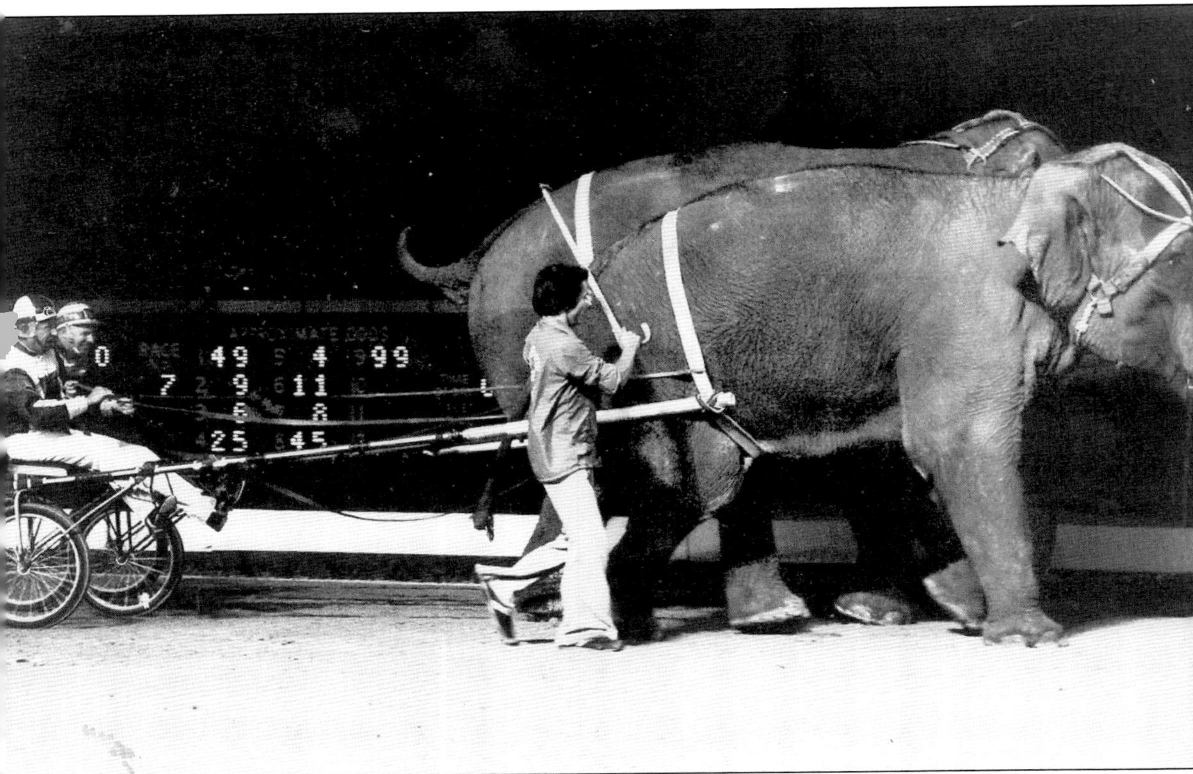

Pompano Park once held a zebra harness race. To top that event, an elephant race was run in the 1970s. "The Elephant Hambletonian" was a match race between Hall of Fame drivers Stanley Dancer, background left, and Billy Haughton, who both enjoyed the novelty of the competition. Each driver won one race. The final race ended in a dead heat.

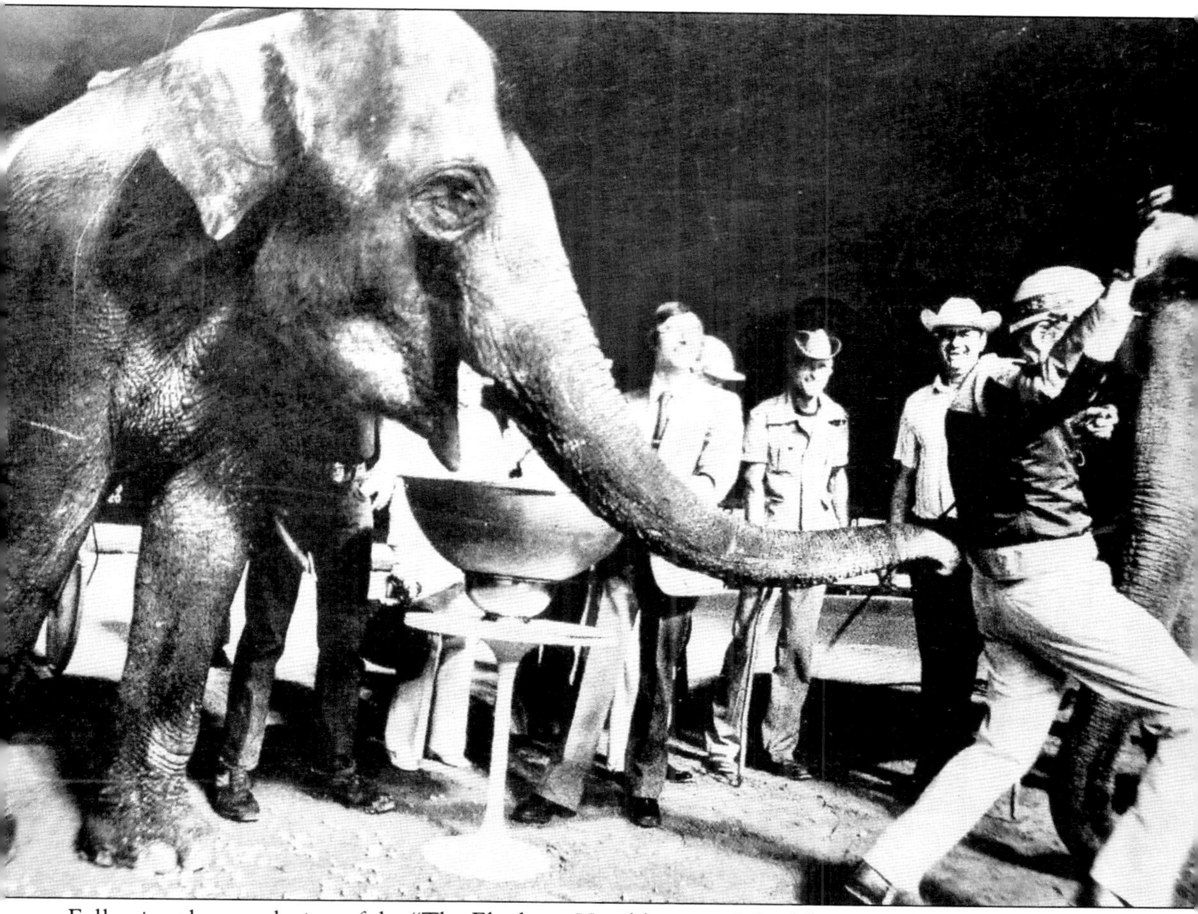

Following the conclusion of the "The Elephant Hambletonian" dead-heat race between Stanley Dancer and Billy Haughton, Dancer's elephant appears to be playful in the winner's circle. The elephant is ignoring the peanuts on the ground while trying to pick Dancer's pocket.

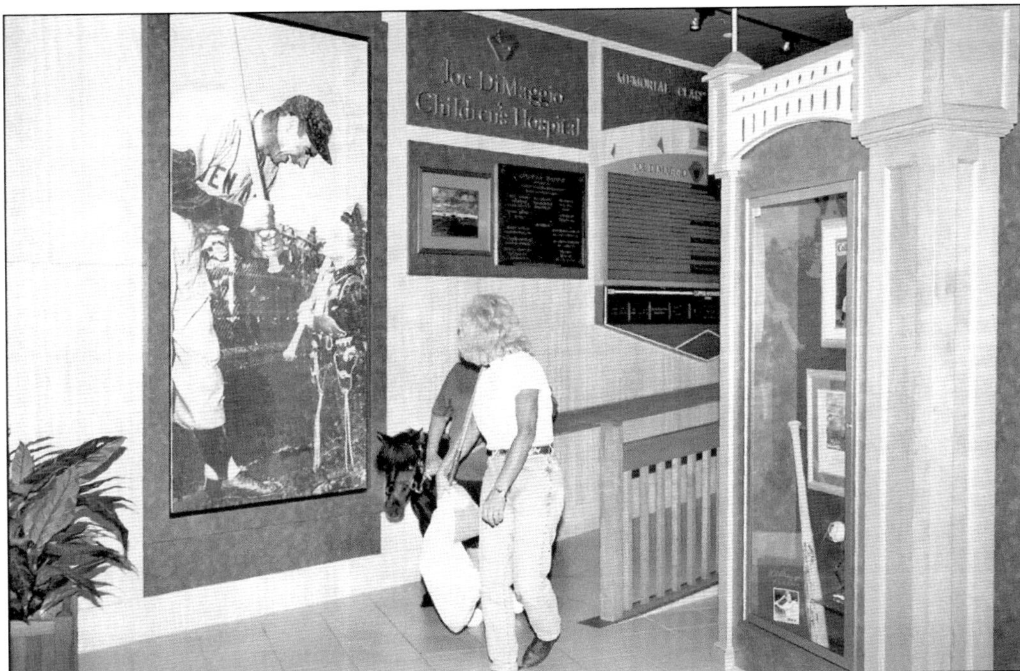

Baseball great Joe DiMaggio appears to be looking down at the Pompano Park American Miniature horse entering the Joe DiMaggio Children's Hospital in Hollywood, Florida. The loveable minis bring comfort and joy to children who are ill. To the right is memorabilia of the Yankee legend.

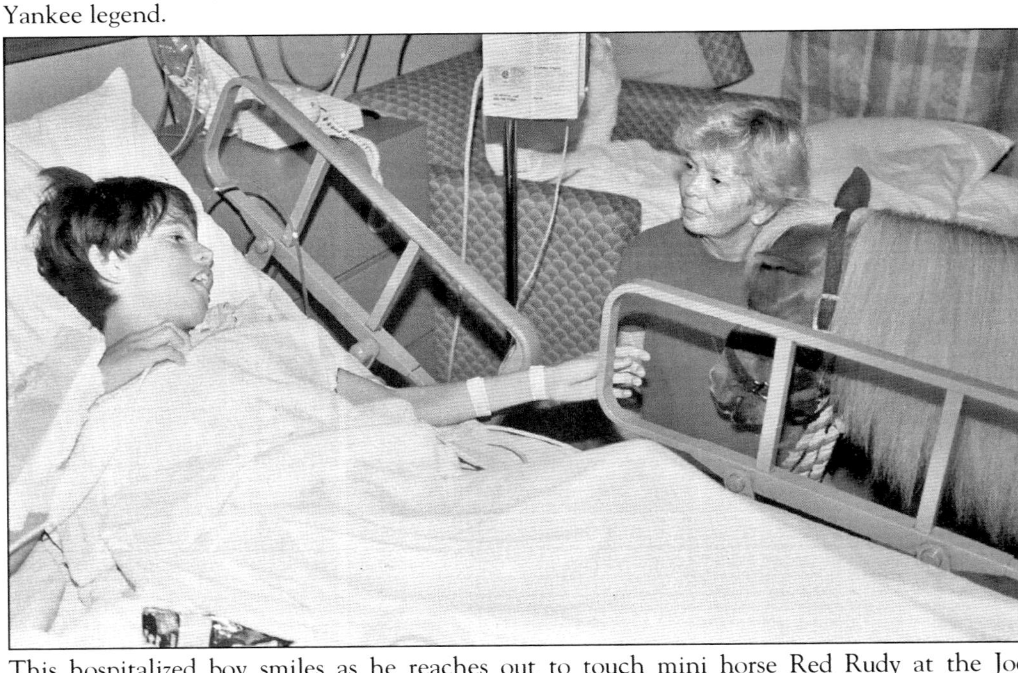

This hospitalized boy smiles as he reaches out to touch mini horse Red Rudy at the Joe DiMaggio Children's Hospital. Officials at Pompano Park make these gentle horses available to the community for charitable and educational events.

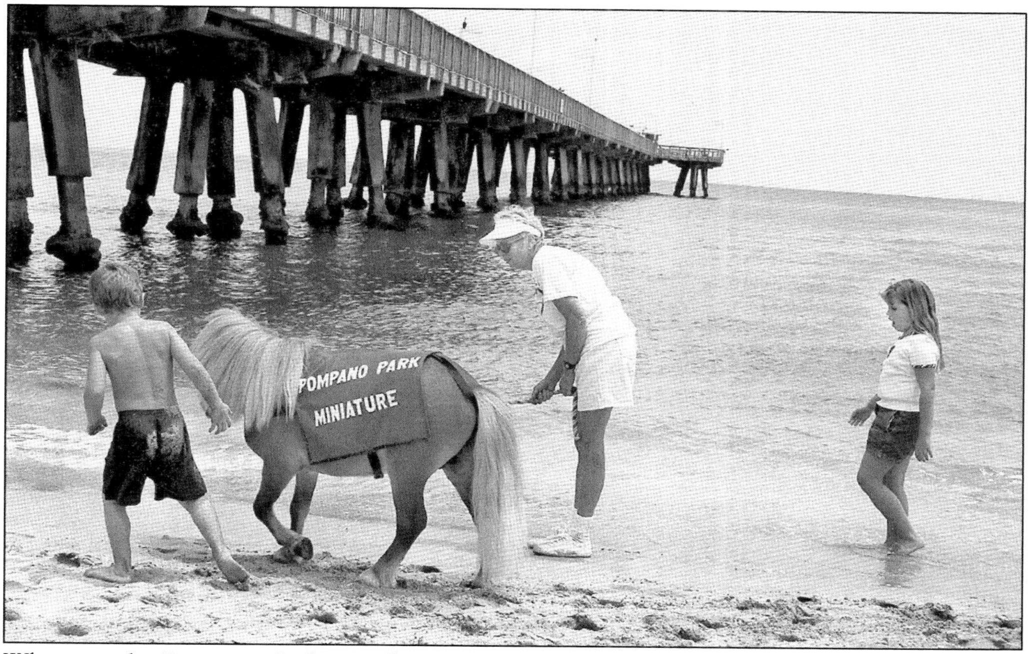

Wherever the Pompano Park mini horses go, they are magnets for horse lovers of all ages. In this image, children and owner Sara Connor play with Red Rudy during the 2001 Pompano Beach Seafood Festival. In the background are the pier and the Atlantic Ocean.

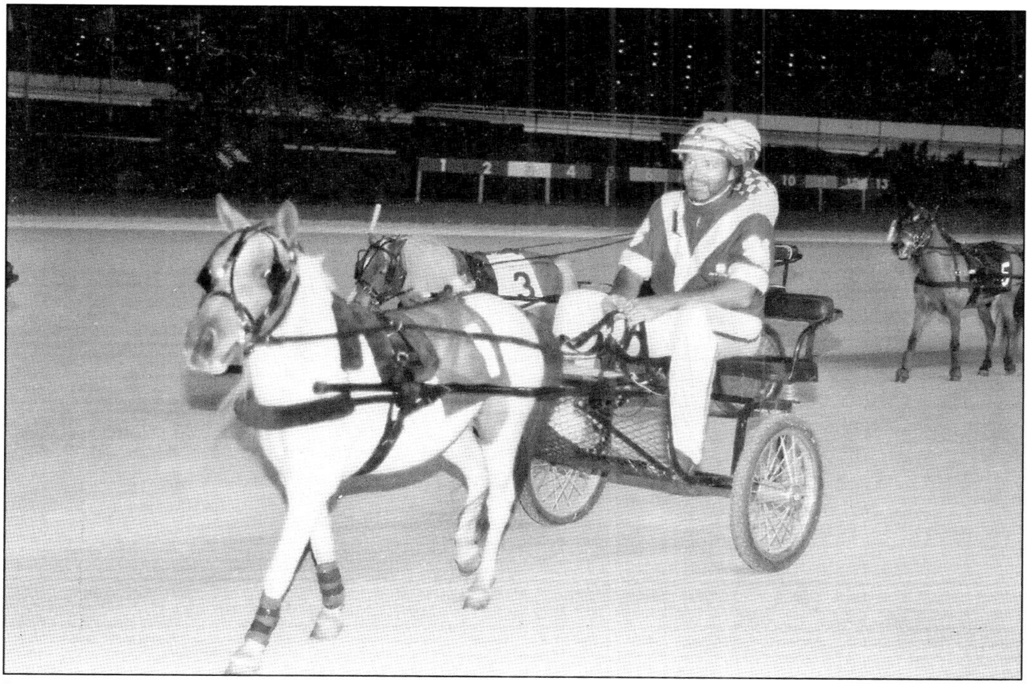

In a promotional mini-horse harness race during the 2000 winter season, driver Mark O'Mara and Polkadot "dash" to the finish line ahead of Red Rudy by a length. Each month the mini horses are featured at Pompano Park.

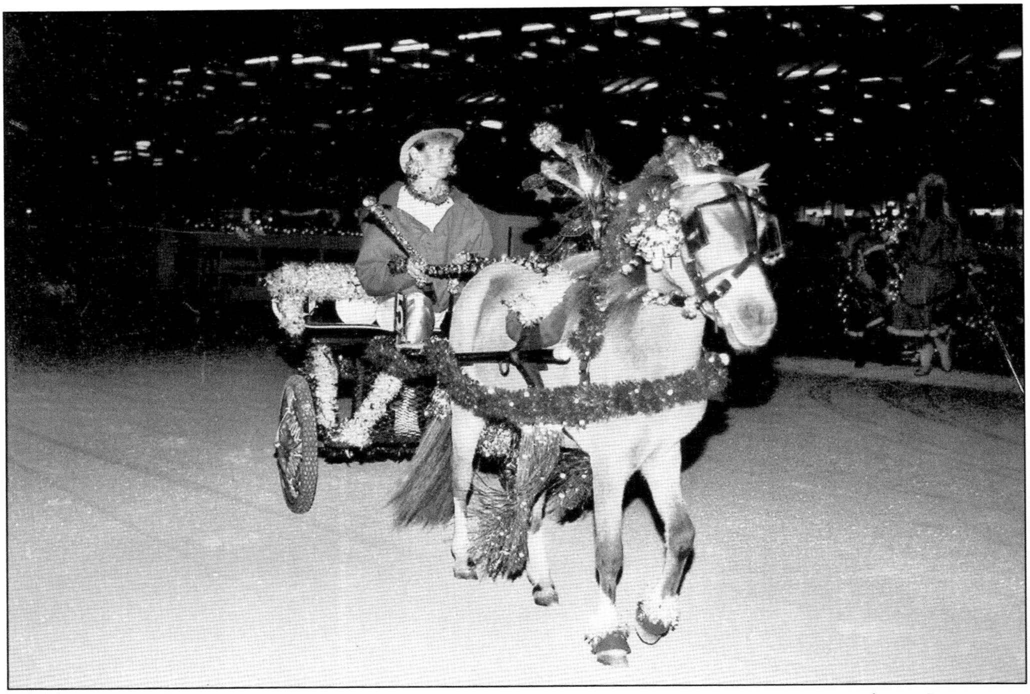

Debbie Schaut and mini horse Moonshine won the Millennium Costume Parade at Pompano Park on New Year's Eve in 1999. The Park celebrated Y2K in grand style, featuring the world's only Millennium Mile race that spanned two decades, starting New Year's Eve at 11:59 p.m. and ending after midnight in 2000.

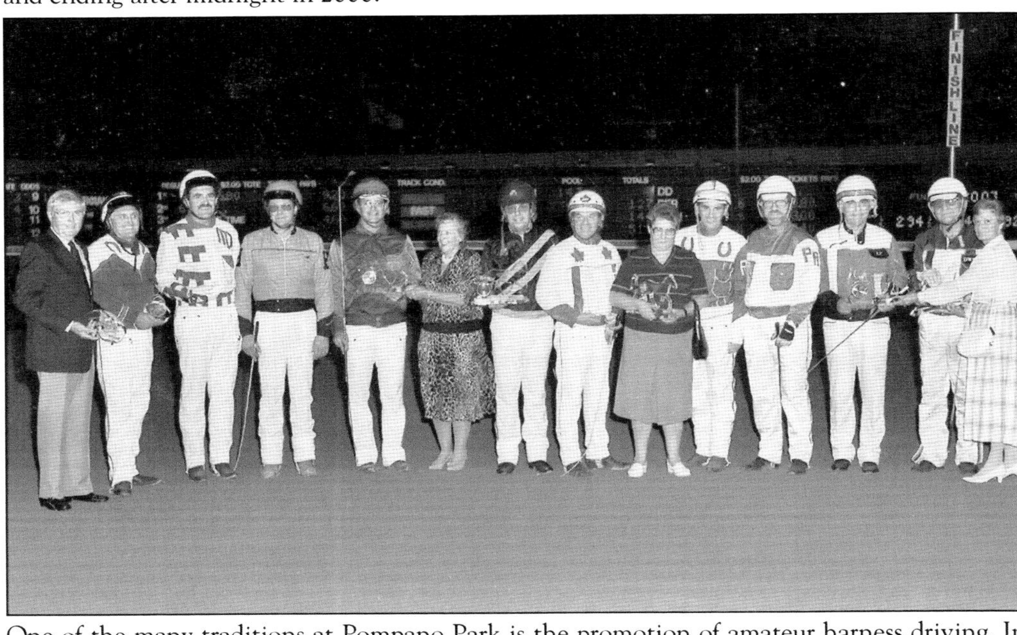

One of the many traditions at Pompano Park is the promotion of amateur harness driving. In this image, a group of Canadian and American drivers pose in front of the tote board in the 1990s after a friendly racing competition.

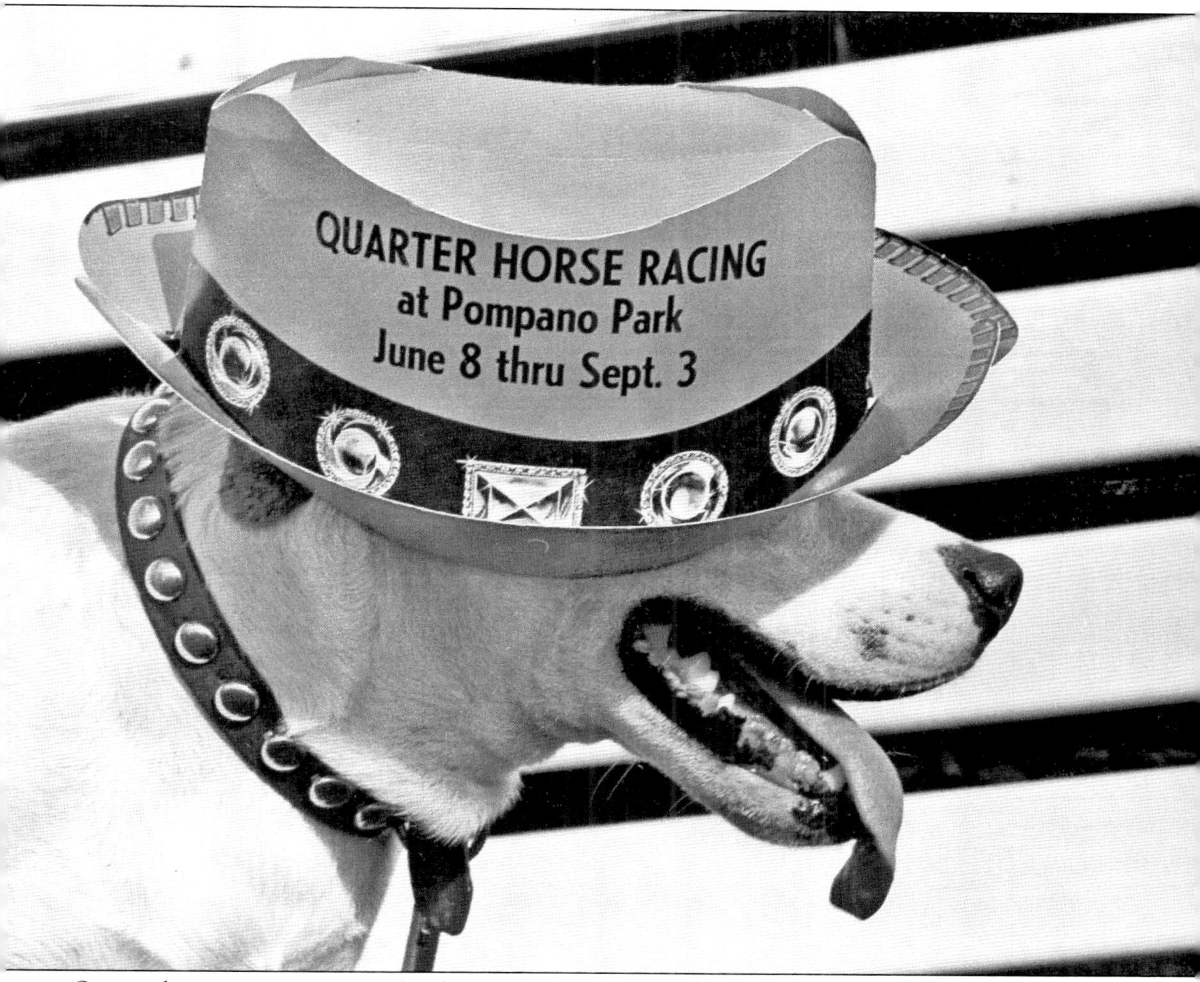

Quarter horse racing was popular during the middle period of Pompano Park history, especially when harness racing was not being conducted. Here "Humphrey the Handicapper" announces the schedule for quarter horse racing: June 8 through September 3, 1972. A quarter horse is an extremely fast breed over a short distance.

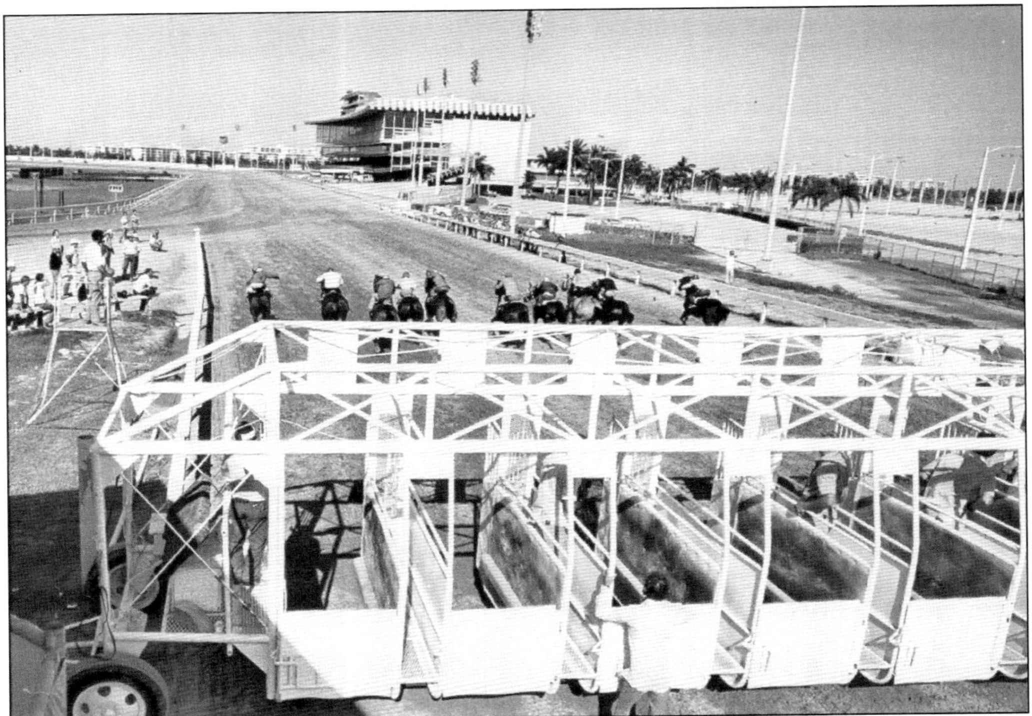

They're off! Jockeys coax their quarter horses to the finish line in less than 20 seconds during the 1972 meet. The Pompano Park grandstand is in the background and the parking lot is to the right.

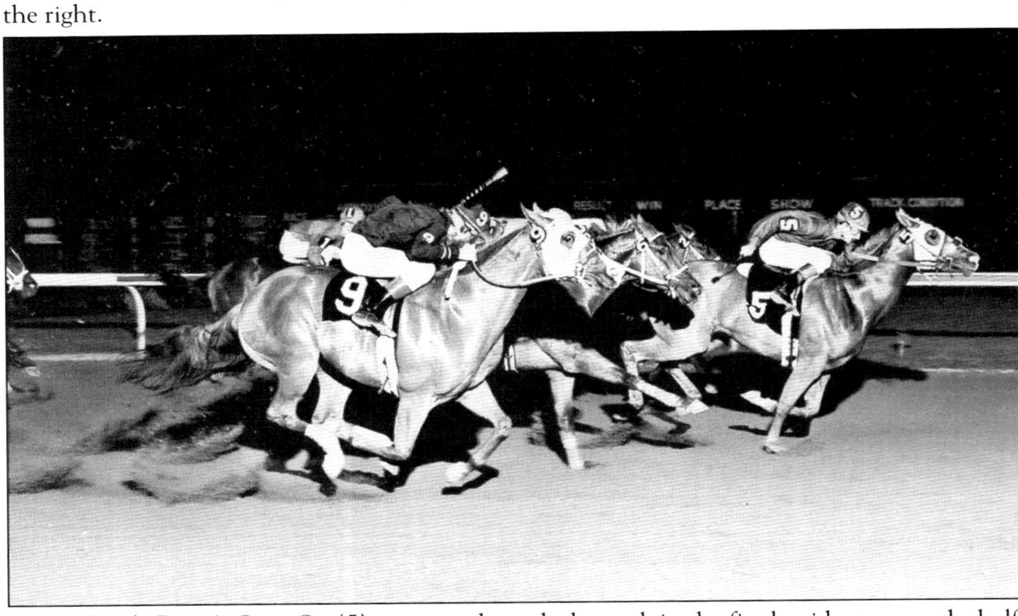

H.J. and Judy Berry's Guns Sis (5) squeezes through the pack in the final strides to record a half-length victory in the $108,615 Florida Bred Quarter Horse Futurity final at Pompano Park on July 5, 1986. Trained by Sam Head and ridden by Ricky Leppala, Guns Sis was clocked in 20.03 seconds for the 400 yards.

Glen Crowe was the recipient of the Leading Trainer Award for the 1980 quarter horse meet. Crowe was out front in the standings throughout the racing season. Here he proudly displays his award.

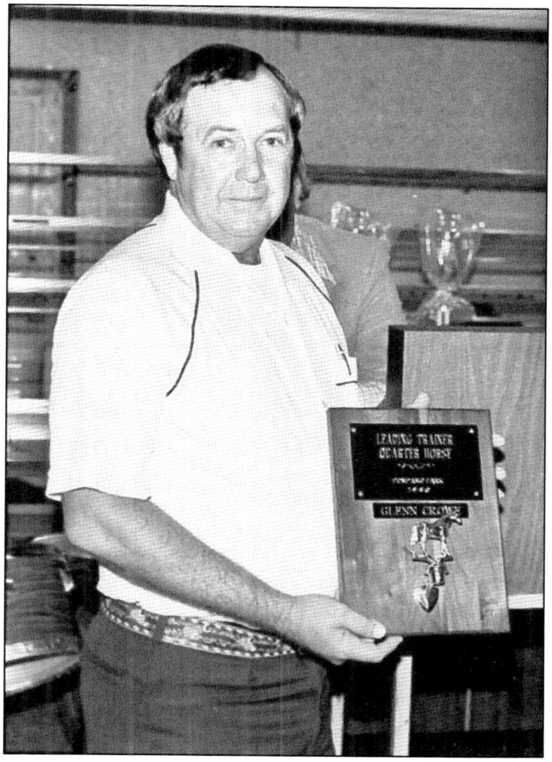

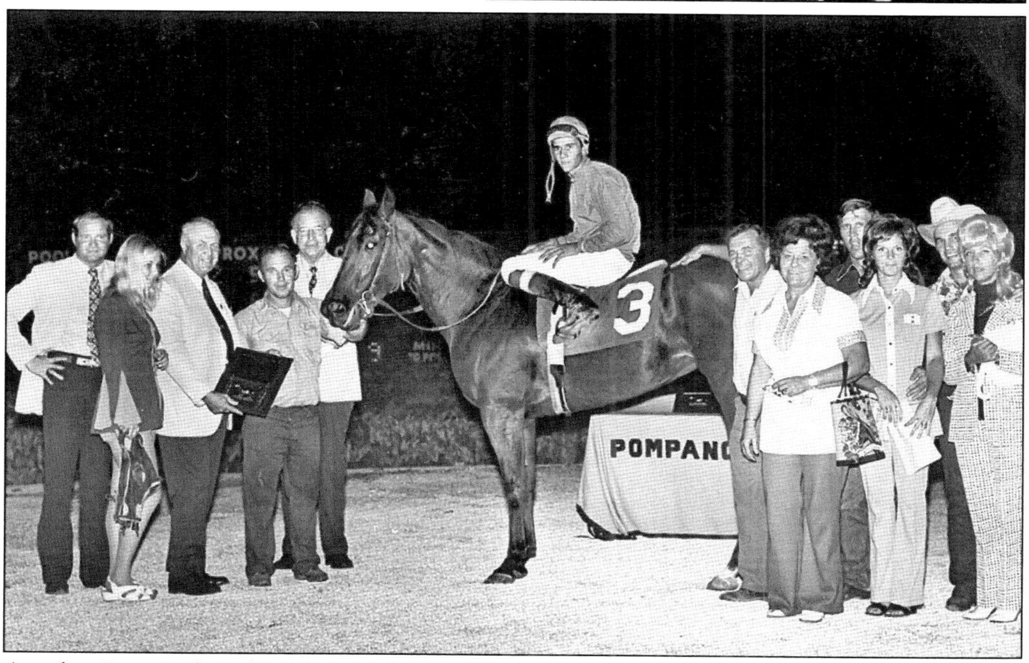

Another Lou, with Mike O'Quinn up, sprinted to a decisive victory in the $10,000 Pompano Park Horse Stake on August 19, 1972. O'Quinn and horse covered the 770 yards in 40.60 seconds. R. Parrish was the trainer of Another Lou, and C.L. Dressel was the owner.

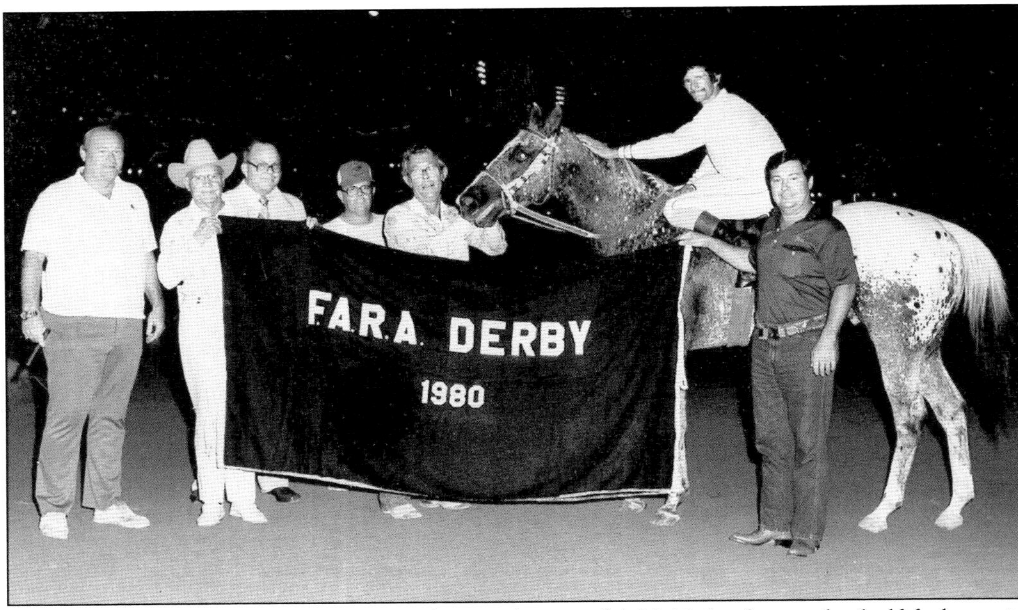

Three-year-old Bar T's Mam set a track record time of 1:08.11 for five-and-a-half furlongs in winning the $10,795 Florida Appaloosa Racing Association Derby at Pompano Park on June 14, 1980. In the winner's circle are, from left to right, Derk Ackerman of Triple Crown horse insurance; Dan Orth, president of Gator Downs Racing; Roy Butler, director of the Florida Appaloosa Association; a Pompano valet; trainer Dan Fussell; jockey LeRoy Allemand; and Kenneth Tackley, owner of the Bar T Ranch.

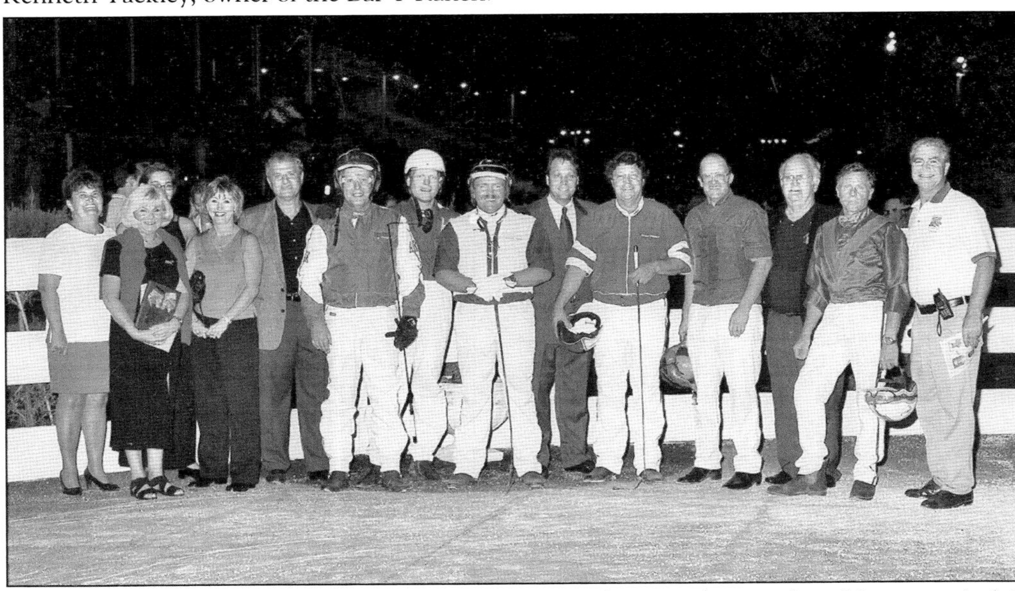

The Amateur Driving Club of Germany poses in 2001 after completing a friendship race. At left is Irene Cole, executive director of the Florida Amateur Driving Club; fourth from left in the suit is Alan Benjamin, president of the Florida Amateur Driving Club; eighth from left in the suit is the club's vice president Dein Spriggs. Larry Albano, director of TV/video productions, is at right.

A typical page from the official February 6, 1989 Pompano Park Racing Program provides basic information for the betting fan, who will be guided with details on trainers, drivers, horses, odds, types of bets, services, etc.

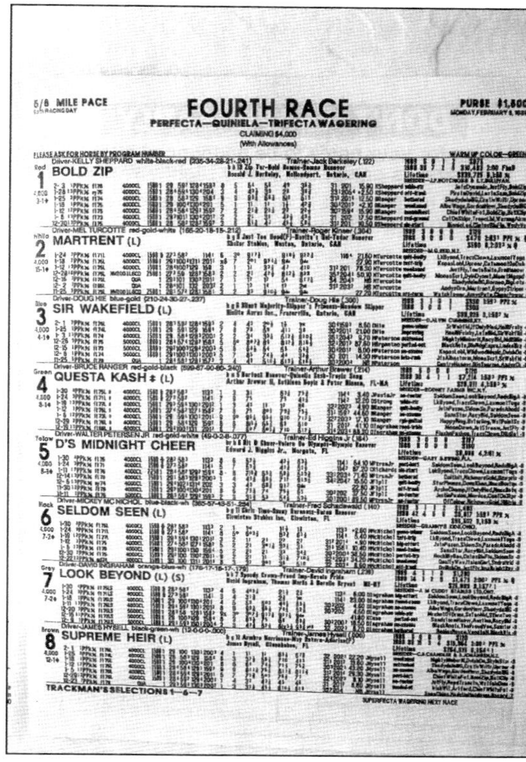

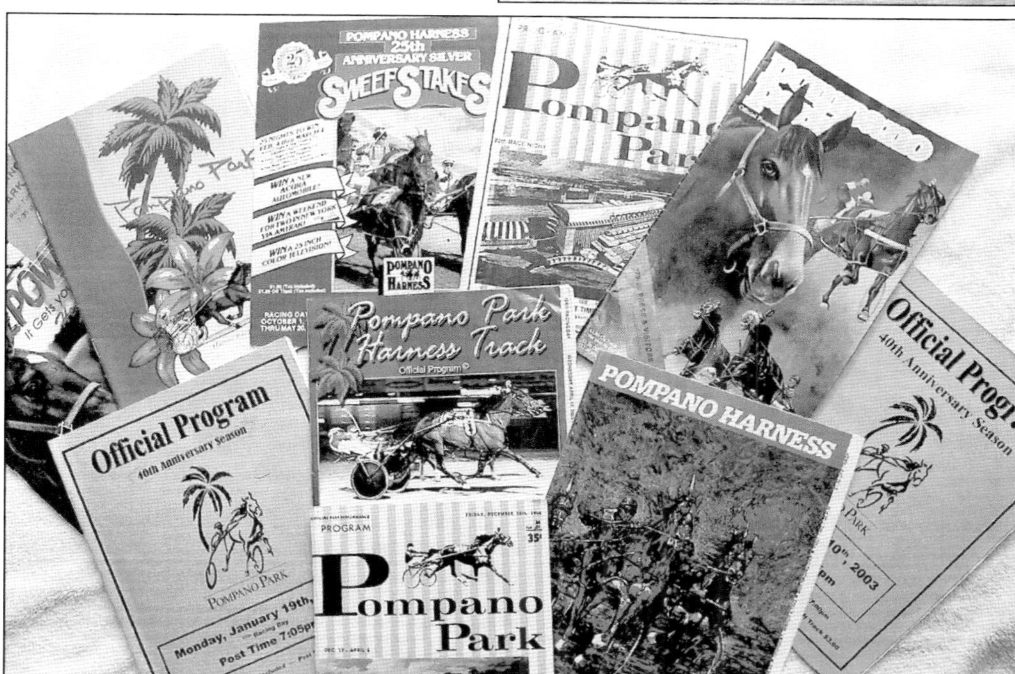

This collection of covers of official programs, both old and recent, reveals the various designs and logos that have been offered to the fans over the years.

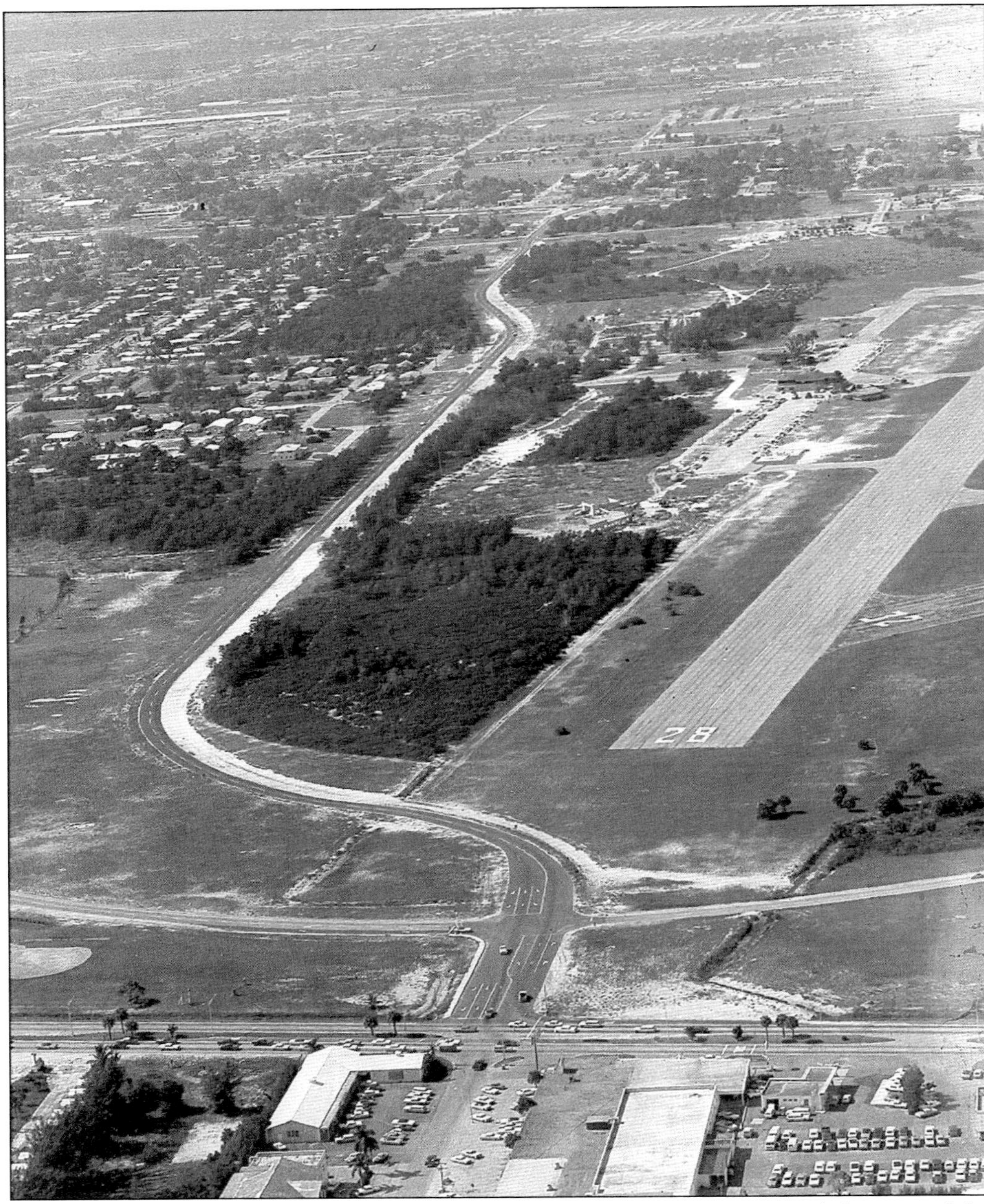

Pompano Park harness racing has benefited from locating in Pompano Beach because of the nearby airfield, seen here in 1968. In the foreground, NE 10th Street crosses U.S. Highway 1 (Federal Highway) and swings to the left of the runway, going west. In the background at the upper left, the long rooftop of the Farmers Market can be seen. Beyond, at the extreme upper left across Atlantic Boulevard, the original training track is barely visible.

Five

Celebrities and More

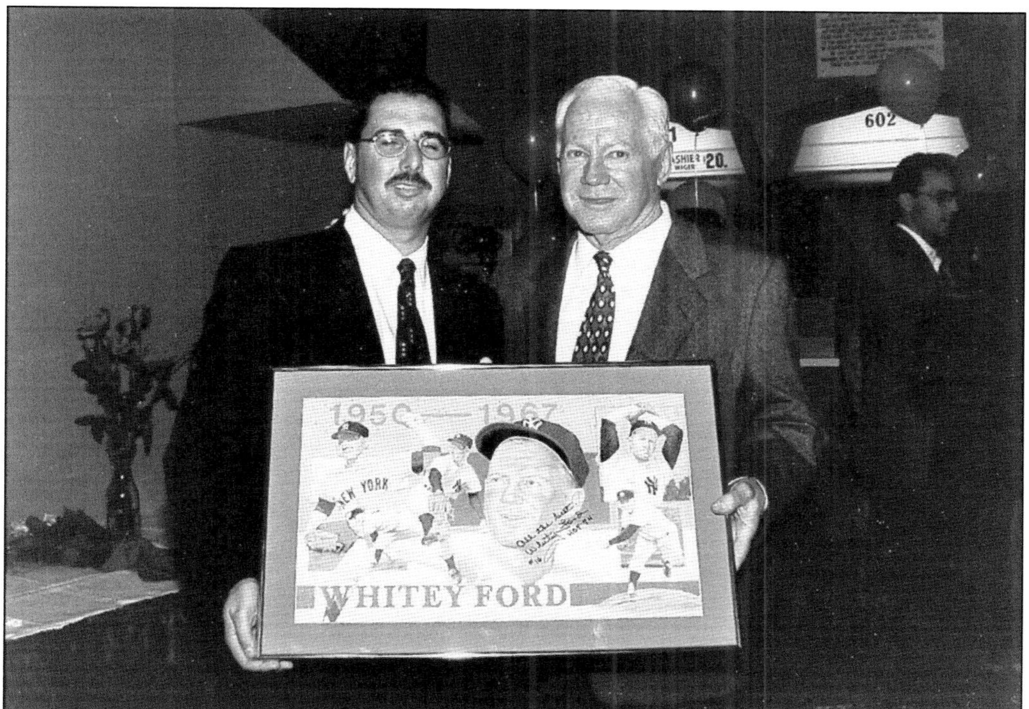

New York Yankees pitcher Whitey Ford, right, joins popular harness driver Joe Pavia Jr. at a recent charity auction at Pompano Park. They display a painting of images of Ford, who was elected to the Baseball Hall of Fame in 1974.

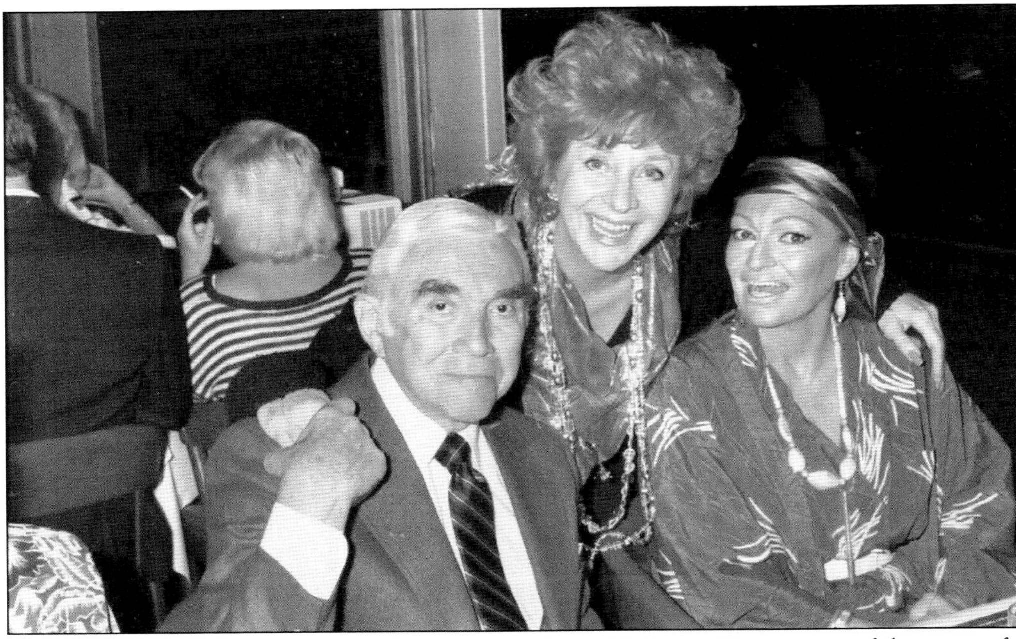

Singer-actress Kay Stevens, center, leans over to chat with Lorne Greene, star of the successful television show *Bonanza*. Seated at right is Green's wife. They are dining at the Top of the Park Restaurant in 1987.

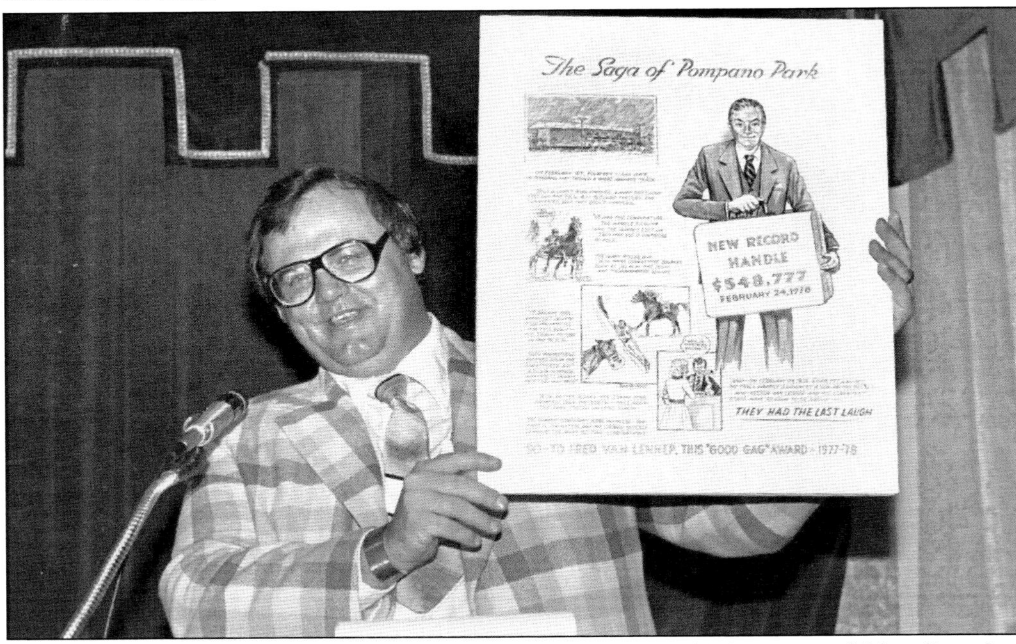

Addressing a group of local business leaders in 1978, General Manager and Vice President Hector van Lennep displays a Pompano Park record of accomplishments in honor of his father. The younger van Lennep himself featured events including all-Jewish, all-Canadian, all-Italian, all-Irish, and all-women races; media races; and a night honoring the New York Yankees, to name a few.

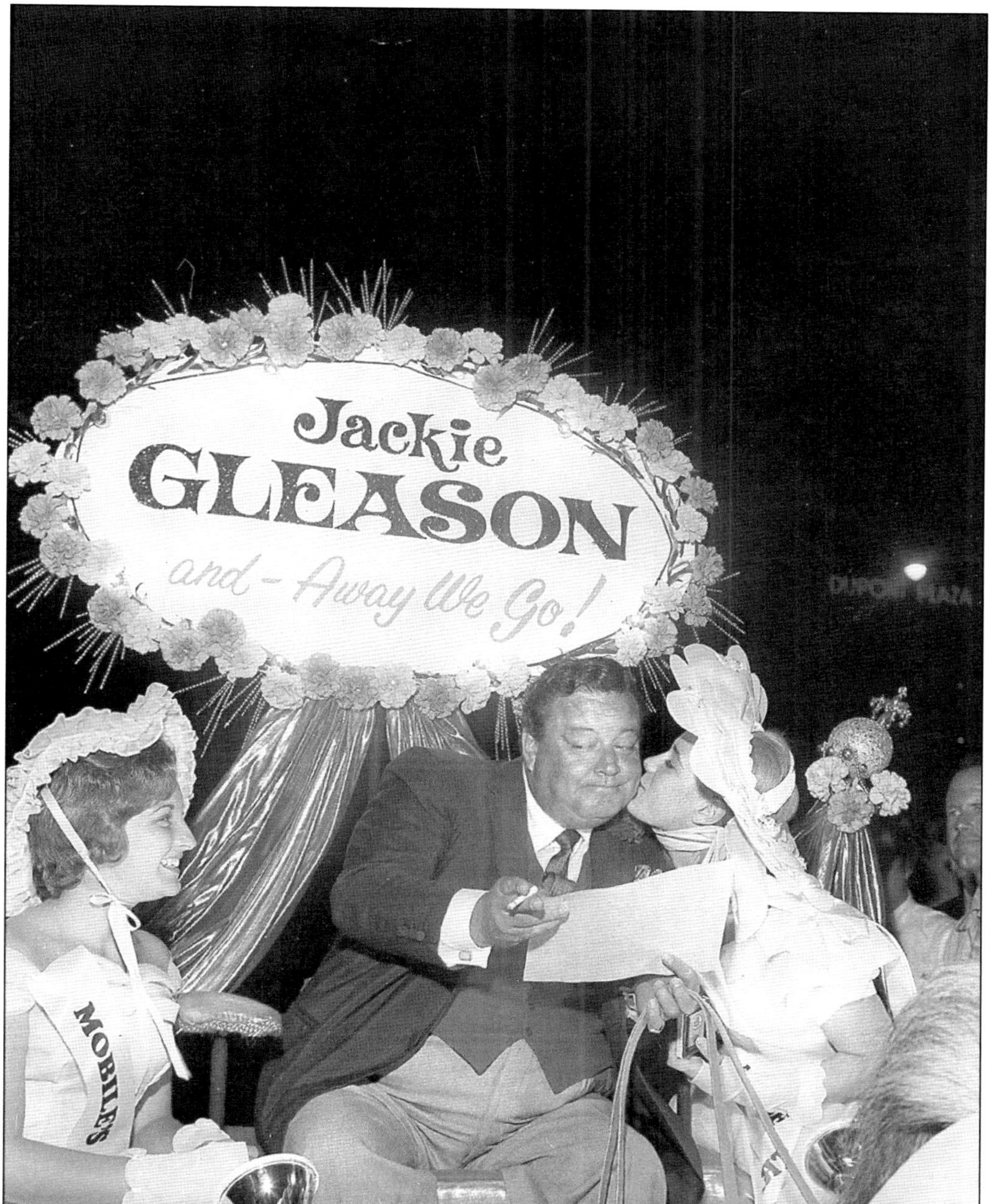

A resident of South Florida, comedian Jackie Gleason was a regular visitor to Pompano Park. Although he had an outgoing personality and loved to clown around, he often had to disguise his appearance in order to maintain his privacy at the Park. He enjoyed handicapping the horses.

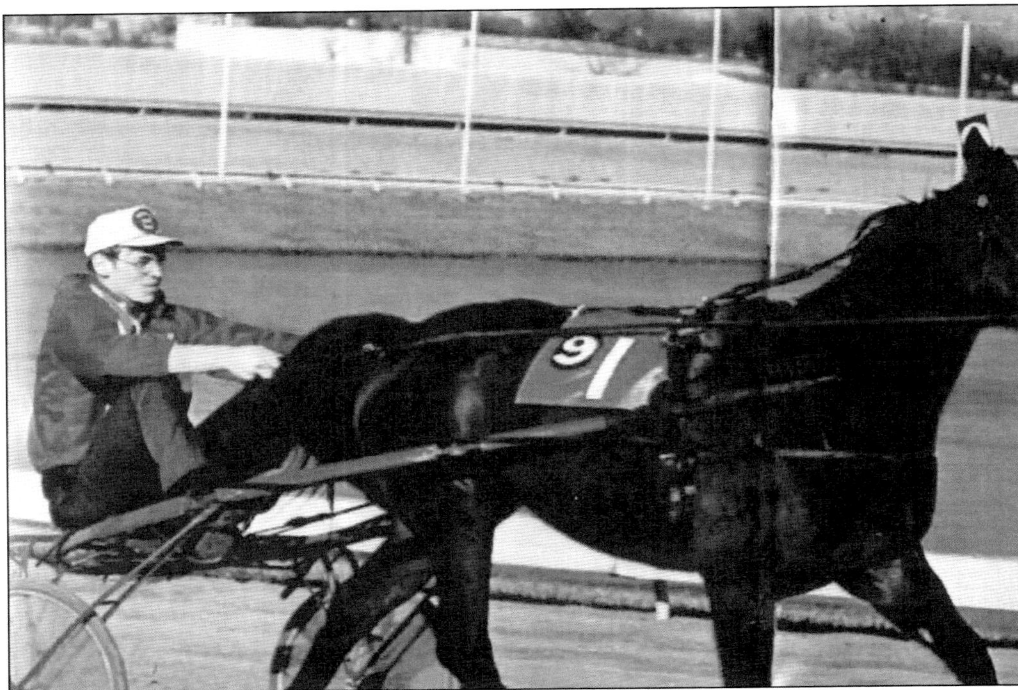

Dan Issel, above, multimillionaire athlete with the Kentucky Colonels of the old American Basketball Association, was a student of harness racing. In 1971, he owned three pacers at Pompano Park. Superstar Wilt Chamberlain also owned harness racehorses, and New Jersey Nets star Sam Bowie raced horses at Pompano Park.

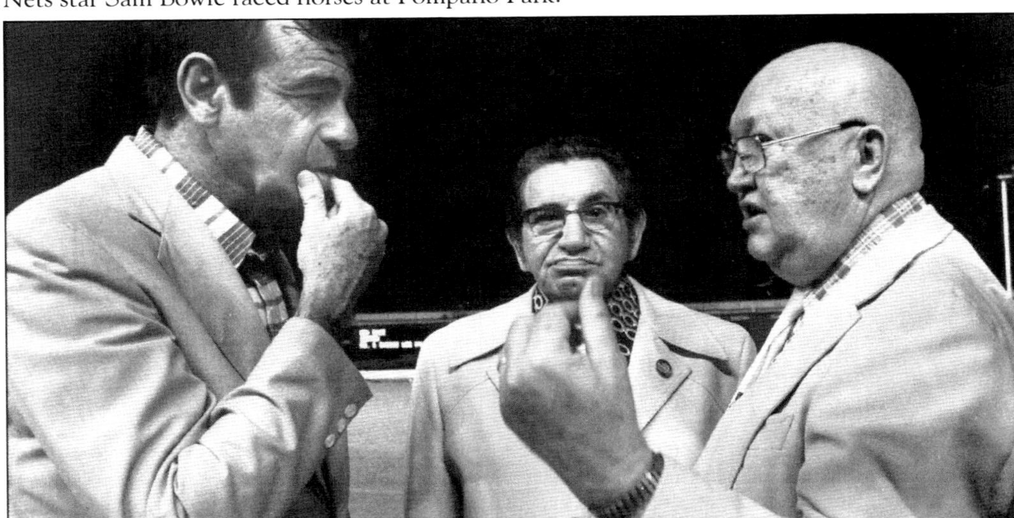

These gentlemen are in deep discussion in the winner's circle at Pompano Park. Famous actor Walter Matthau, left, is debating the fine points of harness racing with park official Bob Cox, right. The man in the center is unidentified.

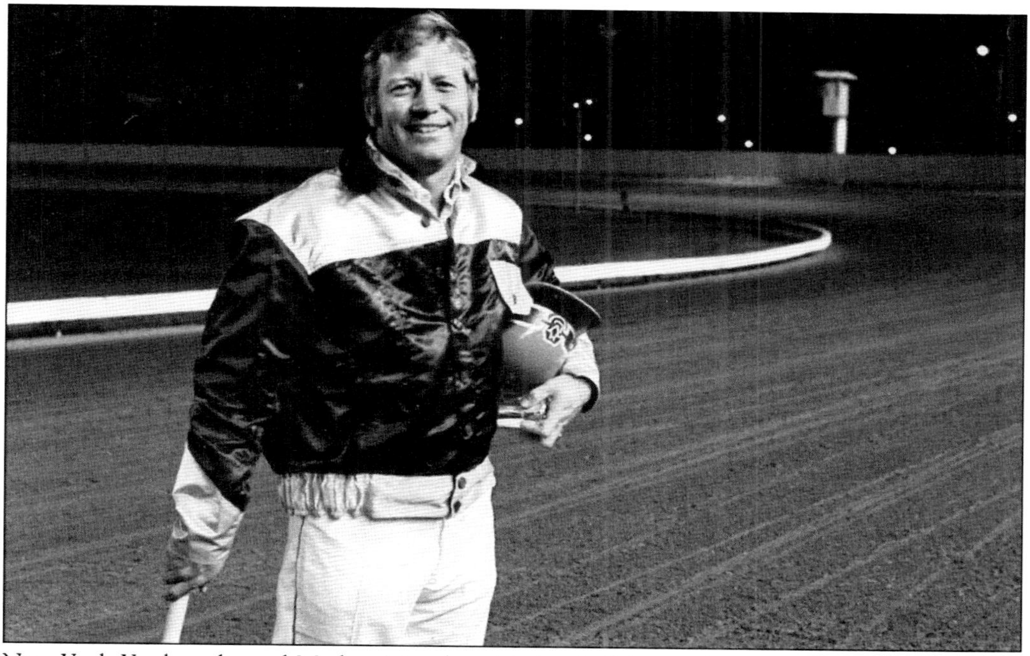

New York Yankees legend Mickey Mantle, with baseball bat and racing helmet in hand, is in his racing colors ready to drive a horse around the track. When the Yankees did their spring training in Fort Lauderdale, Mantle was a regular at Pompano Park.

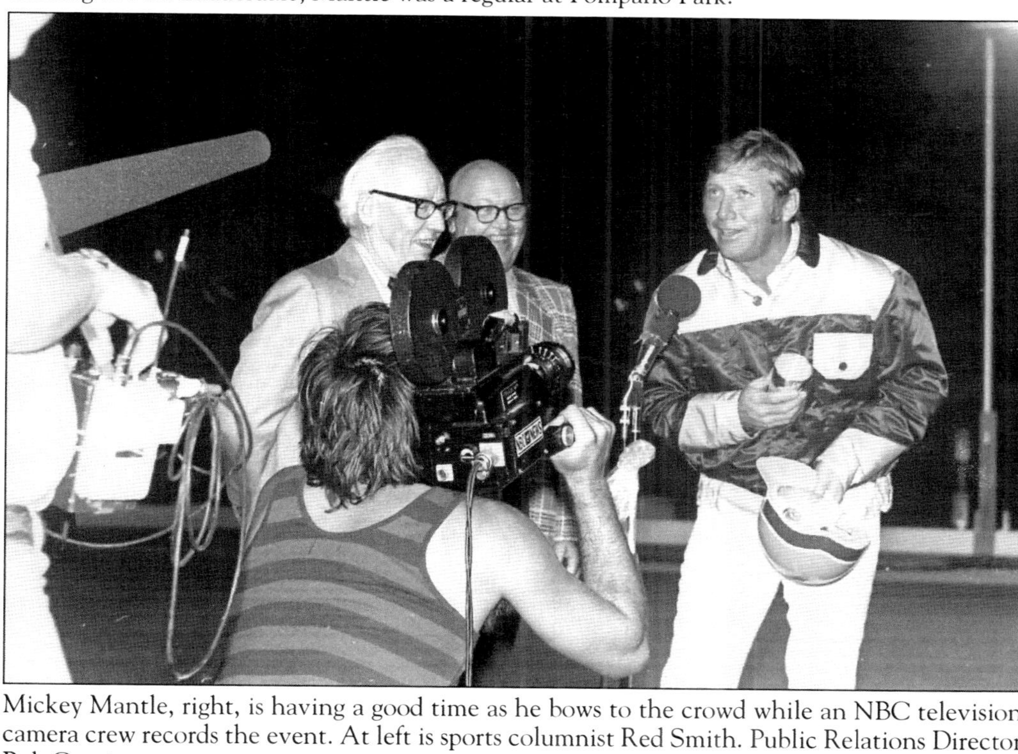

Mickey Mantle, right, is having a good time as he bows to the crowd while an NBC television camera crew records the event. At left is sports columnist Red Smith. Public Relations Director Bob Cox is at center.

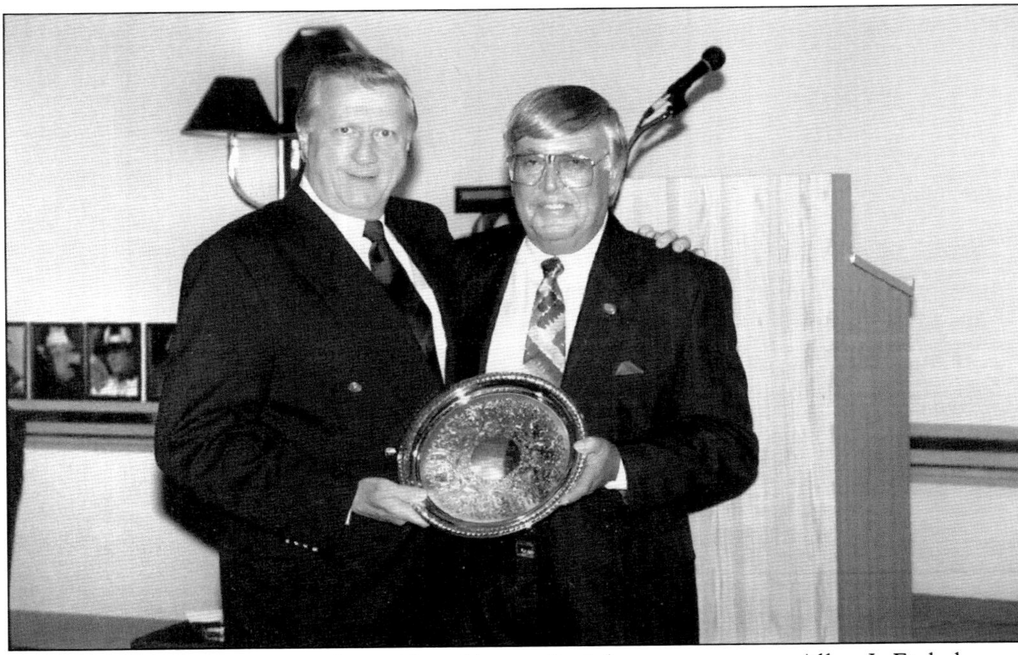

New York Yankees owner and president George Steinbrenner presents Allen J. Finkelson of Pompano Park with an award upon Finkelson's induction to the United States Harness Writers Association Hall of Fame on March 21, 1993. Finkelson also received the USHWA Proximity Achievement Award in 1986 for his contributions to the sport of harness racing.

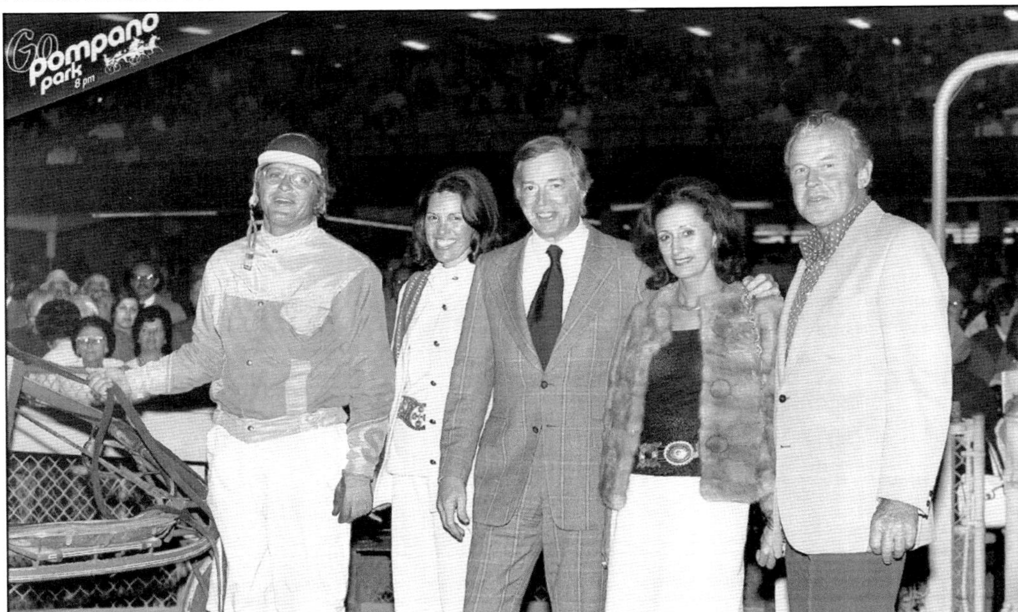

Standing in the winner's circle are, from left to right, an unidentified winning driver, Julie Brown, television announcer Hugh Downs, Ruth Downs, and driver/trainer Roger Brown, who all came down from the Top of the Park Restaurant to enjoy the moment. Note the starting time for harness racing at the track in the upper left corner in 1975.

Tennis star Bobby Riggs made a grand visit to Pompano Park. Here he is in his colors and helmet, being assisted by two women in preparation for a ride in a sulky. Ever the showman, he wowed the crowd when he circled the track.

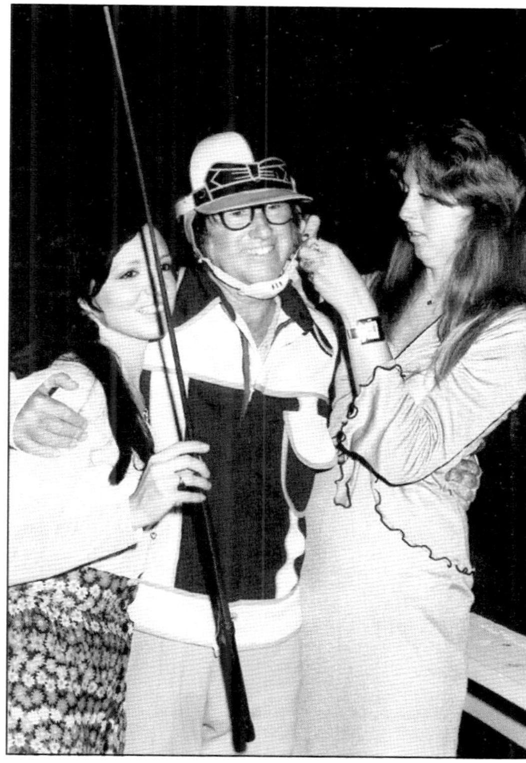

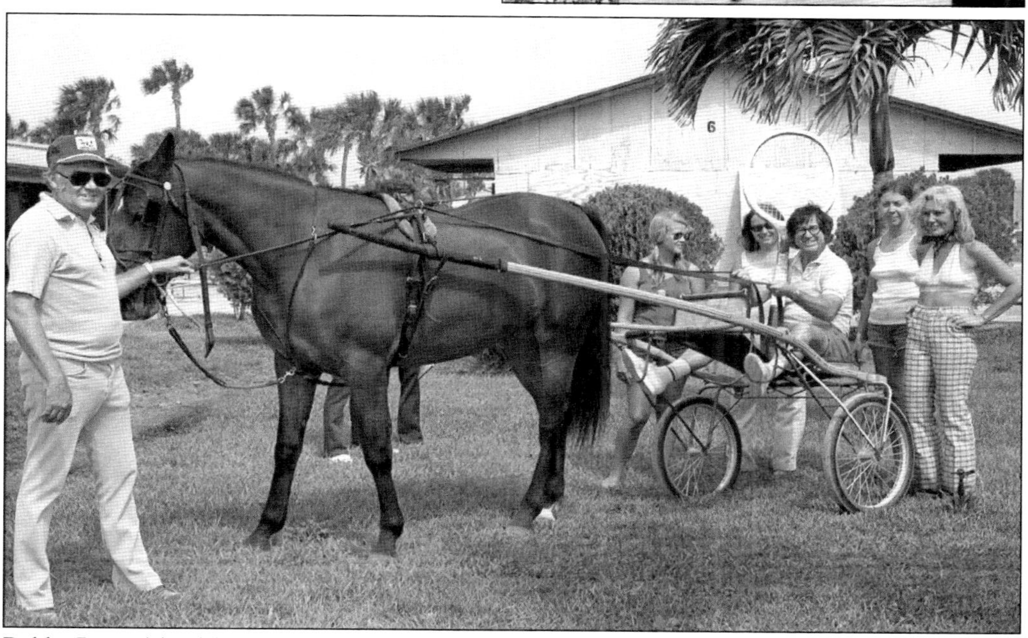

Bobby Riggs (third from left) tries out a sulky amid female admirers. Winner of one Wimbledon tennis title and two U.S. Open titles, he gained even greater notoriety in a nationally televised competition labeled "The Battle of the Sexes" when he challenged Billy Jean King in 1973. He lost to her.

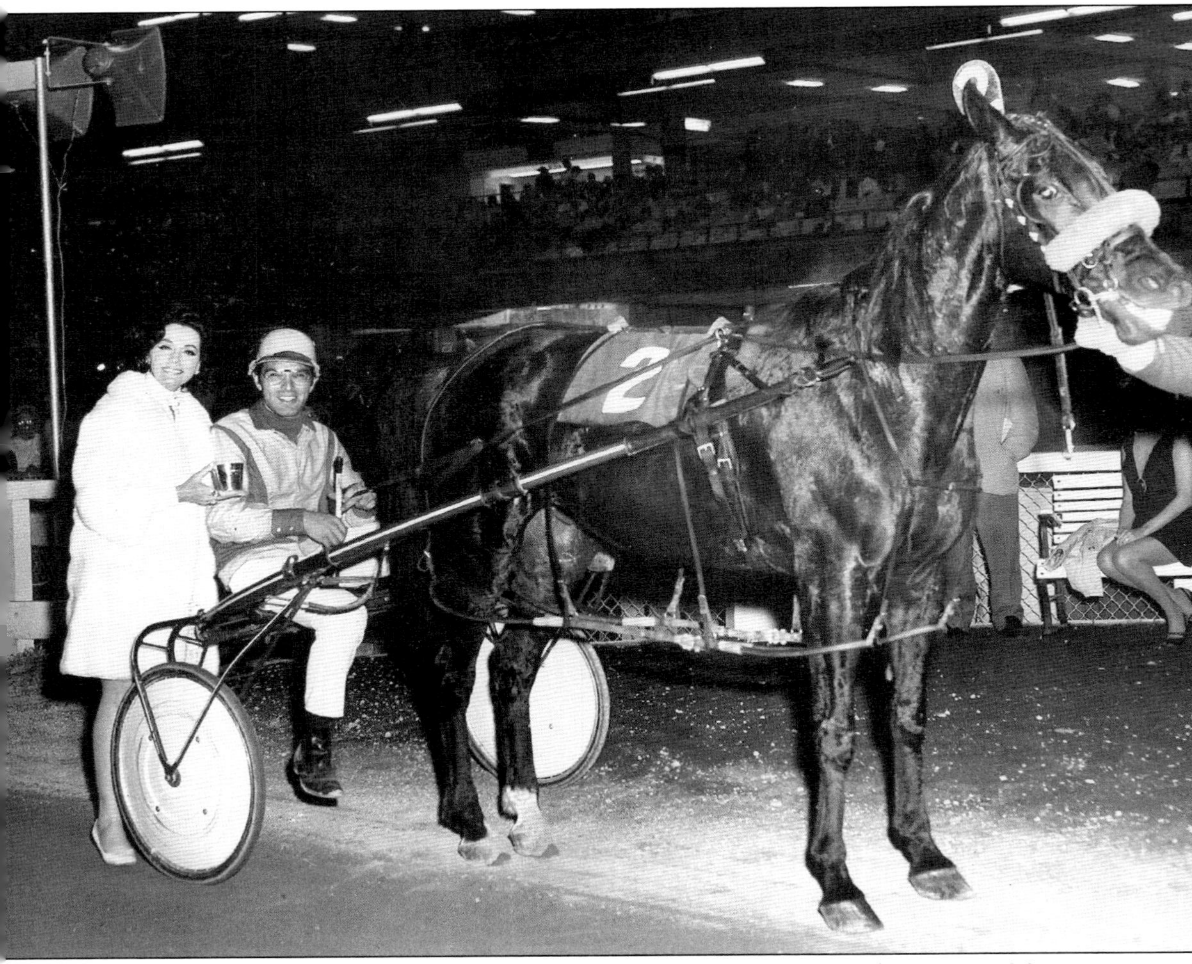

Just back from her recent personal appearance at Super Bowl I, grand opera star Marguerita Piazza attended the races at Pompano Park Harness Track during the winter meet of 1967. Here she congratulates winning driver Larry Rolla.

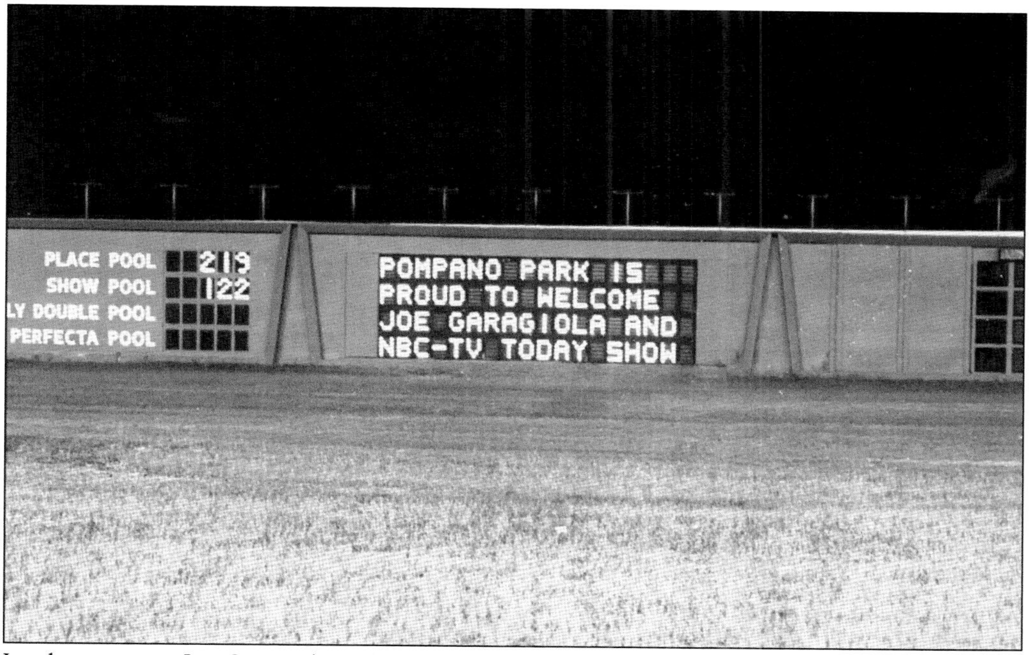

Lead announcer Joe Garagiola and the NBC-TV *Today Show* were extended a special welcome for their visit to Pompano Park. The program originated from Pompano Park in 1970. Garagiola was also famous for being a major league baseball player and sports announcer.

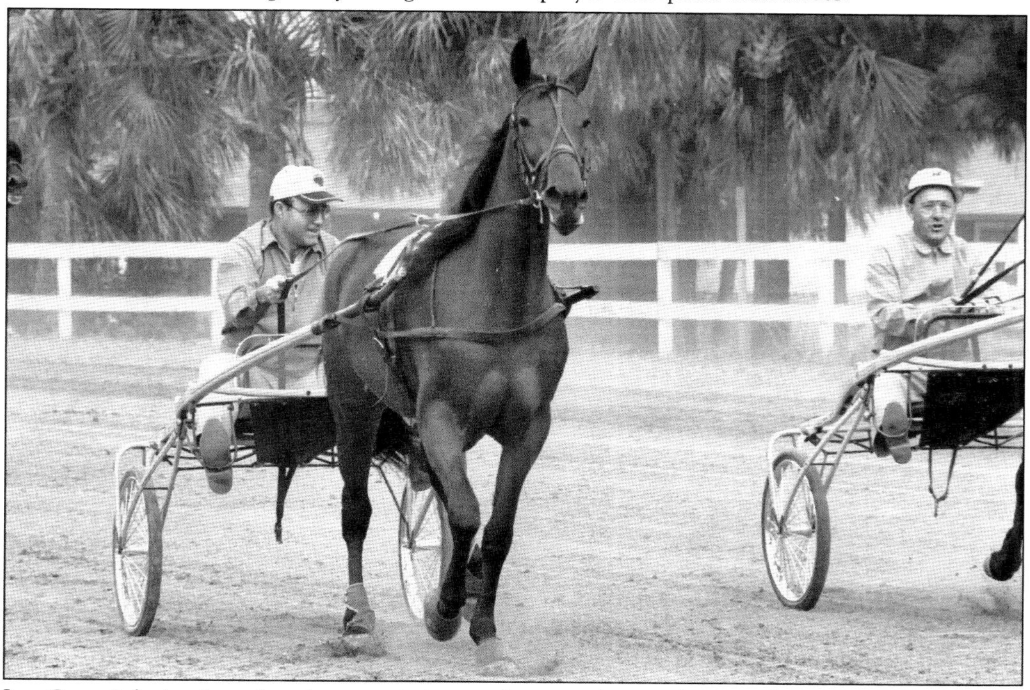

Joe Garagiola is given hands-on training on how to drive a harness horse by Delvin Miller while enjoying a ride in the sulky. Later he donned silks and helmet for an "official" drive. The exposure on national television gave a boost to harness racing in South Florida.

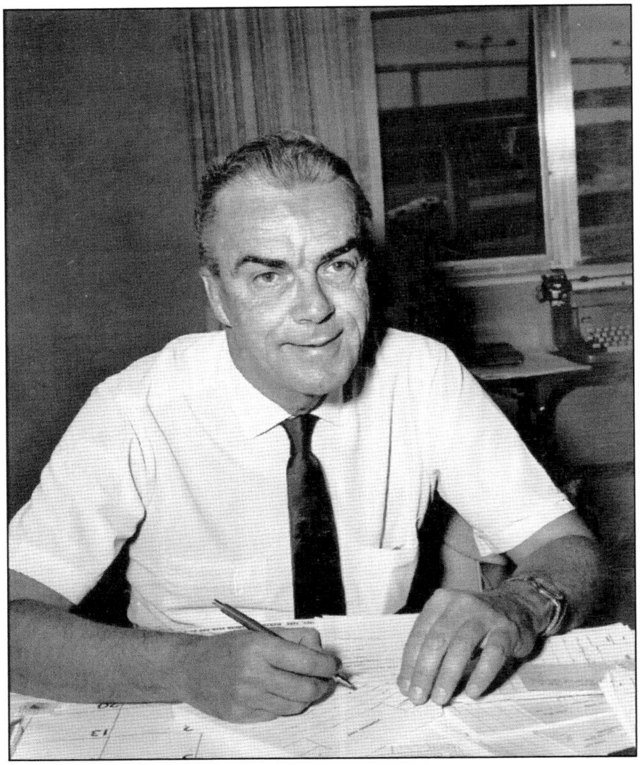

Bill Conners was famous throughout the North American harness racing industry. He was racing secretary for more than two decades at Pompano Park. For his contributions to the sport he was elected by the United States Harness Writers Hall of Fame in 1986. In this image he paused for a moment from his work.

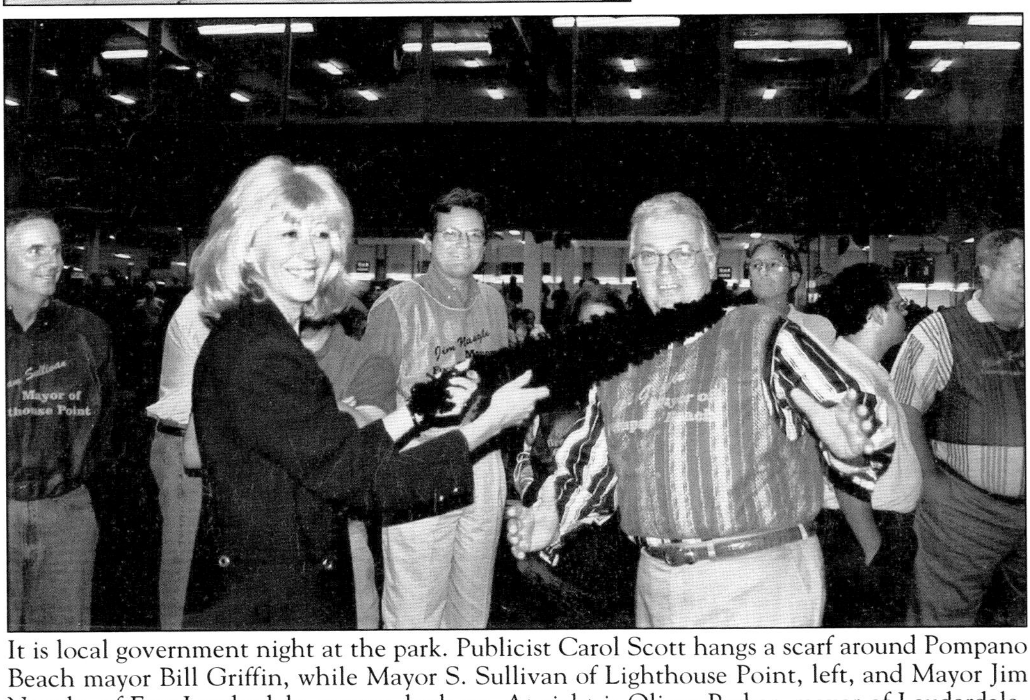

It is local government night at the park. Publicist Carol Scott hangs a scarf around Pompano Beach mayor Bill Griffin, while Mayor S. Sullivan of Lighthouse Point, left, and Mayor Jim Naugle, of Fort Lauderdale, center, look on. At right is Oliver Parker, mayor of Lauderdale-by-the-Sea.

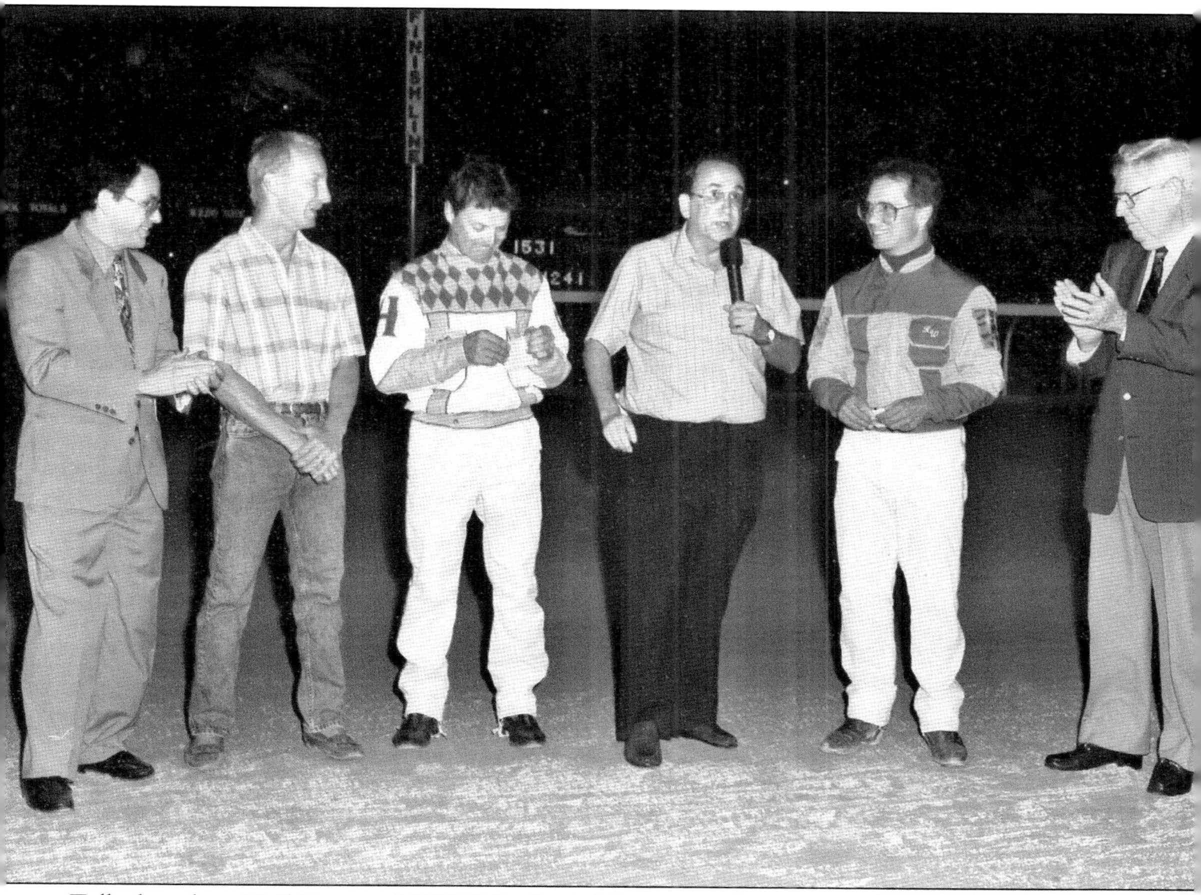

Talk-show host Neil Rogers of WIOD Radio in Miami served as master of ceremonies for the awards presentations following the finale of the April 28, 1993 Pompano Harness Drivers Showdown III competition at the track. From left to right are Mark Loewe, director of racing; Bruce Ranger, semifinalist; Wally Hennessey, runner-up for the second straight year; Rogers; champion Kevin Wallis; and Executive Vice President and General Manager Harold Duris. Joe Pavia Jr., the other semifinalist, was driving at the Meadowlands that night.

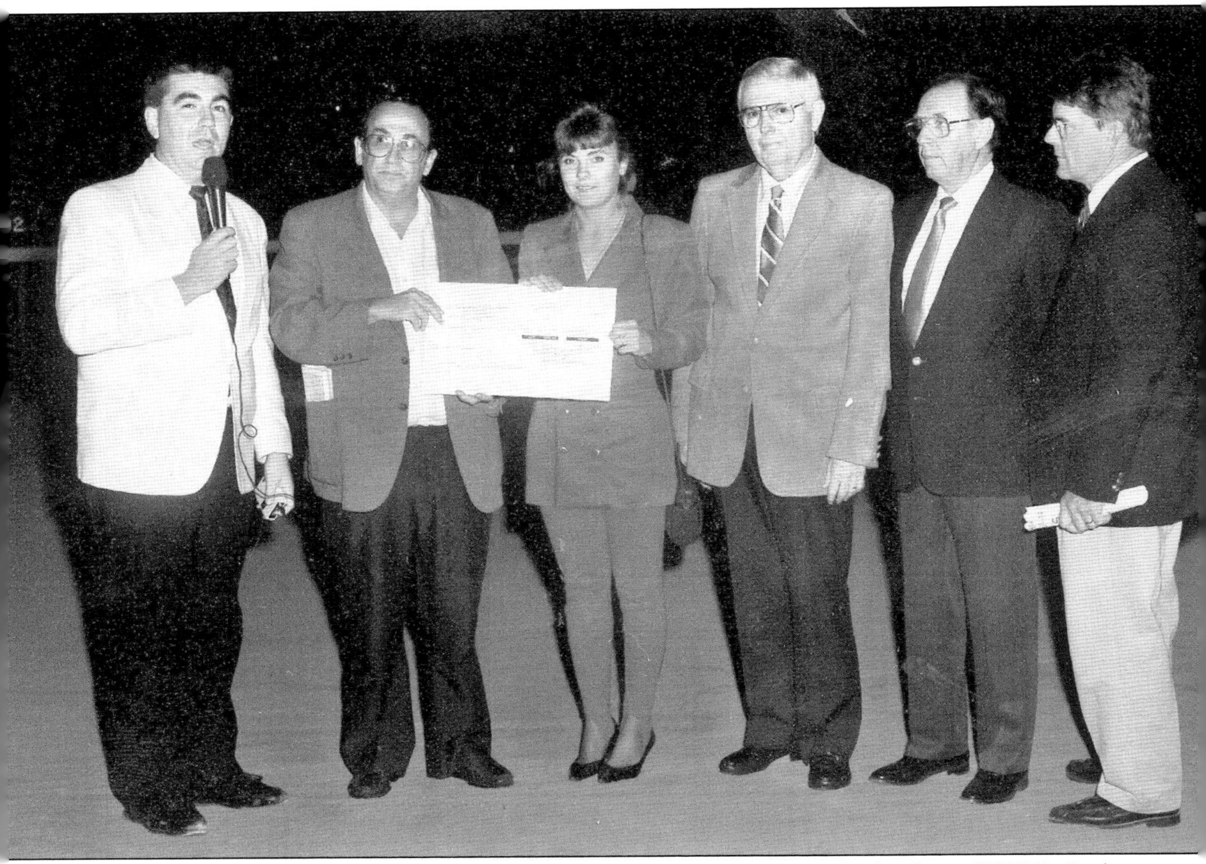

Melanie Wrenn, center, wife of driver Peter Wrenn, presents a check to WIOD Radio personality Neil Rogers for $7,000 on behalf of Pompano's horsemen and horsewomen, as the proceeds for the Camillus House Pace in 1998. They donated the $3,000 purse to the Miami facility for the homeless, while the track donated its on-track operating commissions. From left to right are Kent Williams, race secretary; Rogers; Wrenn; Harold Duris, executive vice president and general manager; Walter Warrington of the Florida Standardbred Breeders and Owners Association; and Jay Sears, FSBOA president.

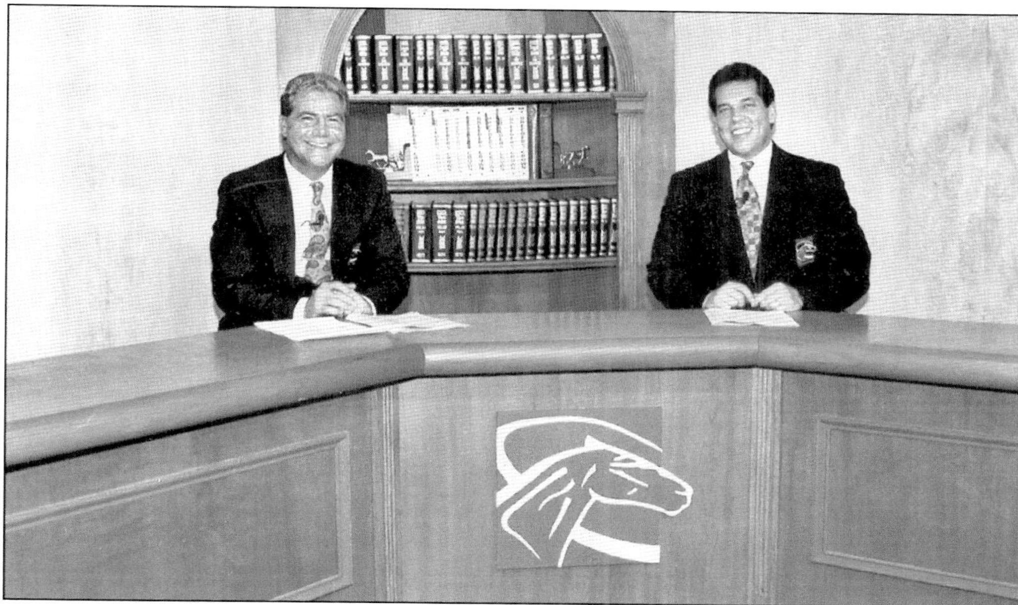

The television and video announcing team of Larry Albano, left, and Gary Seibel presented the racing results nightly on television at the Pompano Park television studio during the 1990s. Seibel is now a broadcaster for the national racing network TVG and for ESPN.

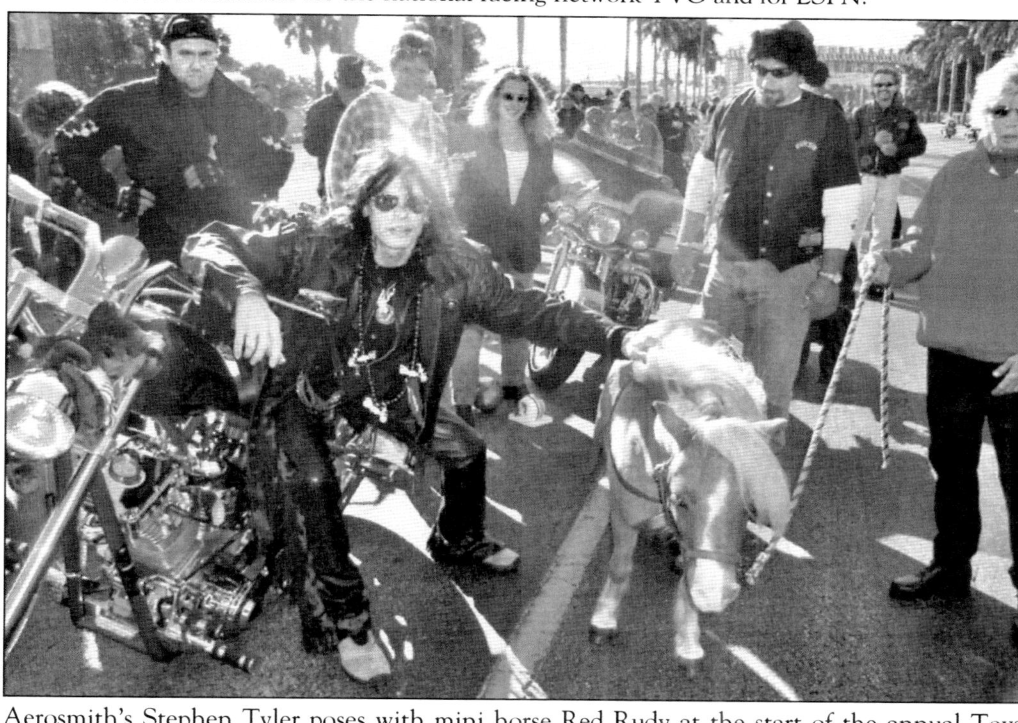

Aerosmith's Stephen Tyler poses with mini horse Red Rudy at the start of the annual Toys in the Sun Fun Run. Tyler was the grand marshal for the event on December 7, 2003, that began at Pompano Park. Thirty thousand motorcyclists participated and raised money for the Joe DiMaggio Children's Hospital in Hollywood, Florida.

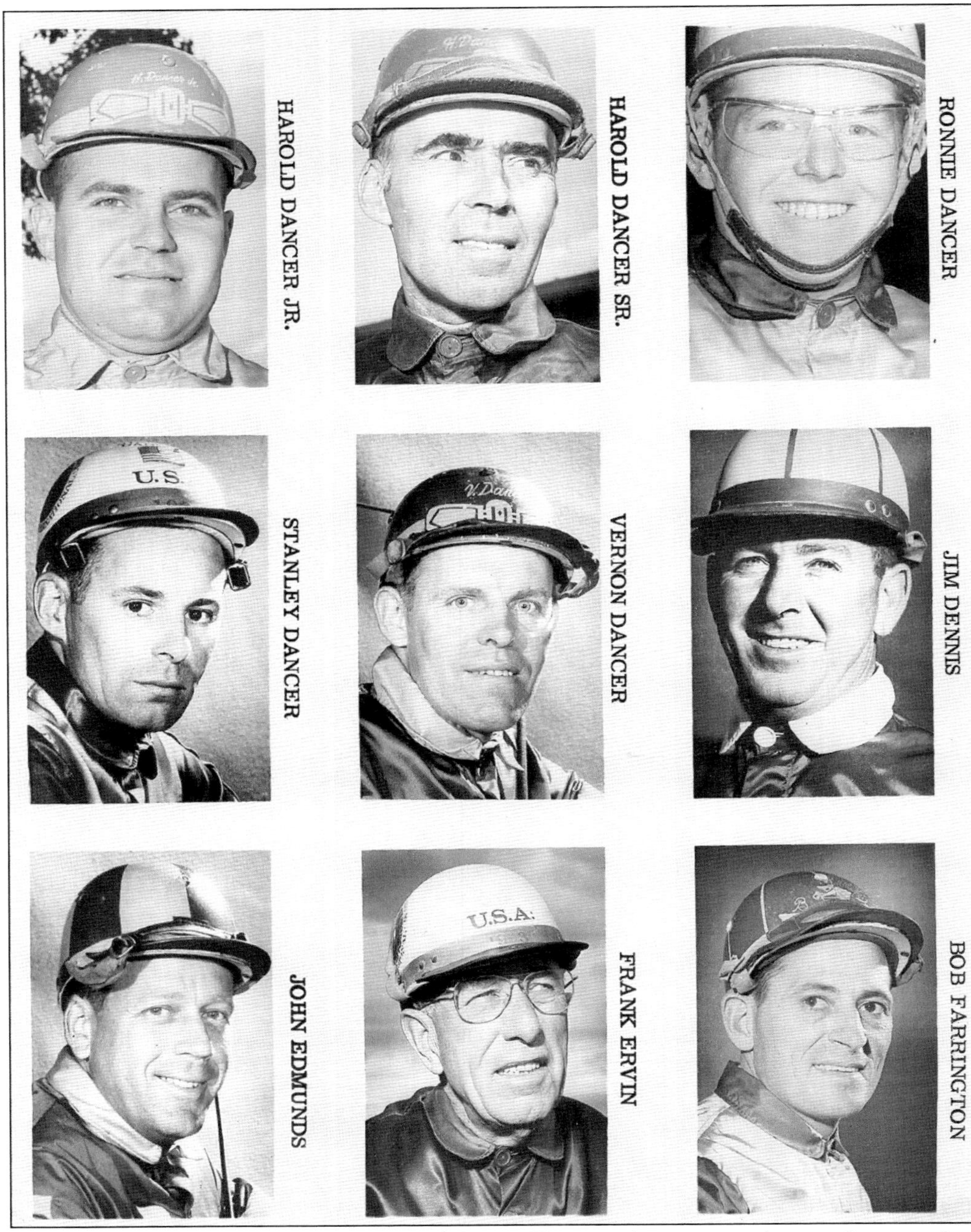

In this unique composite of nine United States Trotting Association drivers, five members of the Dancer family stand out prominently. Four of these nine veteran drivers are members of the Hall of Fame in Goshen, New York: Frank Ervin (1968), Stanley Dancer (1969), Bob Farrington (1979), and Vernon Dancer (2002).

Herve Filion (born 1940 in Quebec), a familiar driver at Pompano Park, achieved an unsurpassed record in his career. He was the first to earn more than 400 wins (407 in 1968), and he did it 14 times more. He received the Driver of the Year Award 10 times. As the all-time leader in races won, he has more than 15,000 wins. He said in 1990, "I let the horse do the work. I guide him. If the horse gets beat, it's not my fault. If he wins, it's not my fault."

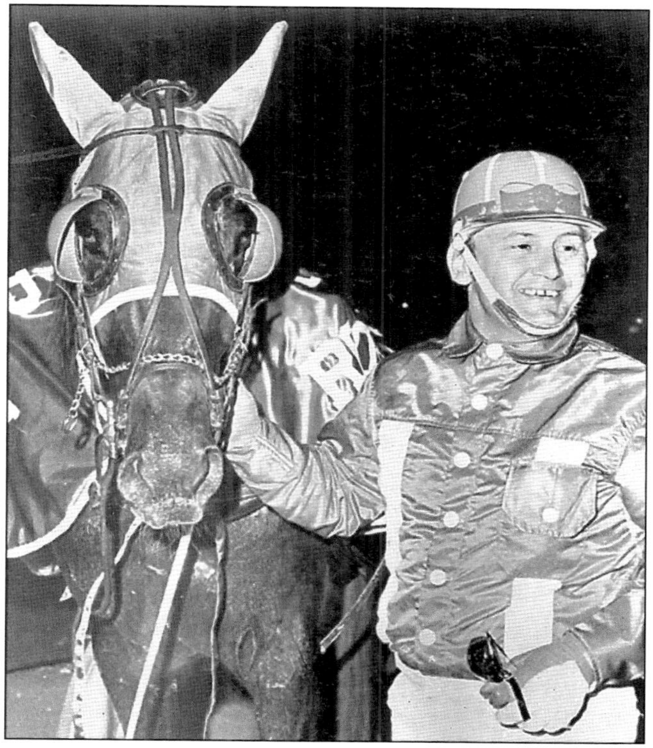

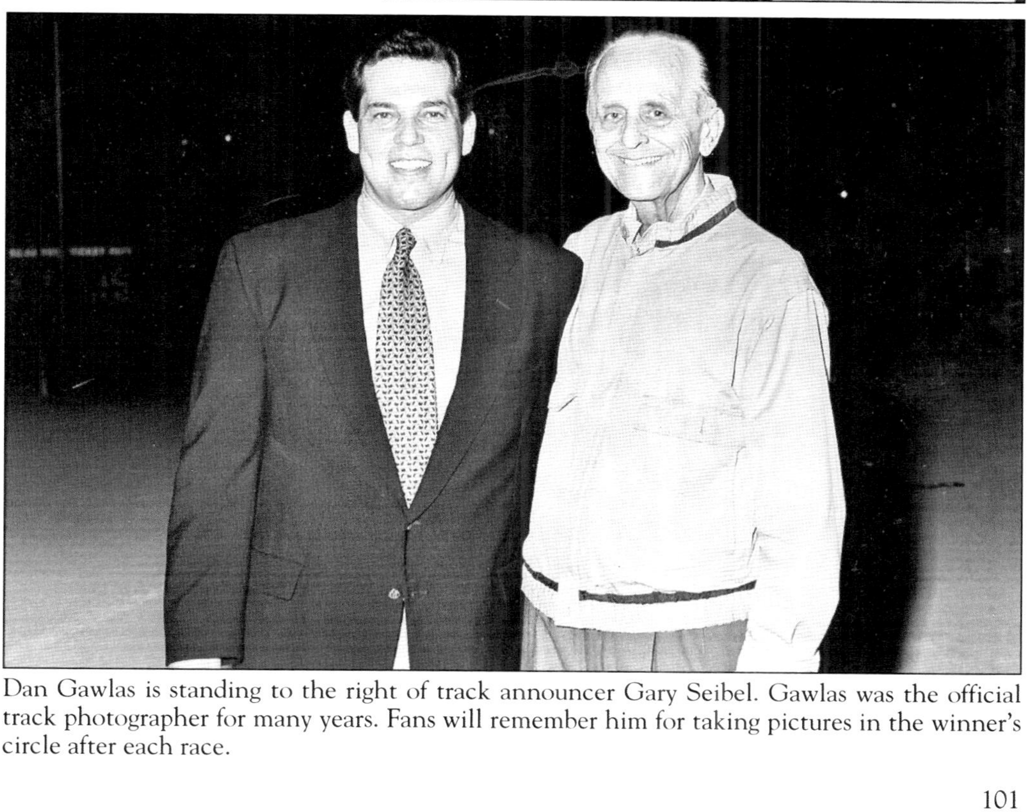

Dan Gawlas is standing to the right of track announcer Gary Seibel. Gawlas was the official track photographer for many years. Fans will remember him for taking pictures in the winner's circle after each race.

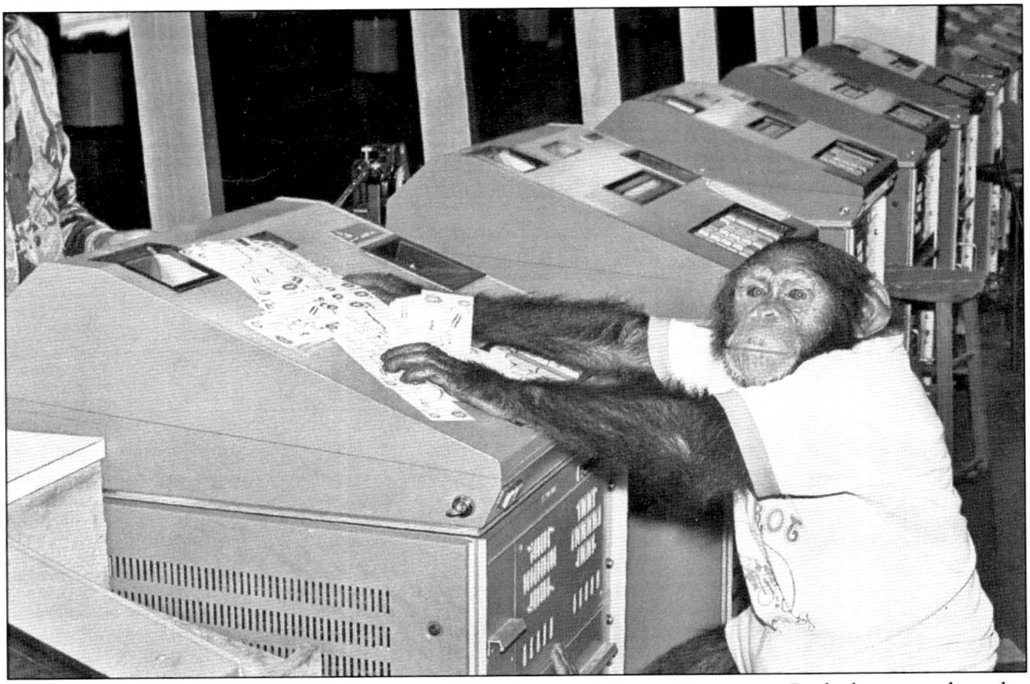

This serious chimp is manning the mutuel betting machine at Pompano Park, but somehow he pushed the wrong button, allowing tickets to spew forth. The chimp eventually left the booth to entertain the youngsters at trackside.

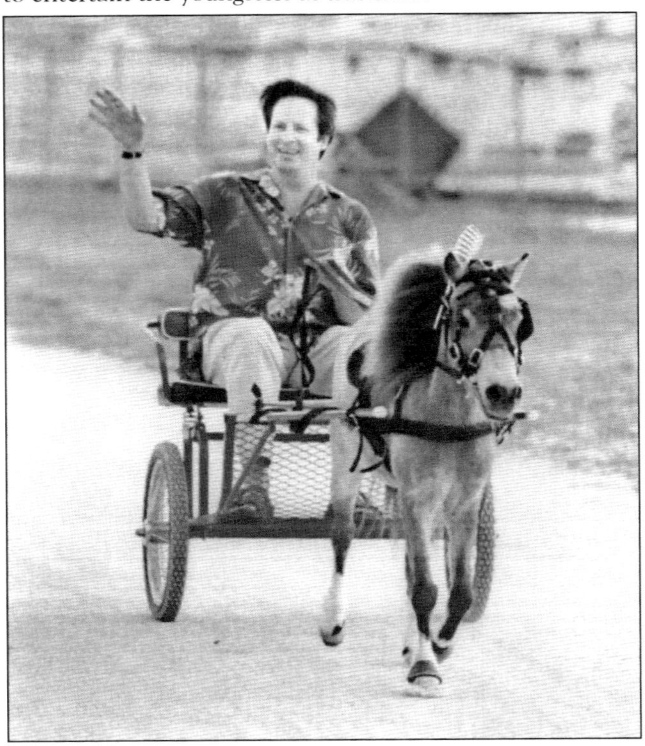

Pulitzer Prize–winning author and *Miami Herald* columnist Dave Barry waves to fans as he practices for a mini-horse charity race at Pompano Park in 2002 guiding Moonshine.

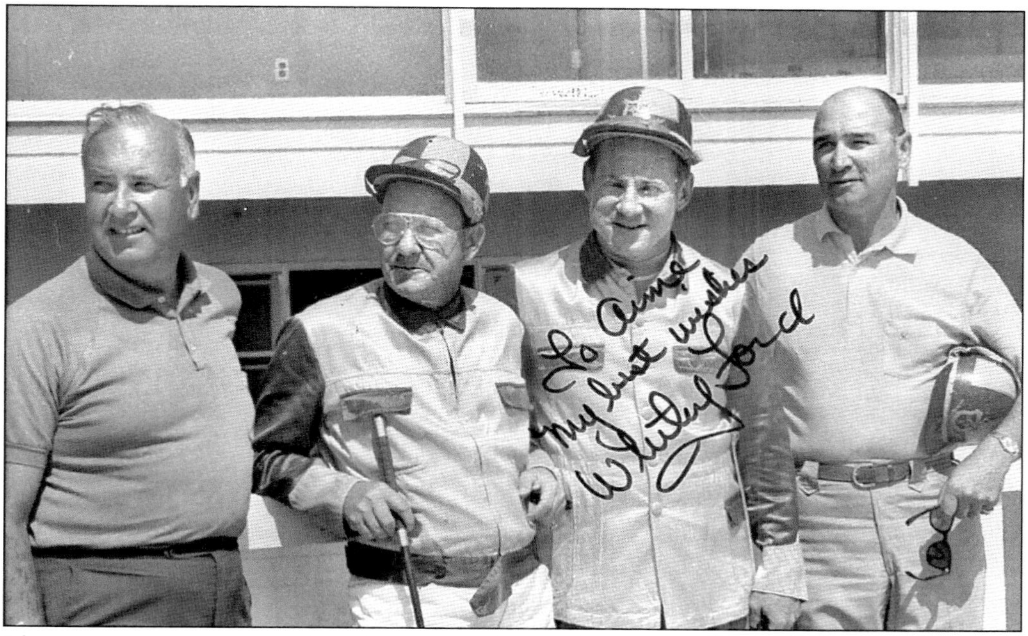

Three sports are represented in this image of these four outstanding performers. From left to right are Canadian hockey player Ivan Dugre, harness driver Del Miller, baseball's Hall of Fame pitcher Whitey Ford, and trainer Aime Choquette, who trained for the Del Miller stable.

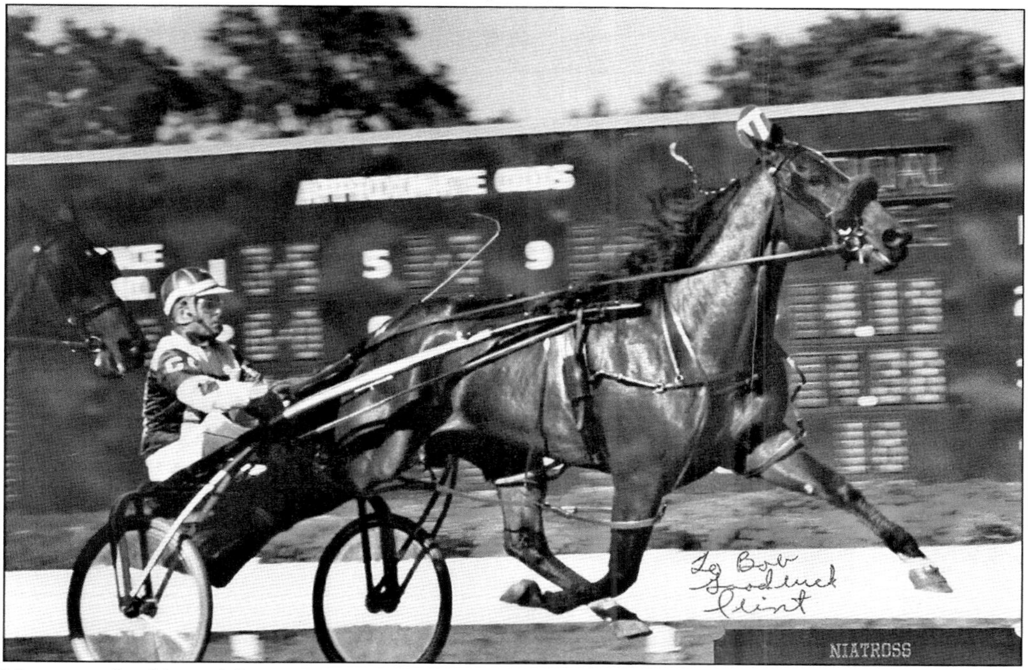

Niatross, the United States Trotting Association Horse of the Year for 1979 and 1980, driven by Clint Galbraith, is seen here winning the Red Mile in Lexington, Kentucky, on October 1, 1980. Soon after, Niatross raced to a record victory at Pompano Park on the biggest night in Florida harness racing history, December 27, 1980, when 18,451 fans witnessed the event.

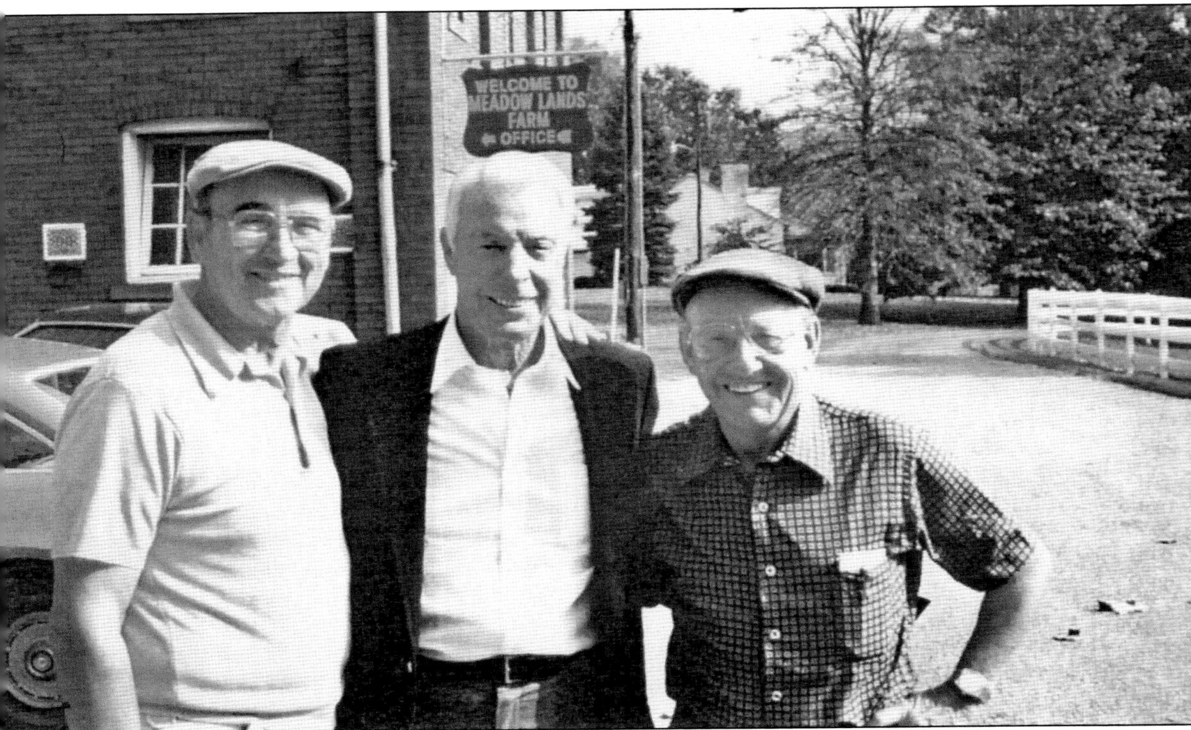

Baseball great Joe DiMaggio, center, was a devoted fan of harness racing. He is flanked by trainer Aime Choquette, left, and Del Miller, right. The scene was taken in 1980 at Del Miller's Meadow Lands Farm, in Meadow Lands, Pennsylvania. The brick building at rear left contained the barn and office. Miller's home is in the background. The track is at right.

The Harness Racing Museum and Hall of Fame is located in the historic town of Goshen, New York, where the spirit of the Standardbred prevails. A scenic half-mile track is located off Main Street. This cover of a recent museum souvenir catalogue contains items of interest to the harness-racing fan.

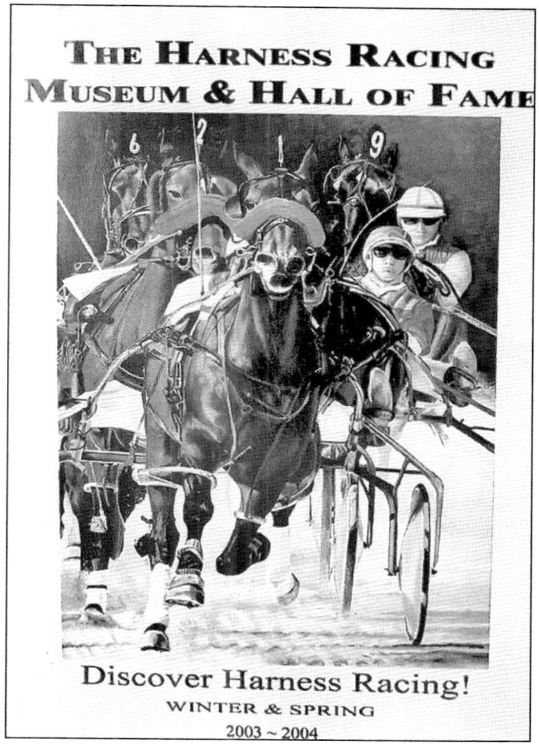

From its inception, Pompano Park has promoted harness racing in various ways to community groups. Here, Park personnel provide a demonstration of the sport to school children. Guided tours are also conducted at the track.

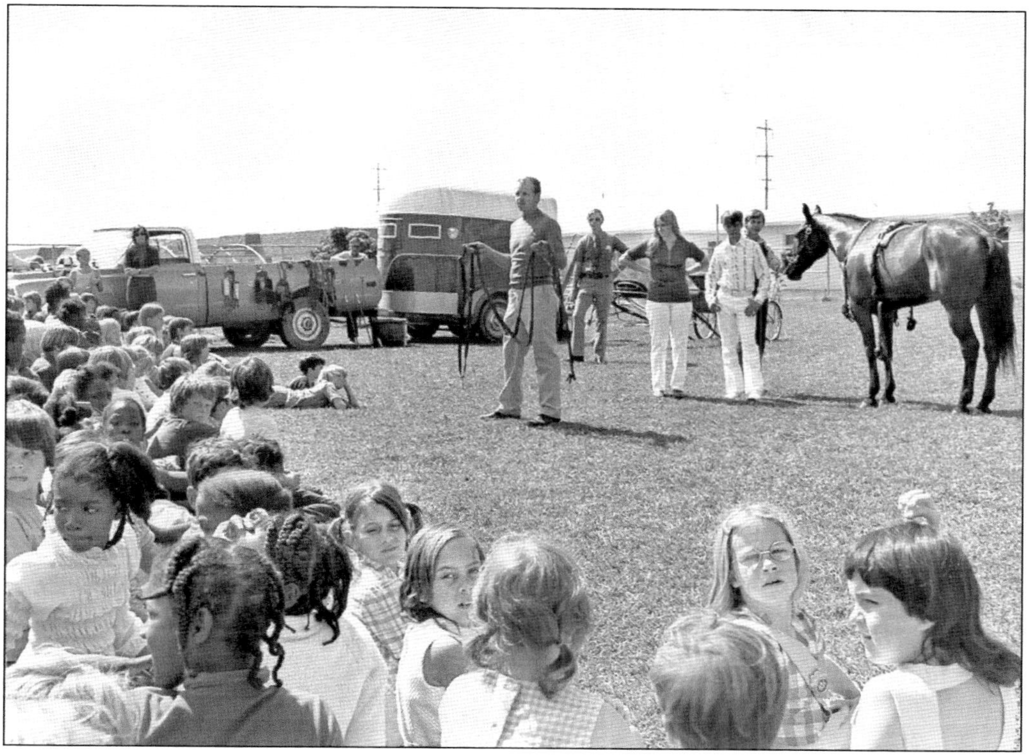

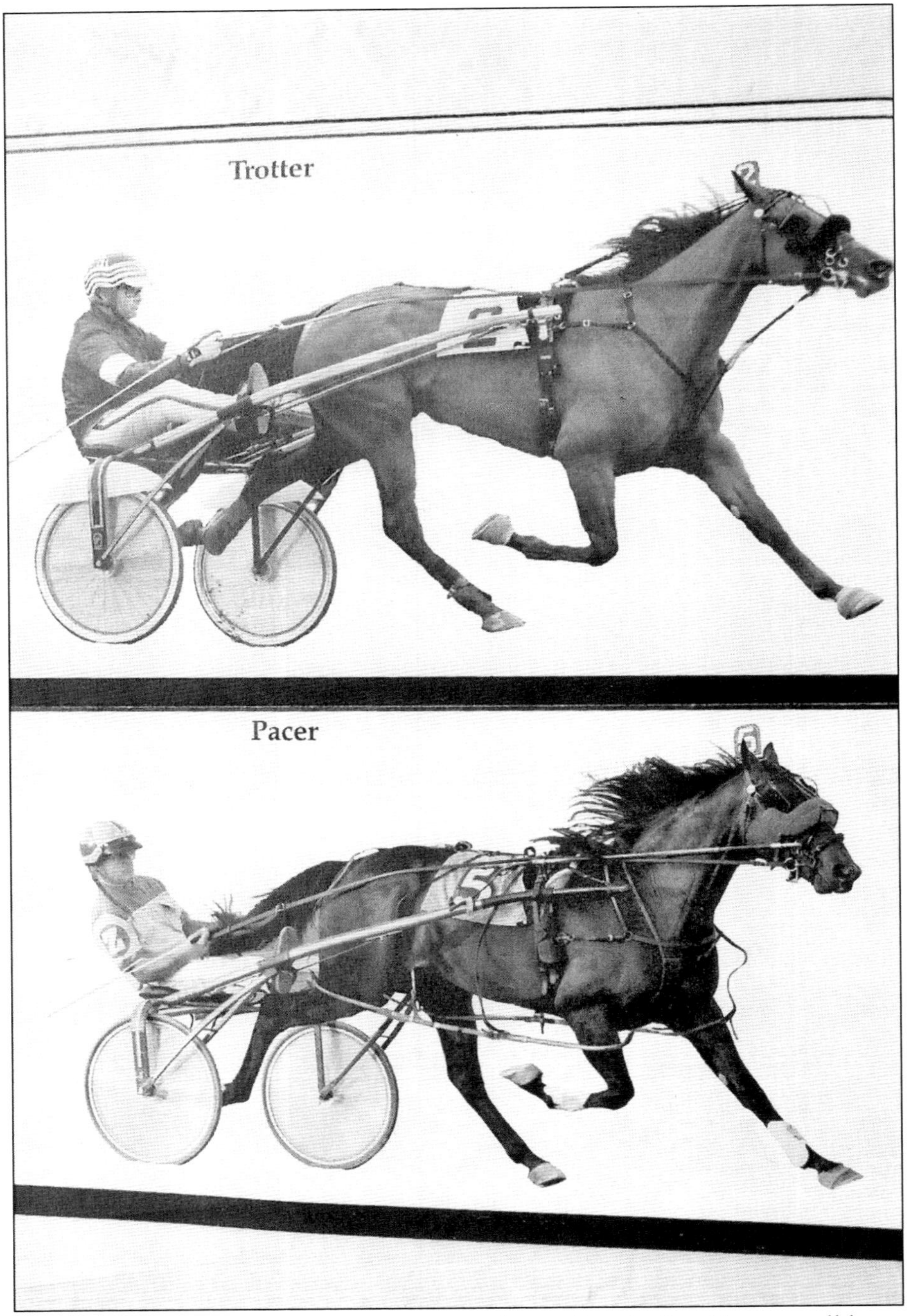

Special breeding and training are necessary to produce a Standardbred because all horses can run but not all can trot or pace. There are two gaits in harness racing. The trotter, at top, moves with a diagonal gait: the left front and the right rear legs move in unison, as do the right front and the left rear legs. The pacer moves the legs on the same side of the body in tandem: left front and left rear, and right rear and right front. Harness racing's Standardbreds offer beauty in motion.

Six

Pompano Park Today

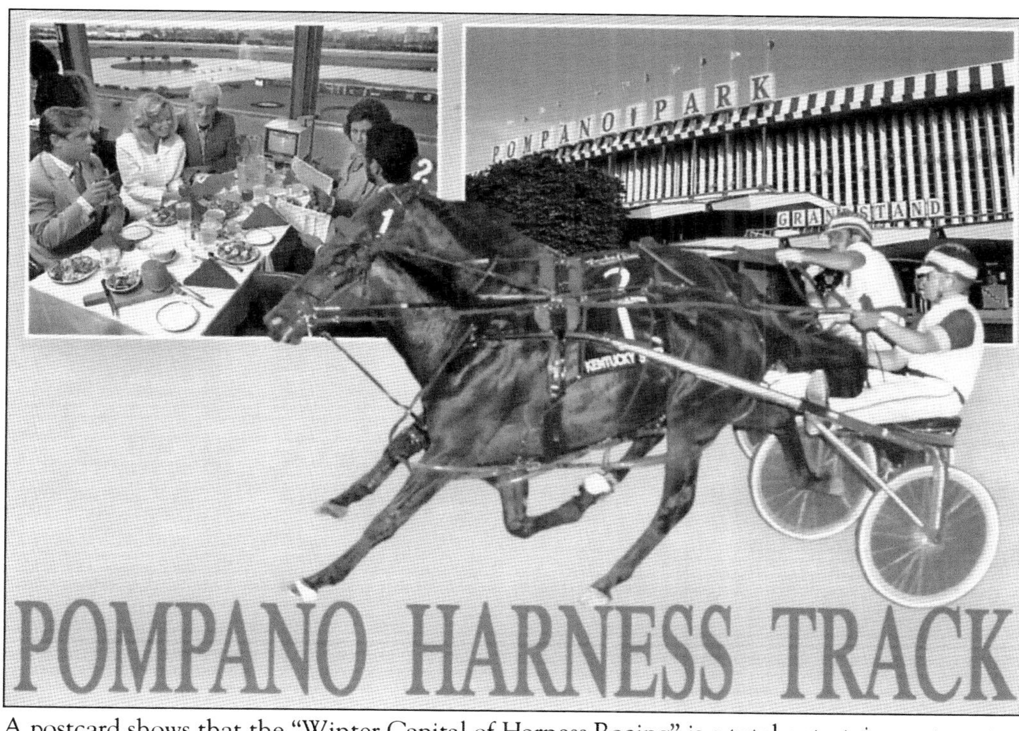

A postcard shows that the "Winter Capital of Harness Racing" is a total entertainment center, featuring pari-mutuel betting on live and simulcast races, poker play, dining amenities in the clubhouse, various other eating and drinking facilities, the mini horses, and special events. The track hosts the greatest horses, drivers, and trainers in North America.

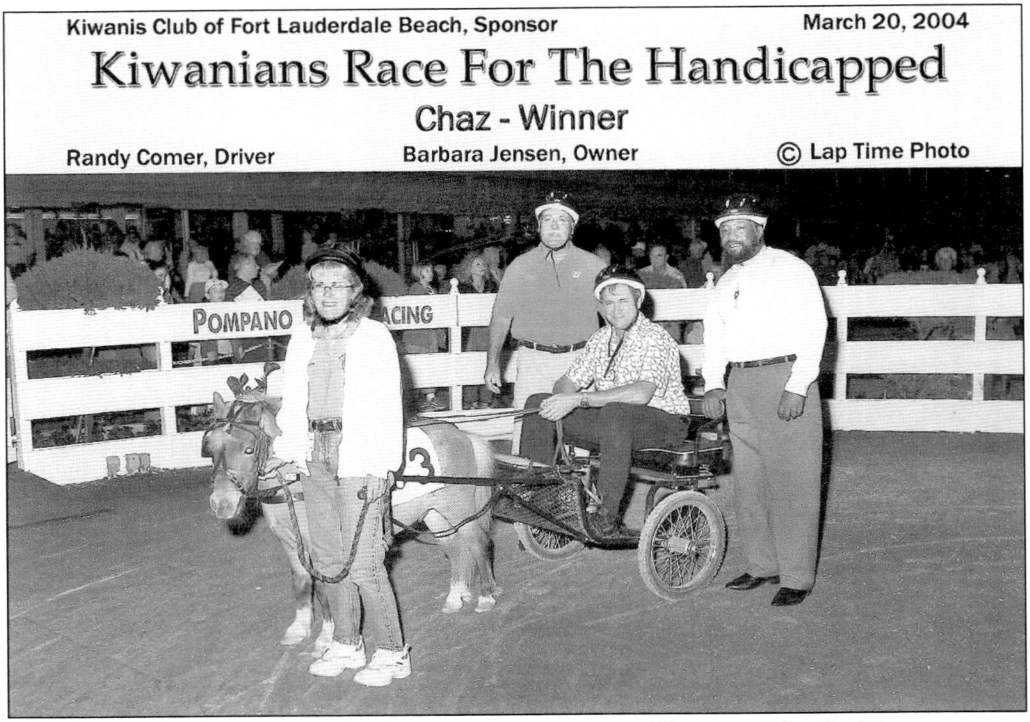

The special fund-raising event, Kiwanians Race for the Handicapped, was won by mini horse Chaz on March 20, 2004. Guest driver Randy Comer sits proudly in the sulky, joined by owner Barbara Jensen and leaders of the Kiwanis Club of Fort Lauderdale.

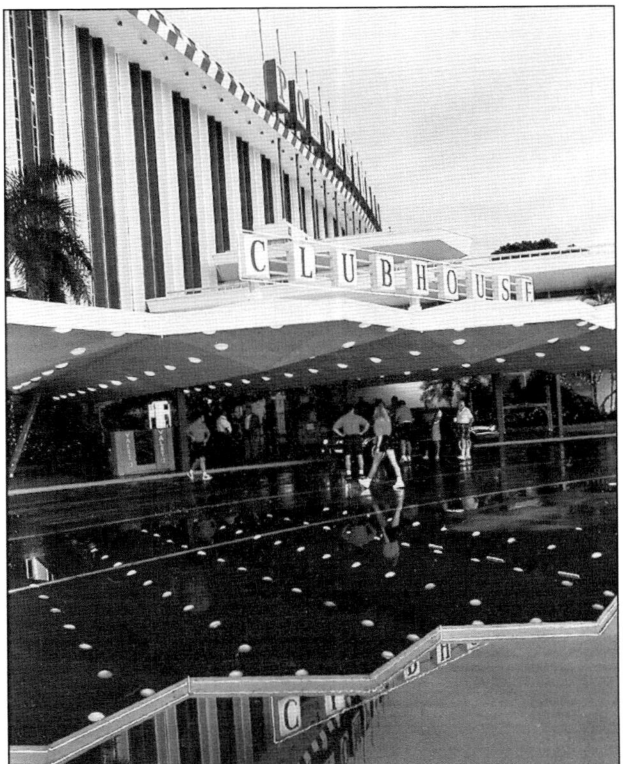

With lights reflecting brightly at the clubhouse entrance, attendants prepare for a busy season's opening night on October 4, 1998. The 34th season marked the first full year of racing. The ageless wonder Rapunzel's Star set the world record for a trotting 14-year-old gelding at the previous meet.

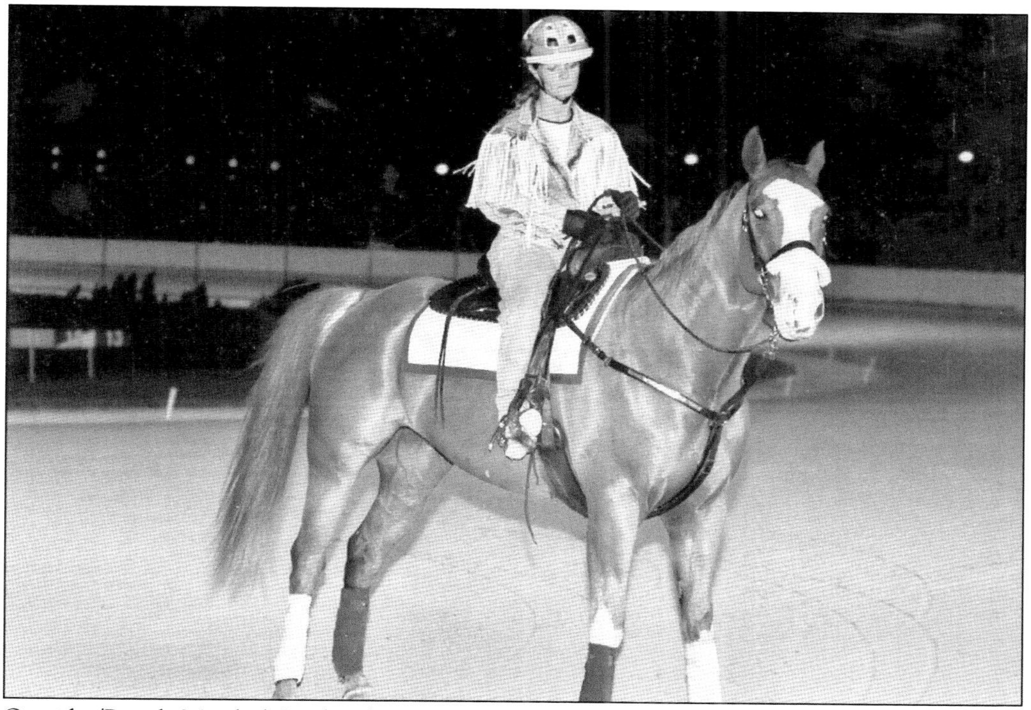

Outrider/Parade Marshal Cindy Johnson rides atop Bo as the track marshal who leads and guides horses and drivers out of the paddock preliminary for the start of the race. The time is early in the 2000 season. Bo enjoys the attention he is receiving.

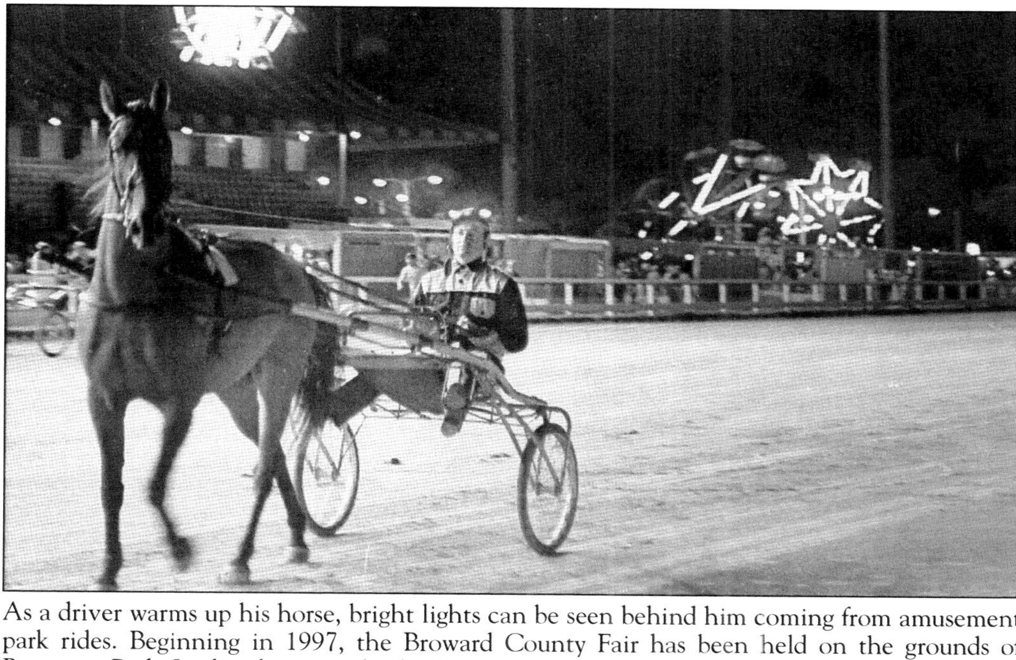

As a driver warms up his horse, bright lights can be seen behind him coming from amusement park rides. Beginning in 1997, the Broward County Fair has been held on the grounds of Pompano Park. In that first year the fair hosted such performers as 'N Sync, Britney Spears, the Village People, Mandy Moore, and Peter Noone.

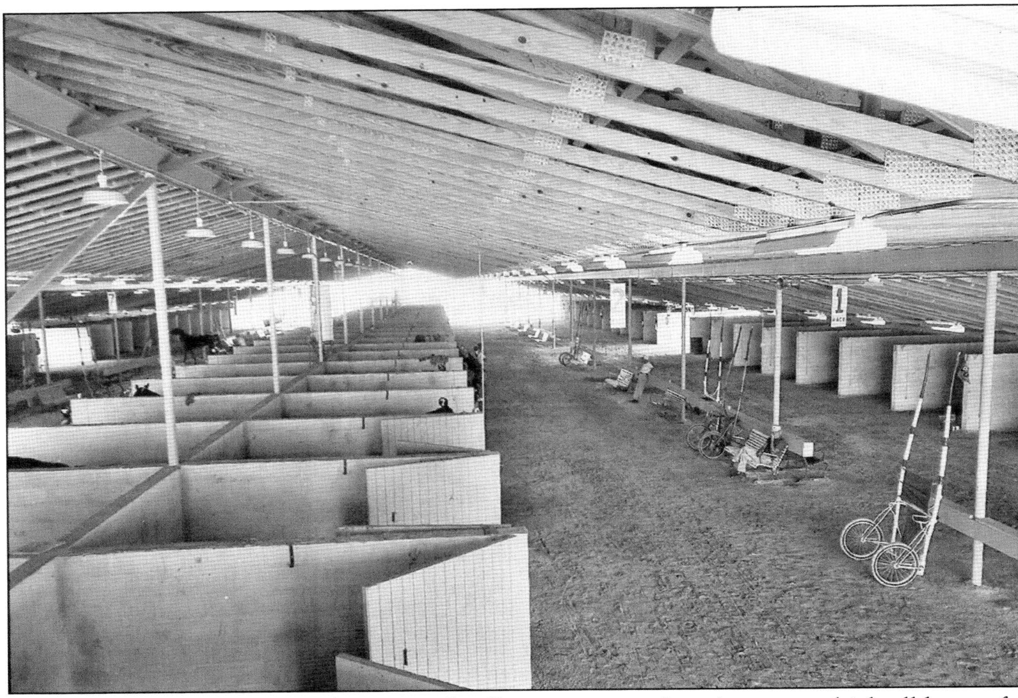

The paddock at Pompano Park is a set of stalls in a restricted enclosure to which all horses for a race must be taken at a specific time before they race. Only owners, trainers, grooms, drivers, and officials are permitted in the paddock.

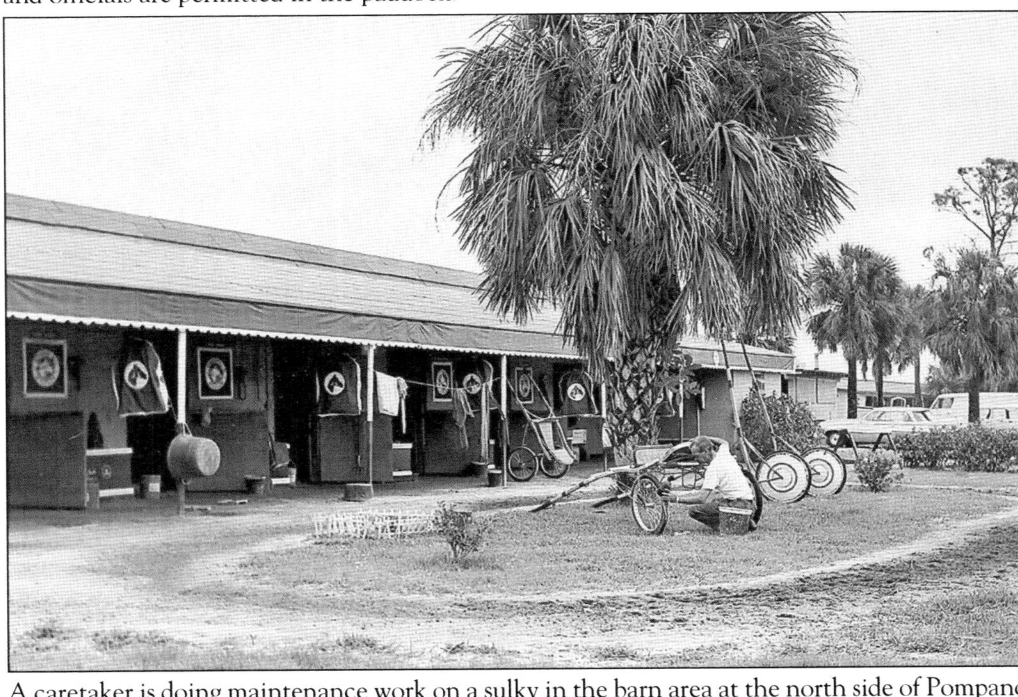

A caretaker is doing maintenance work on a sulky in the barn area at the north side of Pompano Park. The caretaker attends to the horses and stables. The sulky is the driver's bike.

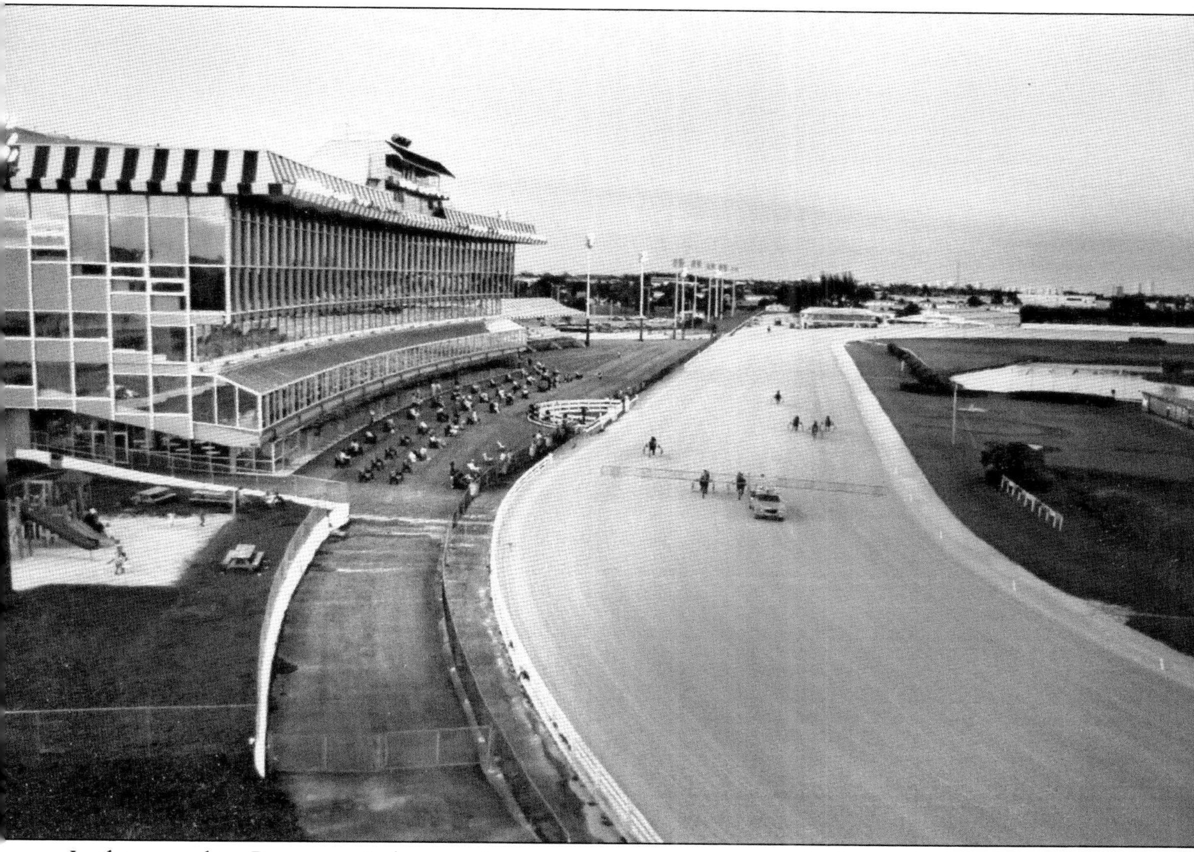

In this sprawling Pompano Park scene during a recent summer meet, the horses have been called to the starting gate. The children's play area is at left, winner's circle in the center, and totalizator board at right. This view is looking north. The track has come a long way since founder Frederick L. van Lennep staged non-betting races on Sunday afternoons five decades ago.

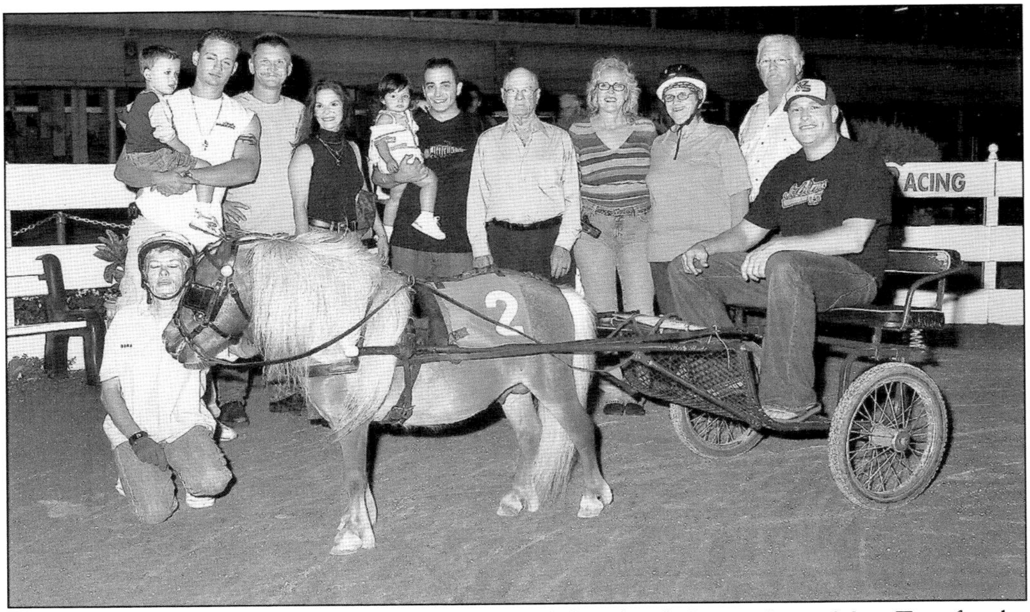

Annie's Pizza of Coral Springs/Margate sponsored the Florida Lions Camp Mini Trot for the Visually Handicapped at Pompano Park on April 24, 2004. Driver Ryan Shannon guided mini horse Red Rudy to victory.

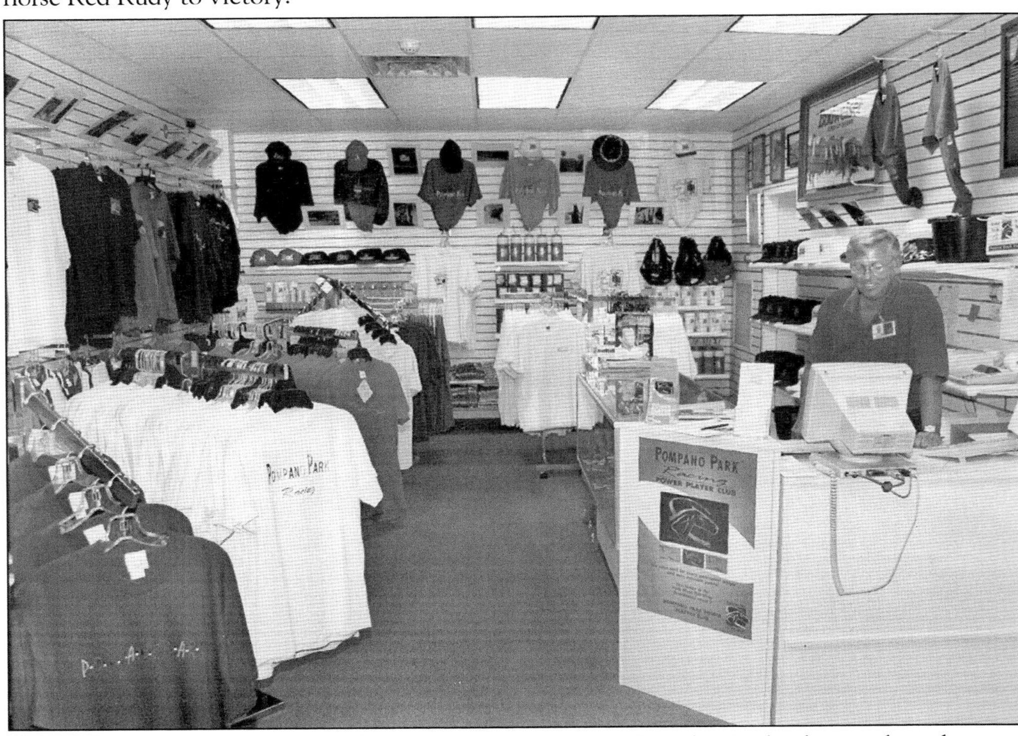

The interior of the gift shop displays harness-racing items for sale. Books that explain the sport are on sale, as well as jewelry, caps, shirts, collectibles, and more. It is located on the second level at the grandstand entrance. Manager Bob Wildman waits to serve.

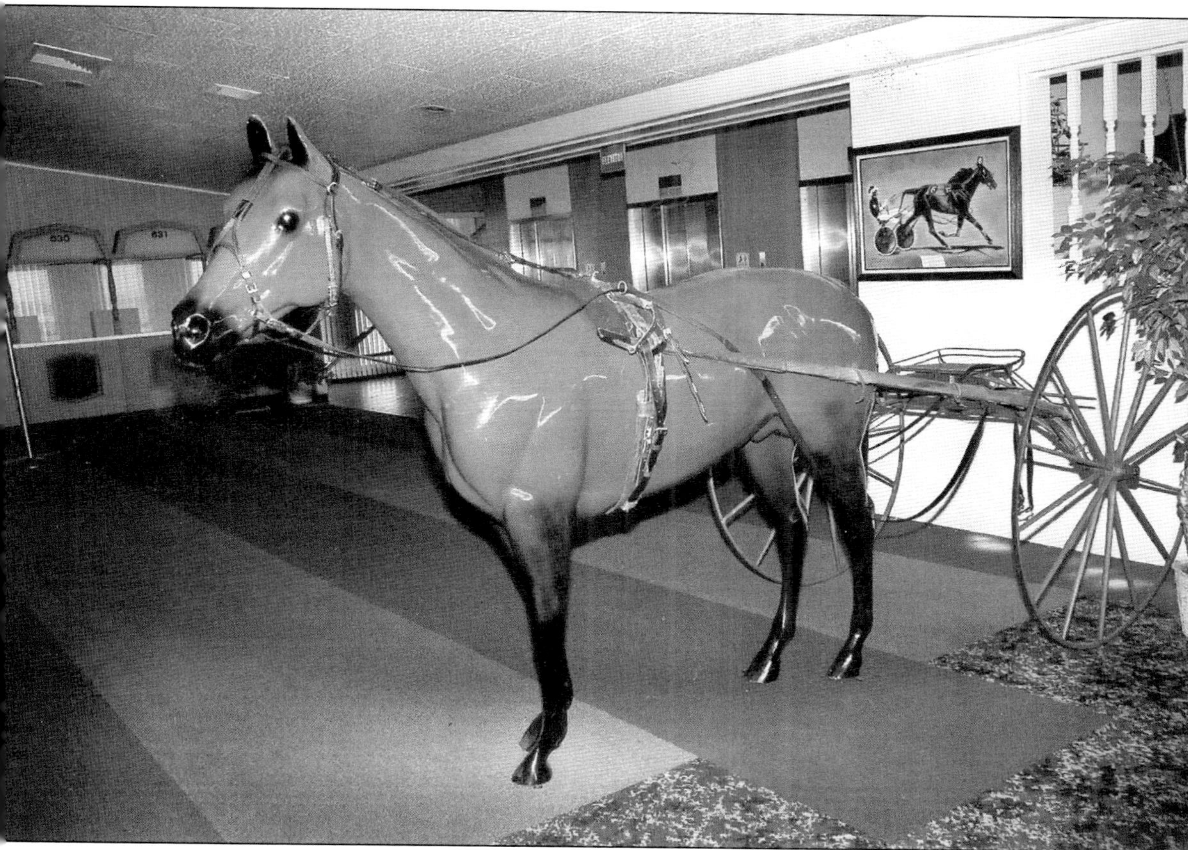

Harness racing is generally considered to be an American sport, with the modern version dating back to 1806, when records began to be kept and a gelding named Yankee trotted a mile in less than three minutes. This representation of a trotter with sulky stands regally on the park's fourth floor. The origins of the Standardbred go back to Messenger, an English Thoroughbred foaled in 1780 and exported to the United States.

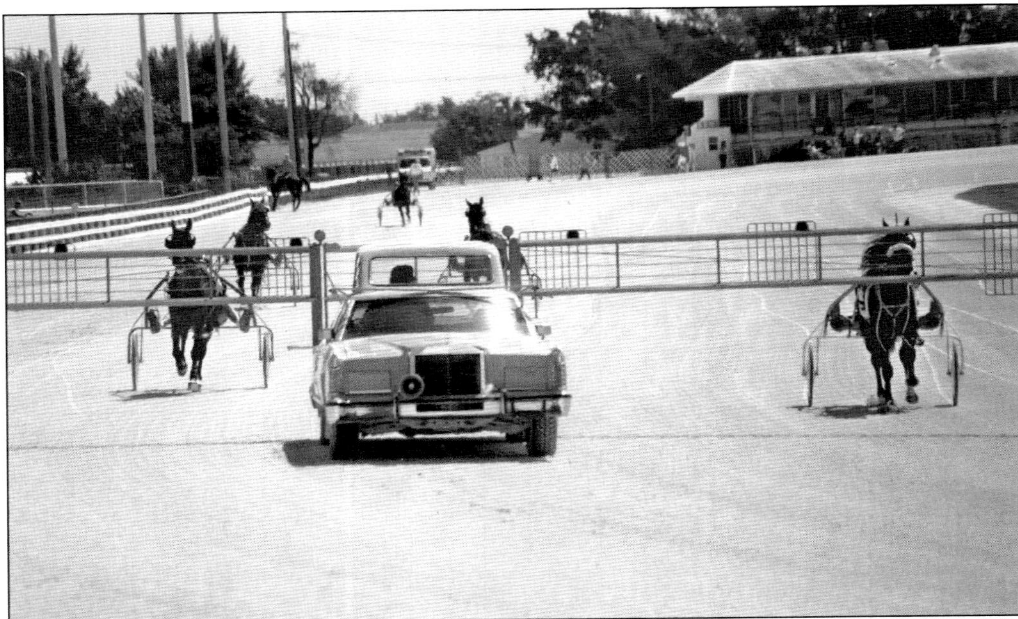

Before harness horses can compete in official races, they must go through a trial period to qualify. On the morning of May 15, 1998, these horses and drivers are approaching the starting gate for a qualifying race. Judges will evaluate their time and gait in the race. The paddock is in the background at right.

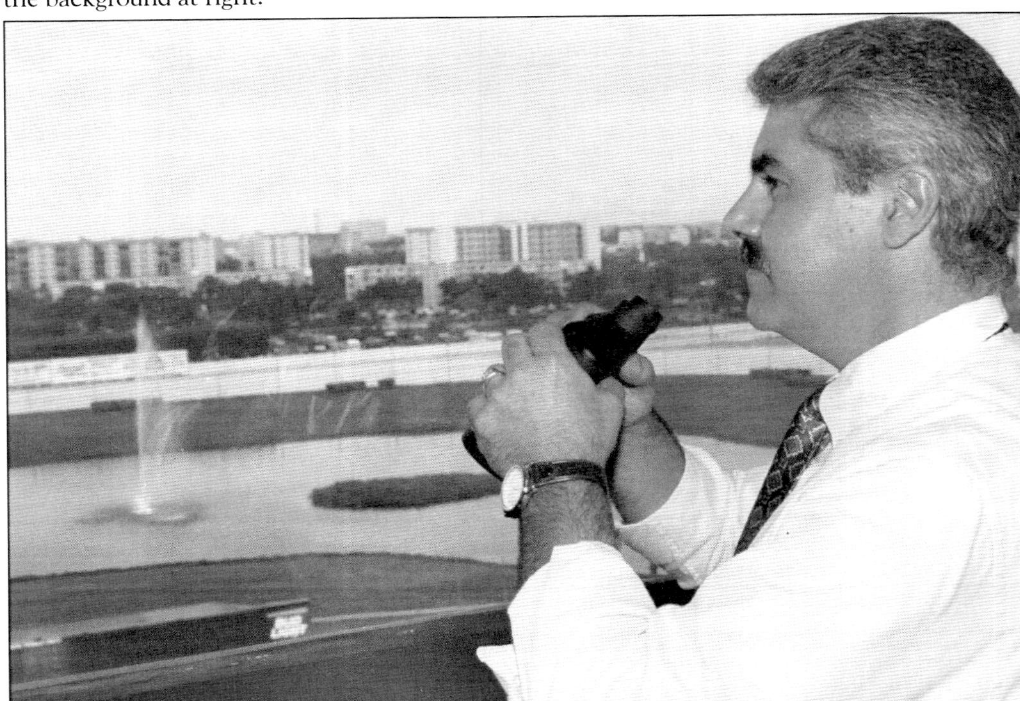

Pompano Park announcer Joe Ricci looks out over the track before calling a race. Ricci has been the track announcer since 1998.

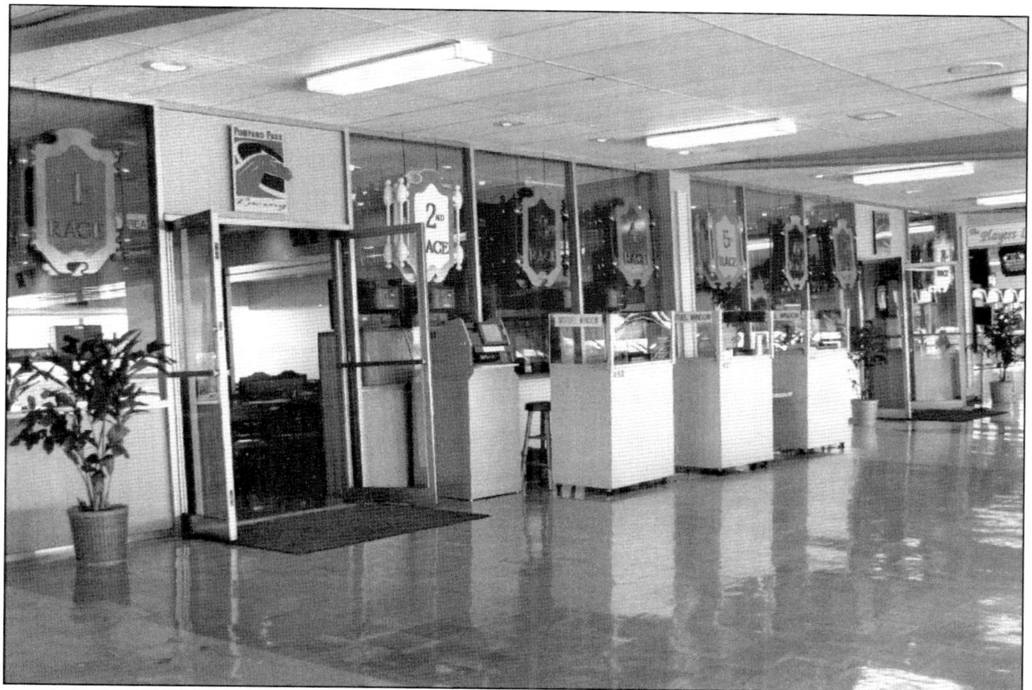

The Winner's Buffet, one of many options for the fan, is served every night of live racing in the Players Lounge on the fourth floor of the clubhouse.

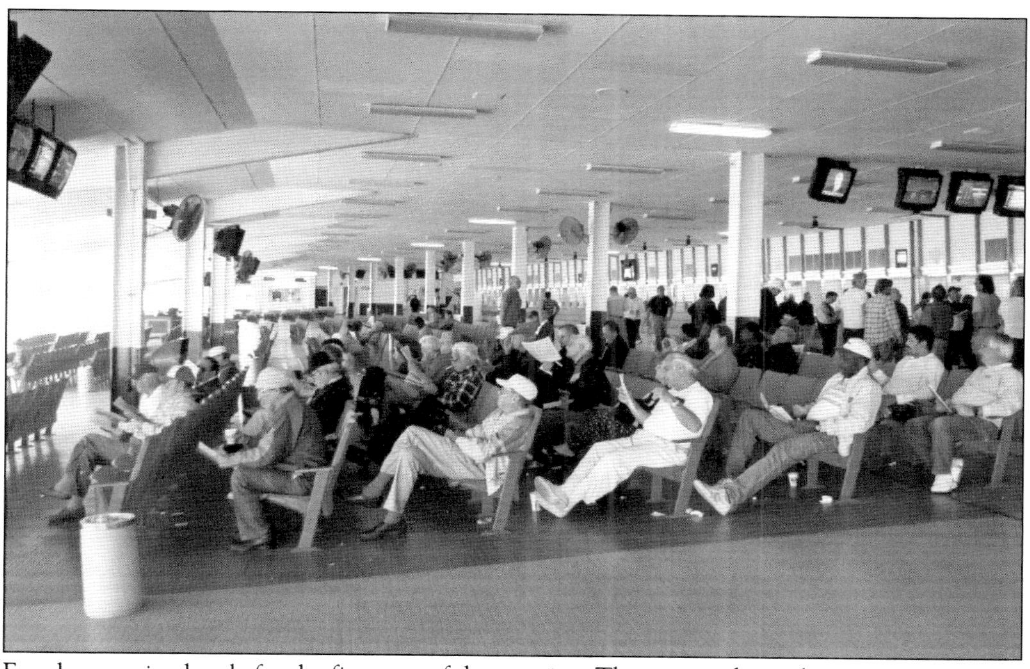

Fans have arrived early for the first race of the evening. They are studying the racing program to help them pick a winner in the handicapping process. The location is at trackside level.

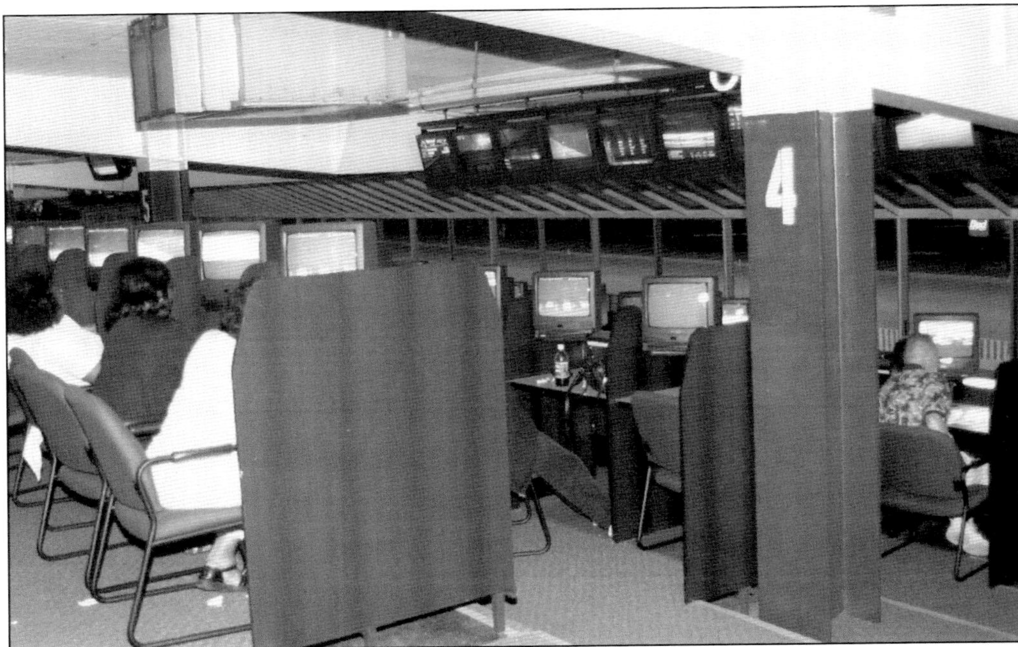

This section on the fourth floor provides individual private television viewing of live and simulcast racing at Pompano Park. The track can be seen through the glass panels at right.

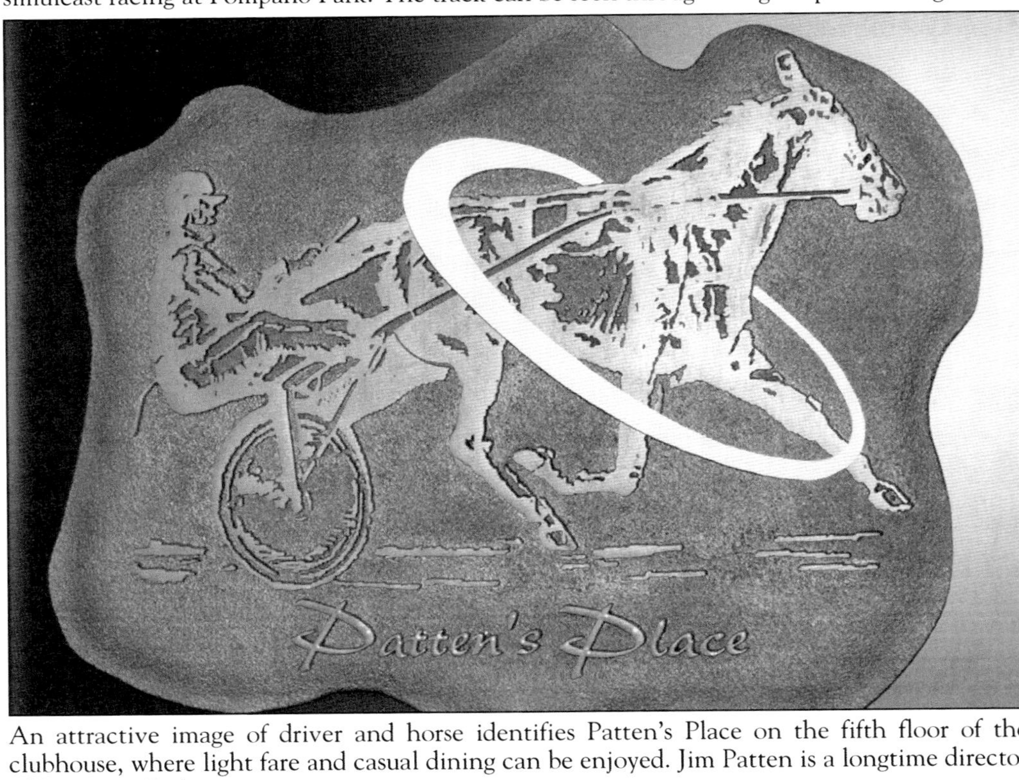

An attractive image of driver and horse identifies Patten's Place on the fifth floor of the clubhouse, where light fare and casual dining can be enjoyed. Jim Patten is a longtime director of Pompano Park.

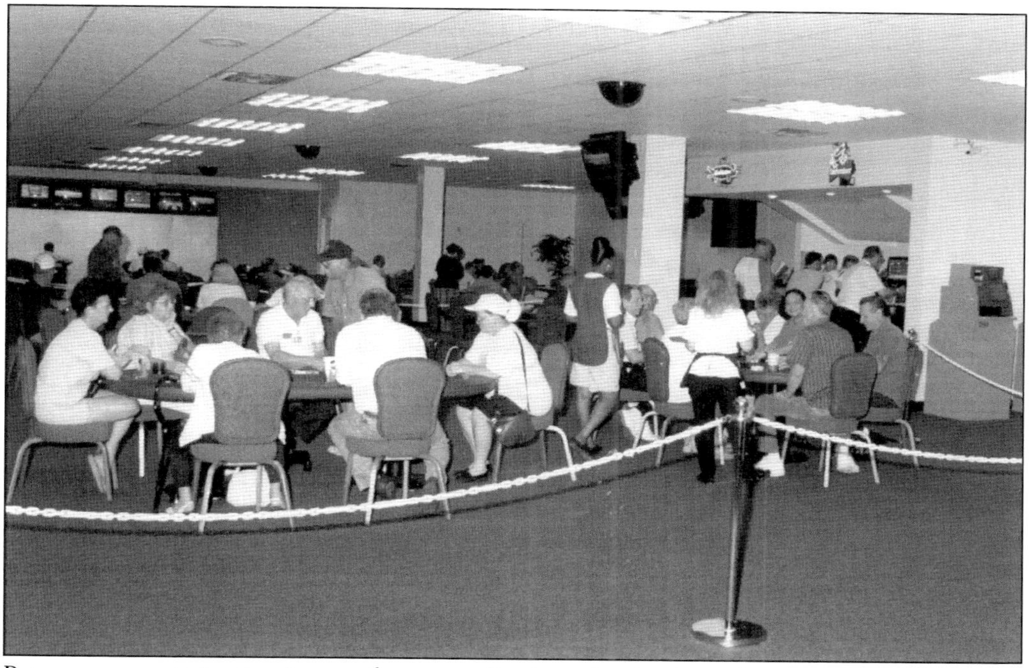

Patrons are participating in an afternoon of poker play in the poker room during a recent Christmas season. As all forms of gambling have expanded across the country, the Park has added this type of gaming for the local and tourist population. Note the betting counters in the background, at left and right, for simulcast racing.

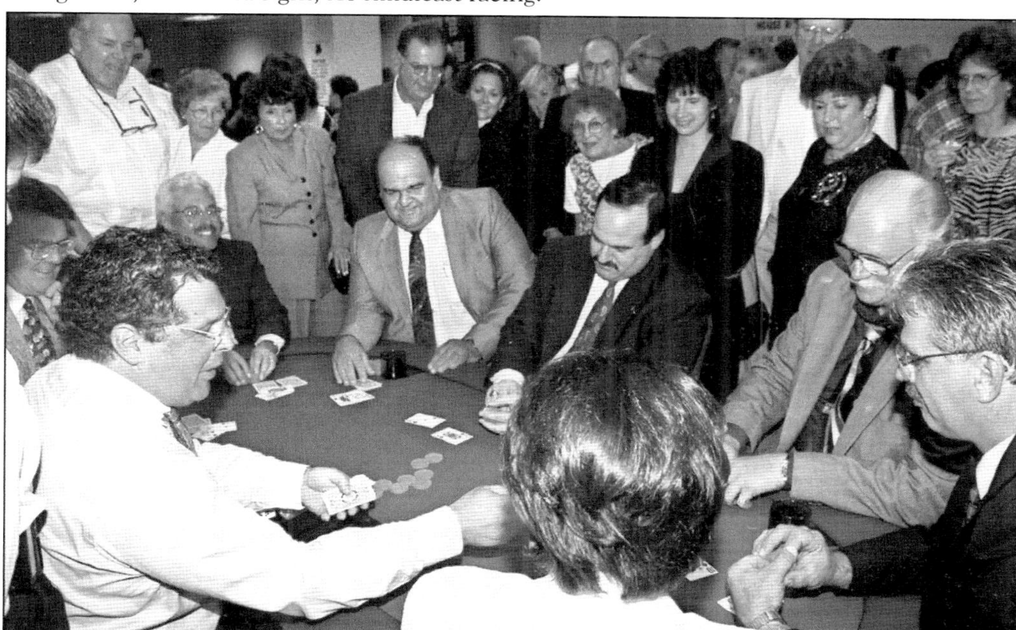

On January 1, 1997, Pompano Park was the first establishment to offer poker play with pot limits of $10 per hand. Poker was later discontinued because of the low dollar pot limits. New legislation in Florida in the summer of 2003 allowed $2 wagers with unlimited pots.

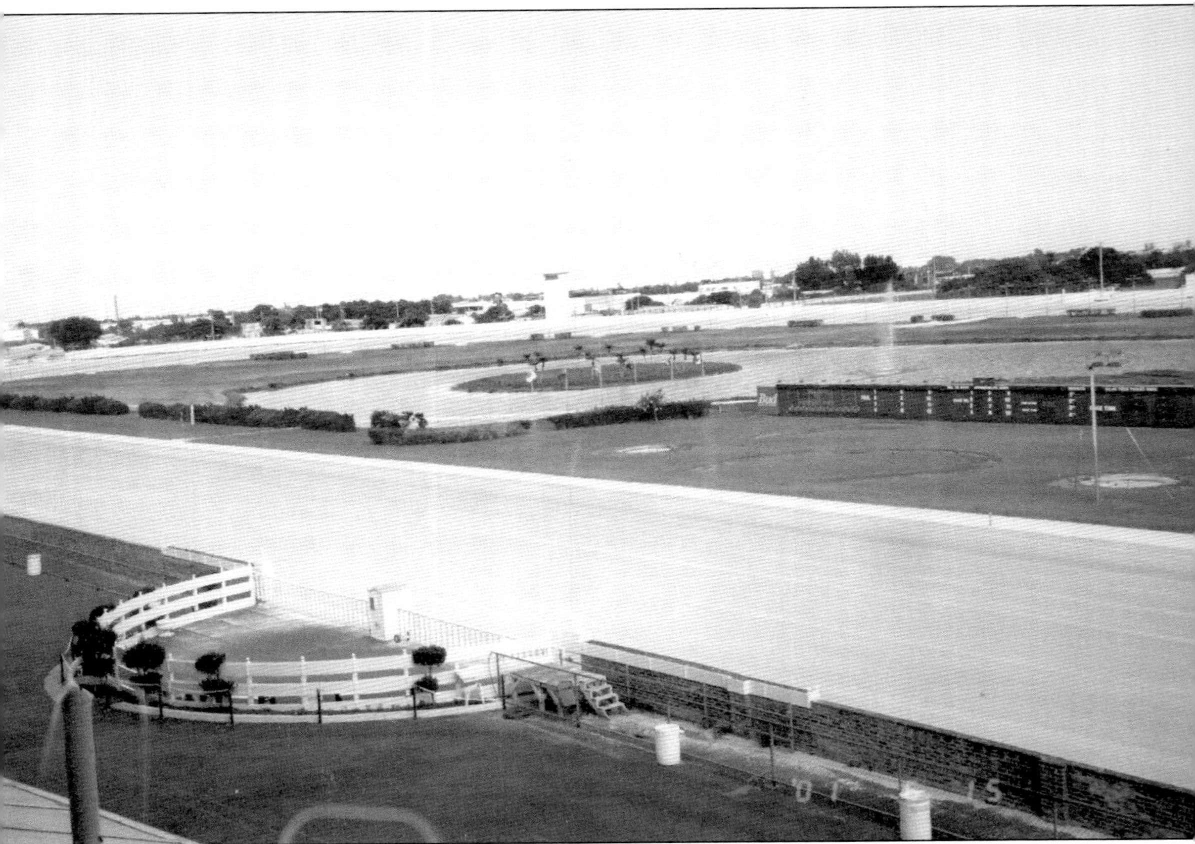

A turn-of-the century contemporary view (June 15, 2001) from the clubhouse captures the extent of the park and beyond. Trackside and winner's circle are at left, the racing track at center, and the totalizator (tote) board and lake are in the background. The totalizator board electronically displays the following data in the infield: time of day, amount of bets in each pool, odds, track condition, post time, an inquiry or objection sign if a foul is claimed, official time, race results, and pay-off prices.

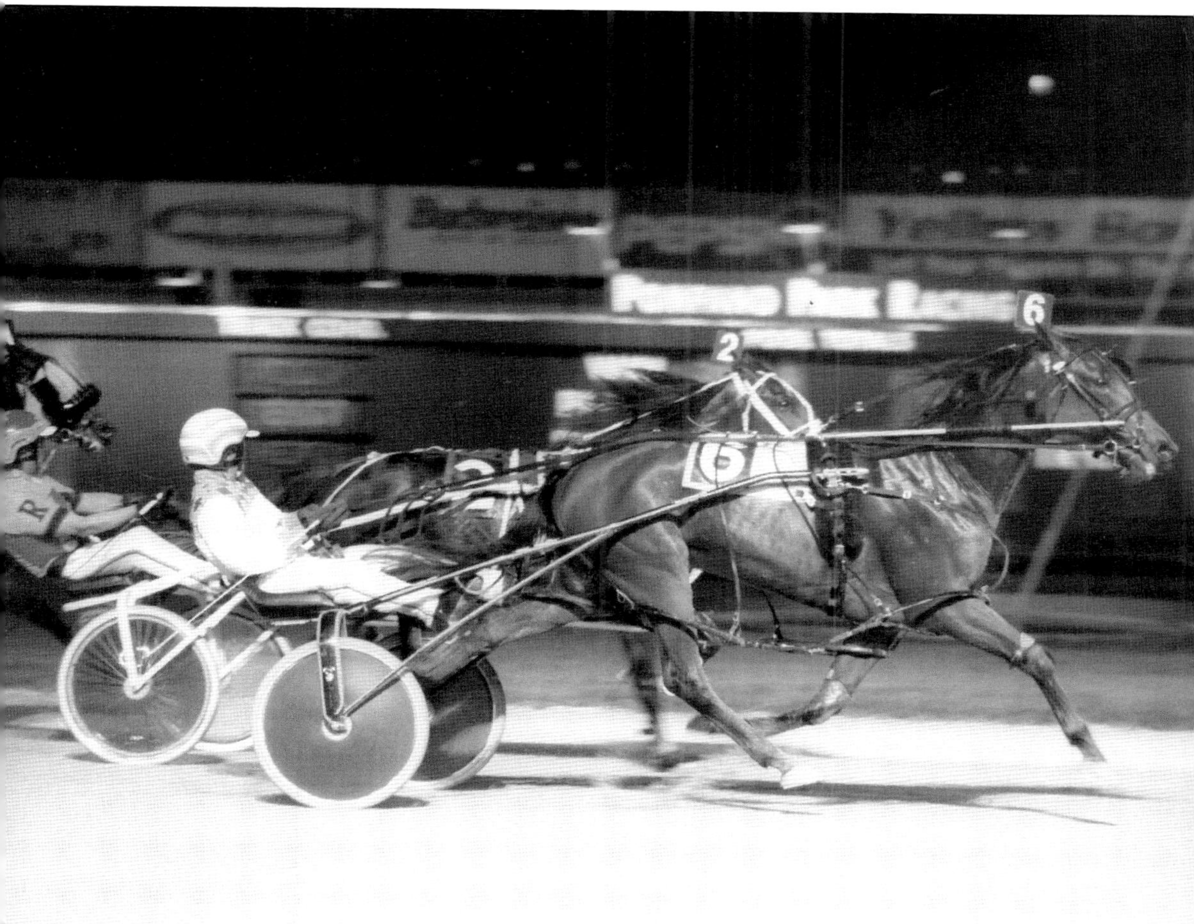

Driver Wally Hennessey (6) drives past Bruce Ranger (2) in a closely contested race during the winter season of 2000. They are looking left to check their time on the tote board. Despite the loss, Ranger has become the winningest driver in Pompano Park history. On September 18, 2004, he won a record nine races on the same card, surpassing Brian Sears's eight victories on February 15, 2003. During the 1998–1999 season, Ranger set an all-time record of 478 victories. As two of the most successful drivers, both Hennessey and Ranger have each won more than 5,000 races.

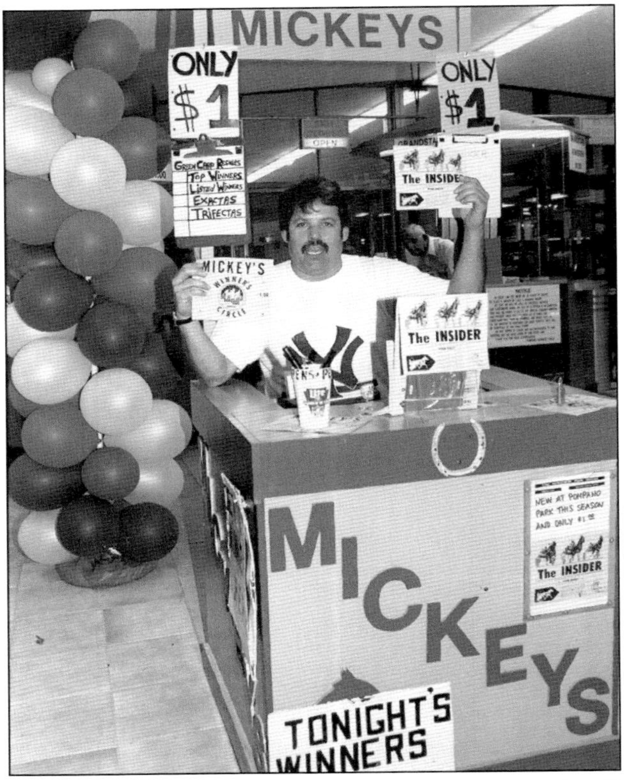

On opening night, October 4, 1996, a fan arriving at the general admission entrance at trackside, is greeted by "Mickeys," who will provide him with a tip sheet for a small fee. Who can resist! However, nothing is guaranteed in racing, where so many variables may defy the logic of the expert handicapper. Also for sale is a newspaper, *The Insider*, which explains detailed information about racing at Pompano Park.

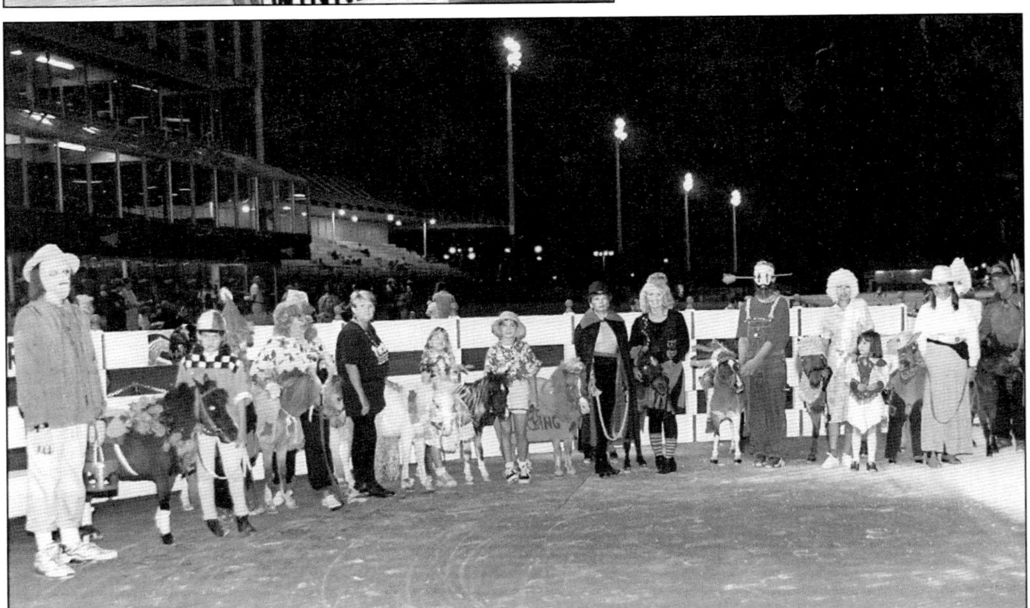

The track traditionally hosts a Halloween party for children, who are presented with gifts and treats. Track personnel assist in the festivities in the winner's circle. The Park's own mini horses participate in the event.

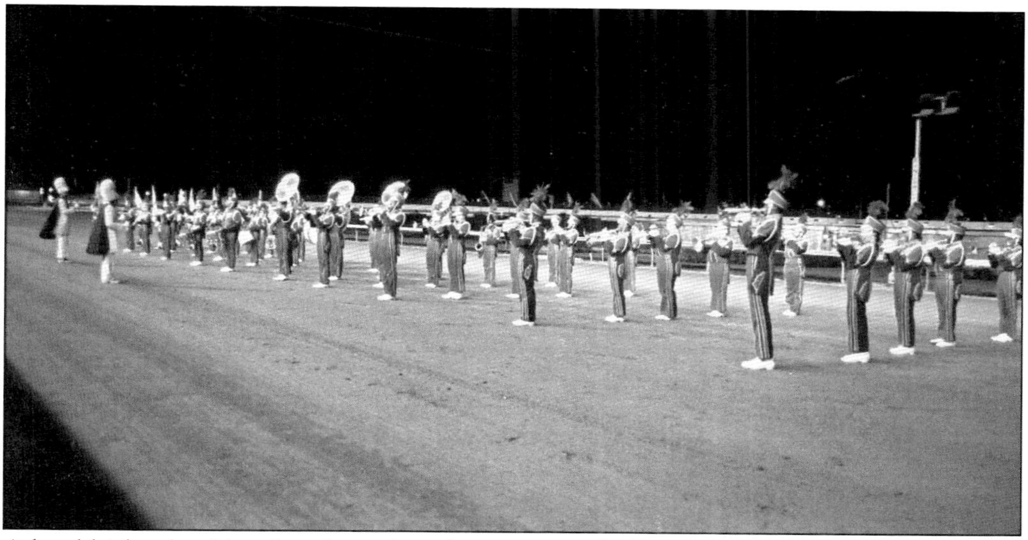

A local high-school band performed on the occasion of a Breeder's Crown race on November 11, 1988. The Breeders Crown three-year-old colt trot produced a new all-age track record by Mack Lobell of 1:51.1, with John Campbell driving. The three-year-old colt pace also produced a new all-age track record by Run the Table of 1:53 in an elimination heat, quickly followed by another 1:53 performance by Call for Rain in the final.

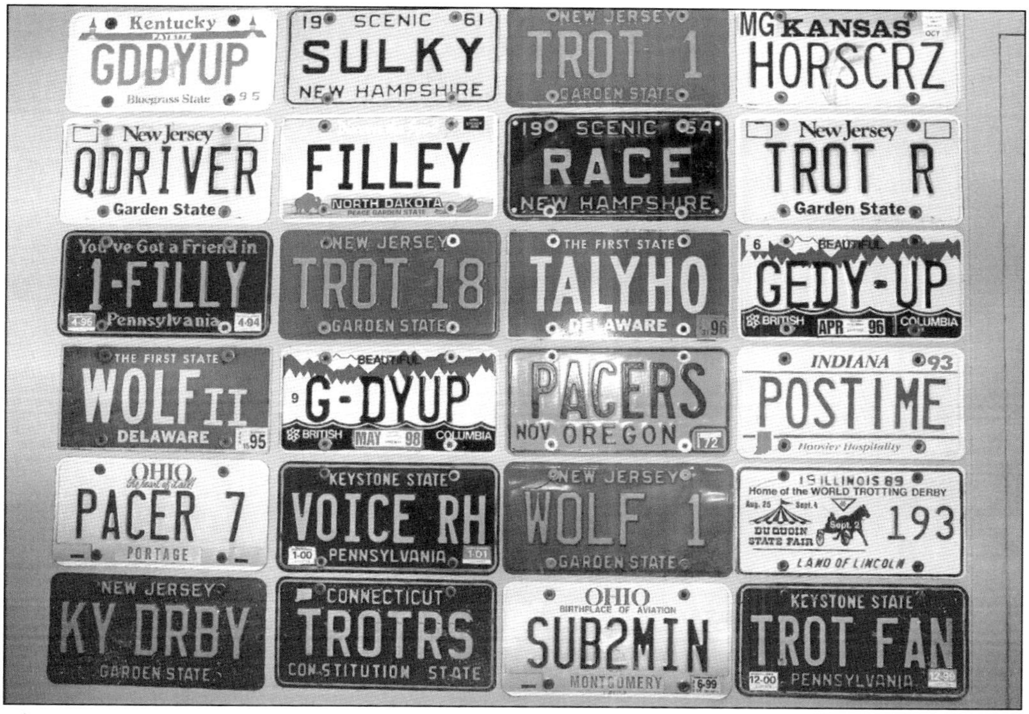

There are many ways to demonstrate one's commitment to the sport of racing. These official license plates from various states feature the harness-racing industry. The collage of images is displayed on the office wall of Steve Wolf, Pompano Park's director of marketing and communications.

POMPANO PARK STAKES SCHEDULE

1/26/04 Monday	The Artsplace	1st leg 3 & 4-yo Pacing Series	$ 6,500
1/28/04 Wednesday	The Miss Easy	1st leg 3 & 4-yo Pacing Series	$ 6,500
2/2/04 Monday	The Artsplace	2nd leg 3 & 4-yo Pacing Series	$ 6,500
2/4/04 Wednesday	The Miss Easy	2nd leg 3 & 4-yo Pacing Series	$ 6,500
2/9/04 Monday	The Artsplace	3rd leg 3 & 4-yo Pacing Series	$ 6,500
2/11/04 Wednesday	The Miss Easy	3rd leg 3 & 4-yo Pacing Series	$ 6,500
2/13/04 Friday	The Mack Lobell	1st leg Open Trot	$25,000
2/14/03 Saturday	The Isle of Capri	1st leg Open Pace	$50,000
2/16/04 Monday	The Artsplace	Final 3 & 4-yo Pacing Series	$17,500 est.
2/18/04 Wednesday	The Miss Easy	Final 3 & 4-yo Pacing Series	$17,500 est.
2/20/04 Friday	The Mack Lobell	2nd leg Open Trot	$25,000
2/21/04 Saturday	The Isle of Capri	2nd leg Open Pace	$50,000
2/28/04 Saturday	The Isle of Capri	Final Open Pace	$150,000
2/28/04 Saturday	The Mack Lobell	Final Open Trot	$75,000
2/28/04 Saturday	The Red Bow Tie	FL Bred Invitational Pace	$50,000
3/5/04 Friday	FL USHWA Memorial	Invitational Trot	$20,000
3/12/04 Friday	The Valley Victory	1st leg 5-yo & under Trot	$ 6,500
3/19/04 Friday	The Valley Victory	2nd leg 5-yo & under Trot	$ 6,500
3/26/04 Friday	The Valley Victory	3rd leg 5-yo & under Trot	$ 6,500
4/2/04 Friday	The Valley Victory	Final 5-yo & under Trot	$17,500

The 40th anniversary season attracted the leading trainers, drivers, and horses, especially with its stakes schedule during the high season of 2004. This impressive list of pacing and trotting series represents a tradition started in the early history of Pompano Park Harness Track.

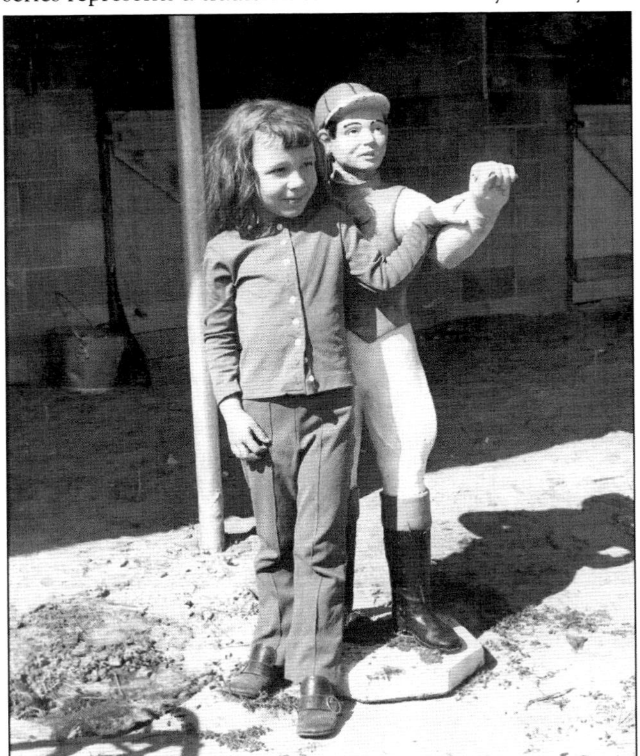

This young girl is fascinated with the lawn jockey still standing in the barnyard area in front of Gordon Norris's stable on the north side of the track. Pompano Park is child-friendly, offering many events geared to their interests.

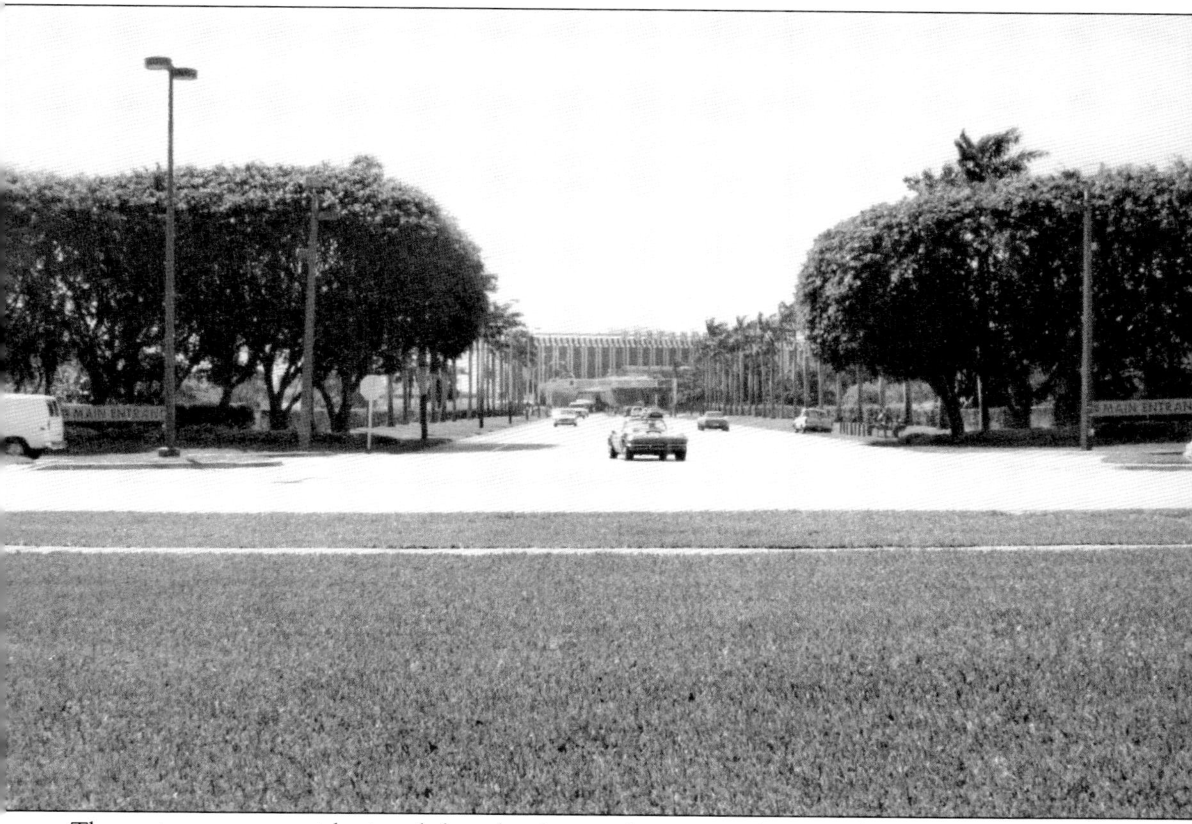

The main entrance, with signs left and right, can be seen at the time the old training track (not shown), north of Racetrack Road (SW 3rd Street), was purchased in 1995 by the Isle of Capri Casinos, a publicly traded company based in Biloxi, Mississippi. The grassy area in the foreground has been replaced by a road that leads north to the Wal-Mart Super Center and other businesses and connects to Atlantic Boulevard.

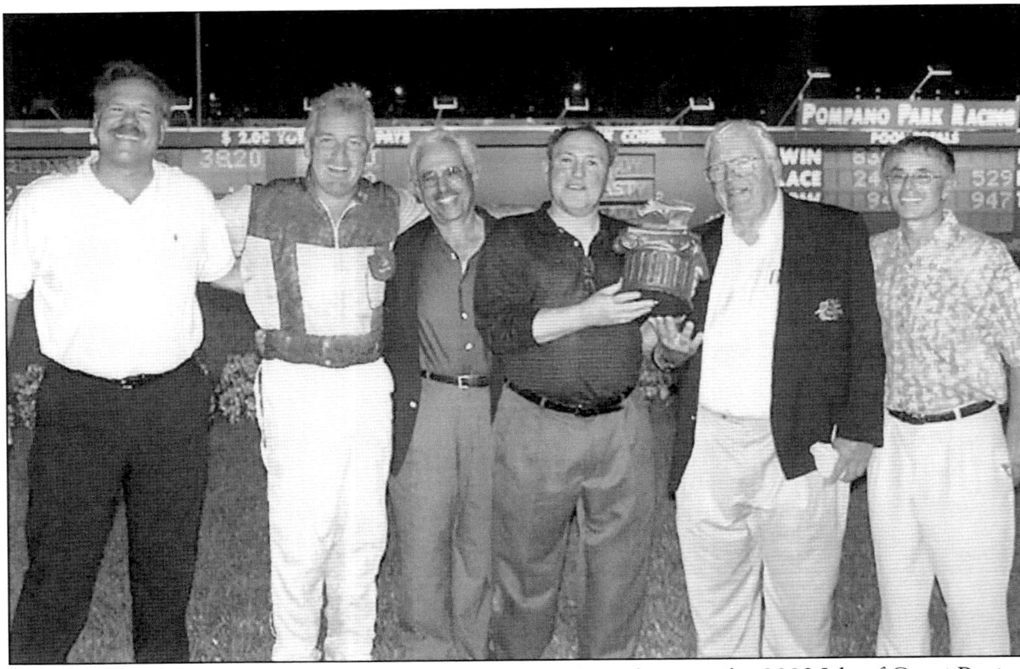

Smiles abound in the winner's circle after Corporate Rrraider won the 2003 Isle of Capri Pacing Series Final. From left to right are Corporate Rrraider's co-owner Daniel Courtemanche, driver Peter Wrenn, Isle of Capri secretary Allan B. Solomon, Corporate Rrraider co-owner Thomas Courtemanche, Isle of Capri founder and president Bernard Goldstein, and Pompano Park general manager Dick Feinberg.

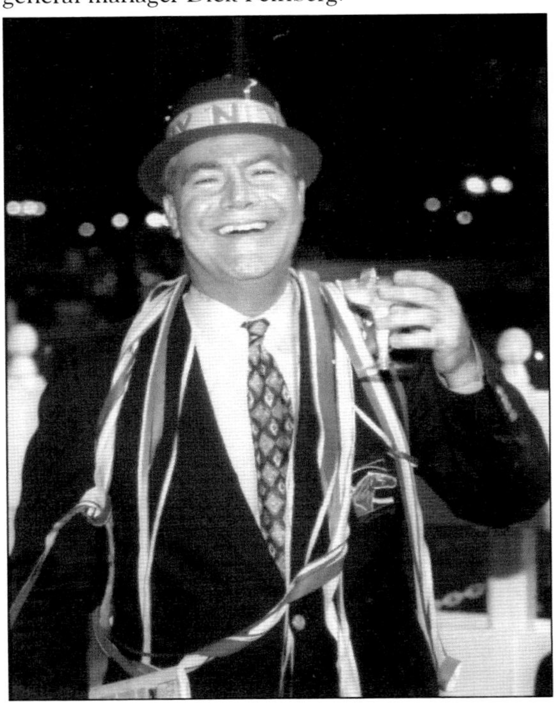

TV host Larry Albano leads in the celebration of the Millennium New Year at Pompano Park. For the occasion, the Millennium Race started in 1999 and was completed after midnight in 2000.

The official program for May 27, 2000, shows Helsa's Sam, driven by Rich Schaut, top left, racing to victory in the Artsplace Pacing Series. At bottom left is world champion pacer Red Bow Tie, who set a track record of 1:52.3 as a two-year-old gelding on October 18, 1998, with Terry Kerr driving, in the Florida Stallion Stakes.

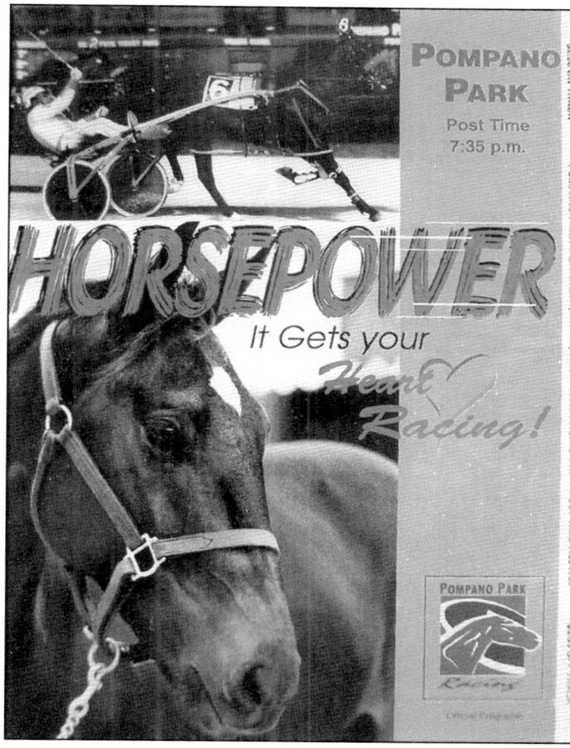

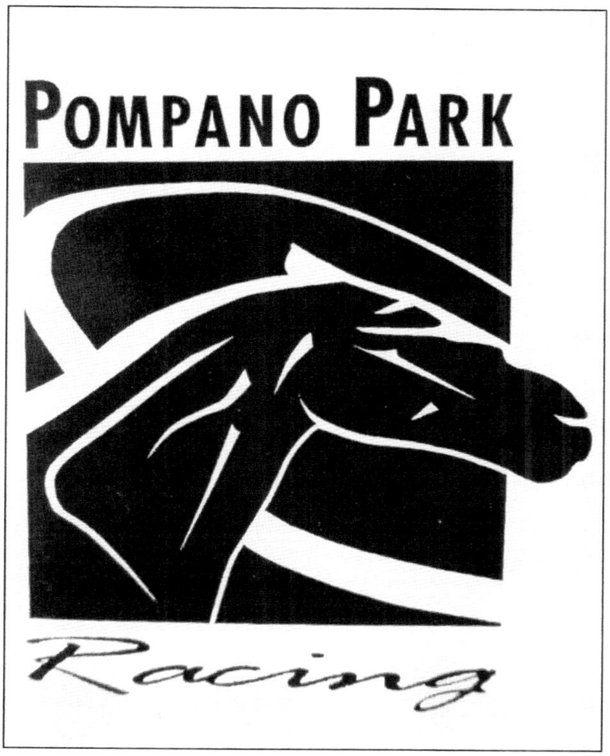

An artist's rendering of a harness horse was used as the Pompano Park logo during the 1990s. In a realistic black and white image, it symbolized the racing action of the sport. The logo was one of many used over the years.

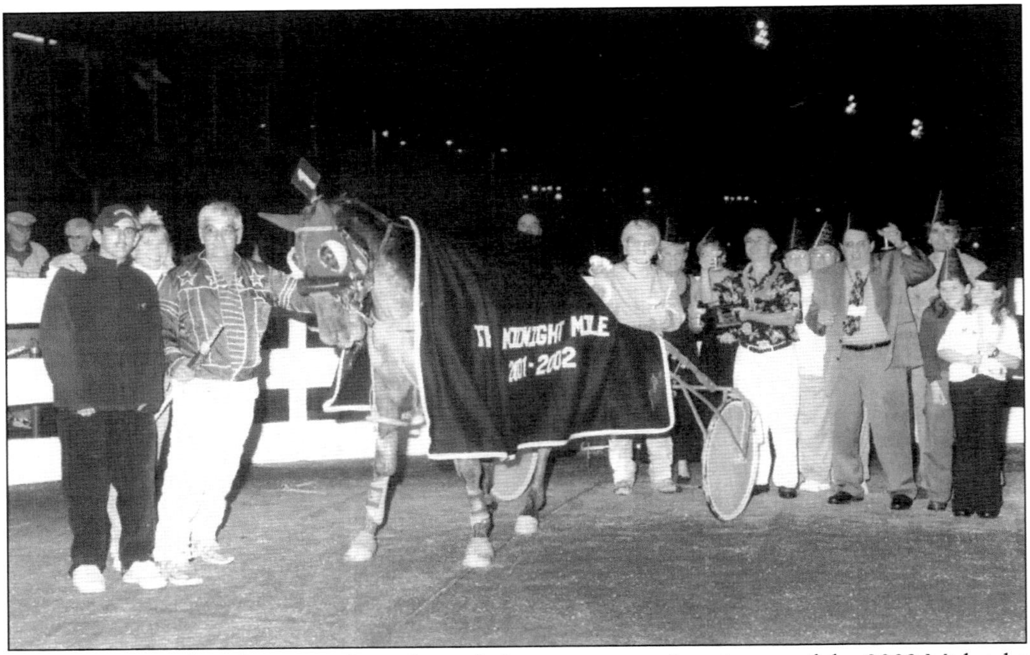

All smiles prevail in the winner's circle, and champagne too, for winners of the 2002 Midnight Mile at Pompano Beach in 2002. The annual race on New Year's Eve starts right before the stroke of midnight and ends in the next year!

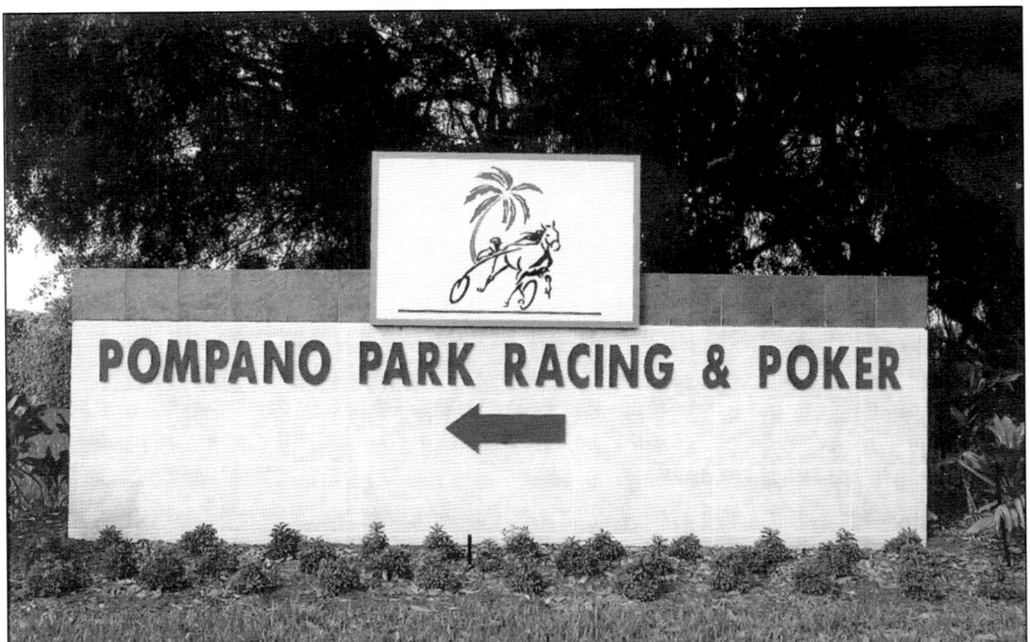

A contemporary sign guides fans to the main entrance of Pompano Park Racing and Poker. It is located on Racetrack Road (SW 3rd Street), east of Powerline Road. Note the impressive Park logo above the sign.

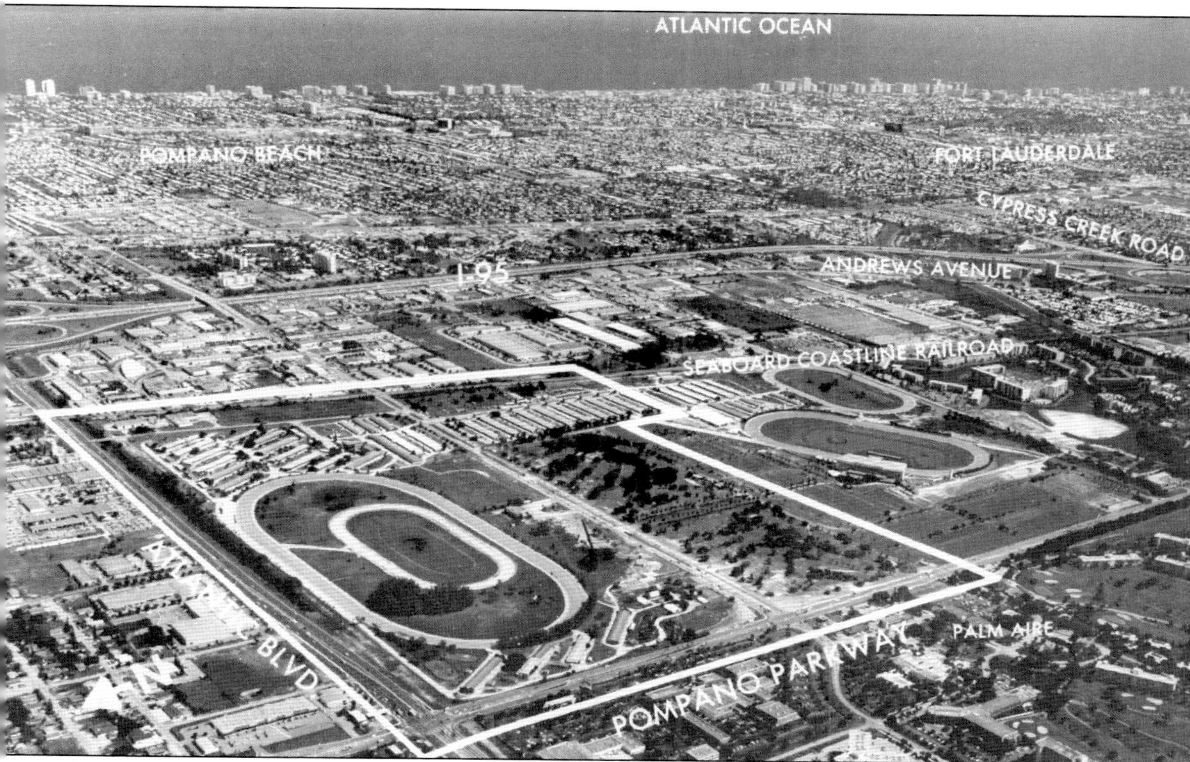

A panoramic aerial view eastward to the Atlantic Ocean captures the original training track (built in the 1950s) in the foreground, left, south of Atlantic Boulevard. Palm Aire, lower right, is west of Powerline Road. The training track no longer exists; it was sold to developers in 1995, and the land now contains a Wal-Mart Super Center and other businesses. The main entrance road, south of the training track that contained a golf course and is still part of Pompano Park, connects the present track with Racetrack Road (SW 3rd Street). The Seaboard Coastline Railroad is now the CSX Railroad. This photo, taken several years earlier, shows the growth of Pompano Beach and environs.

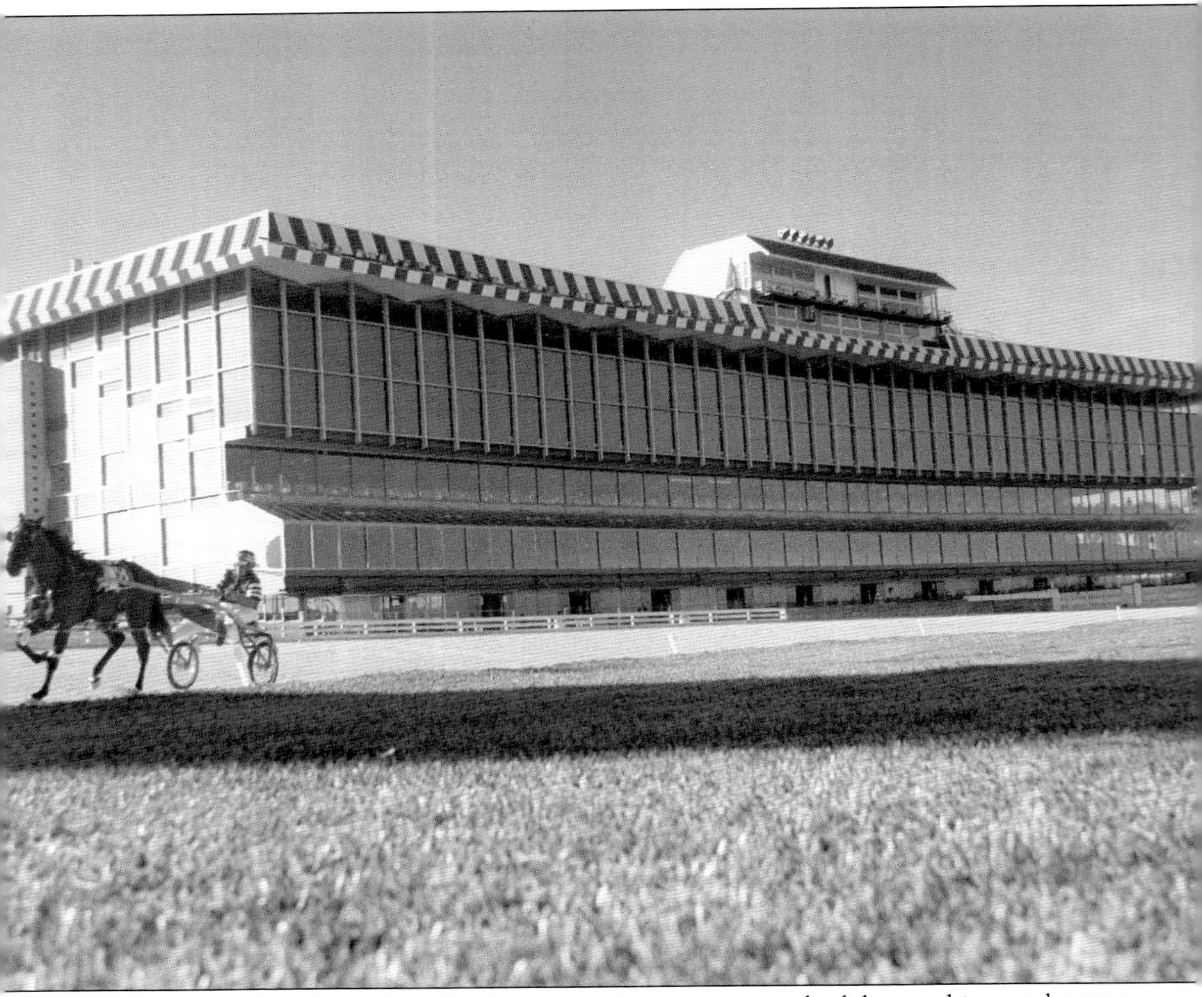

With the track and grandstand/clubhouse serving as a majestic backdrop, a driver and trotter work out during a recent early-morning exercise. At the top of the building is where judges record and assess the races. Pompano Park is a tribute to Frederick L. van Lennep, the Kentucky sportsman, and his wife, Frances Dodge van Lennep, who together brought harness racing to South Florida. They believed that winter visitors, accustomed to seeing harness racing at home, would want to see their favorite sport in a mild climate. They were right!